Lermontov's Narratives of Heroism

Lermontov's Narratives of Heroism

Vladimir Golstein

NORTHWESTERN UNIVERSITY PRESS / EVANSTON, ILLINOIS

Northwestern University Press
www.nupress.northwestern.edu

Printed in the United States of America

10 9 8 7 6 5 4 3 2 1

ISBN 978-0-8101-2872-9

The Library of Congress has cataloged the original, hardcover edition as follows:

Golstein, Vladimir.
Lermontov's narratives of heroism / Vladimir Golstein.
p. cm. — (Northwestern University Press studies in Russian literature and theory)
Includes bibliographical references.
ISBN 0-8101-1611-1 (cloth : alk. paper)
1. Lermontov, Mikhail I͡Ur 'evich. 1814–1841—Characters—Heroes.
2. Heroes in literature. I. Title. II. Series: Studies in Russian literature and theory.
PG3337.L47C484 1998
891.71'3—dc21

98-47237
CIP

∞ The paper used in this publication meets the minimum requirements of the American National Standard for Information Sciences—Permanence of Paper for Printed Library Materials, ANSI Z39.48-1992.

Had I to crave an inscription on my grave, I would ask for none other than "the individual."
—Søren Kierkegaard

Contents

Acknowledgments

Even though this book takes an unabashedly pro-individualistic position, the writing of it was truly a collective affair. My gratitude to those who helped me along the way is extensive and profound.

First of all I would like to thank all the great teachers of literature whom I was fortunate to encounter, and whose personal example has shown me that the study of literature can be a serious and rewarding experience: such are my Moscow teachers, Leah and Genrikh Gorchakov, my Columbia University professors, Edward Tayler and Richard F. Gustafson, and Yale Graduate School mentors, Robert Louis Jackson and Tomas Venclova. This book is a modest proof that their efforts to educate me were not totally wasted.

Yale University's Morse Junior Faculty Research Fellowship provided the time badly needed for the completion of this project.

I am grateful to all my wonderful colleagues at both Oberlin College and Yale University for their encouragement and understanding. My particular gratitude goes to Sibelan Forrester, Tom Newlin, and Vladimir Alexandrov for their careful reading and criticism of various parts of the manuscript.

There is hardly a page in this book that did not benefit from the expertise of Dr. Thomas Epstein of Boston College, who not only helped me to place definite and indefinite articles where they belong, but frequently encouraged to sharpen and reformulate my argumentation.

Susan Harris and Susan Betz of Northwestern University Press were extremely helpful and efficient during all the stages of the book production. This book clearly benefited from extensive and profound commentary, as well as from elegant and felicitous formulations that were provided by Caryl Emerson, the general editor of the Studies in Russian Literature and Theory series. I am immensely grateful to Professor Emerson for her wisdom, warmth, and generosity.

And finally I would like to acknowledge a tremendous contribution of my wife and colleague Svetlana Evdokimova who not only had to read the manuscript more times than she cared but also had to defend her criticism against a furious author who—of course—would incorporate all of her suggestions as his wounded pride would eventually give in to reason.

Chapter One

Heroism and Individualism: The Russian Context

MISREADINGS OF HEROISM

"I want a hero: an uncommon want / When every year and month sends forth a new one." So declared Byron in his immortal satire *Don Juan*. This statement from the creator of what later became known as the "Byronic hero" highlights the paradoxical situation that existed during the Romantic period, when a burgeoning cultural demand for new heroes was met by a correspondingly growing supply.

Lermontov's own celebrated novel *A Hero of Our Time* (1839) underscores his readiness to meet Byron's challenge and reveals his own concern with social, philosophical, and artistic aspects of heroism. One of the goals of my study is to demonstrate that the demand for heroic personalities was even more urgent in Russia than it was in the West, and that Lermontov's oeuvre successfully met this demand.

Nevertheless, because Lermontov's heroes responded to cultural needs rather than cultural expectations, his work encountered considerable resistance. Pechorin, the controversial protagonist of *A Hero of Our Time,* has been the object of constant misunderstanding, criticism, and attack since the book's publication. Was he to be taken for a hero or a villain? Did he speak for Lermontov or not? Many were ready to condemn Pechorin and Lermontov together. In fact, no Russian writer of similar stature has been the object of such a degree of hostility and misreading as Lermontov. Accusations of demonism, of lack of originality, of being as obnoxious as his own characters, or of simply being a shadow produced by the West accompanied Lermontov long after his death, which occurred at the age of twenty-seven as a result of a duel.

In the preface to his novel, Lermontov implied that his critics' hostility was fueled by their resistance to unpleasant truths: "People had been fed enough sweetmeats, it has given them indigestion: they need some bitter medicine, some caustic truths" (2). What were the sweets that the public expected to find in the novel, entitled *A Hero of Our Time,* and what bitter truths did they find instead?

I suggest that it was precisely his portrayal of a new kind of heroic personality, his presentation of characters who fully embodied the individualistic spirit of the Romantic age, that Lermontov's readers found difficult to accept. Lermontov—and this is my central thesis—was not just a renowned Romantic poet: he was also a serious social and ethical thinker who explored with sympathy and understanding the liberating as well as tragic dimensions of heroism and individualism. Sadly, his complex treatment of these issues has frequently been maligned or misperceived, making it difficult to understand either his art or his thought. Dostoevsky, for example, insists that there is only one solution to the problem of proud Romantic heroes: "humble yourself, proud man" (1972–90, 16:139), the solution that Dostoevsky rather simplistically attributes to Pushkin and to Pushkin's own complex treatment of the issue. Referring to frequent Russian appeals for humility, the Symbolist poet Dmitry Merezhkovsky explains Lermontov's achievement, and the hostility that it caused, in the following way:

> Where in Russia is that "proud man" who has to humble himself, after all? One sometimes feels like answering this constant call for humility with: How much further? And the only man in Russian literature who did not fully humble himself was Lermontov. . . . And it is this refusal to humble and surrender, a refusal which metaphysically and religiously asserts itself, that Russian literature cannot forgive Lermontov. (1991, 384)

While the main body of this study analyzes Lermontov's depiction of autonomous, independent, and self-reliant characters, who "metaphysically and religiously" assert themselves, here I shall survey the dominant cultural expectations connected with the issues of heroism and individualism as articulated by Lermontov's contemporaries and by some of his later opponents (Slavophiles, Dostoevsky, Solov'ev, Berdiaev, Vladimir Lossky).[1] This survey will reveal the reasons behind the persistent misreading of Lermontov and delineate the true scope and insights of his project.

Commenting on the genre of the novel, Jacques Barzun remarked that the undermining of heroism has always been part and parcel of the Western novel: "from its beginnings in *Don Quixote* and *Tom Jones* [the genre of the novel] has persistently made war on two things—our culture and the heroic" (quoted in Trilling 1972, 84). Russian literature, with its fixation on such values as unity, harmony, and self-sacrifice, seems to take up this project with a vengeance. Indeed, Tolstoy's *War and Peace* is explicit about its rejection of a Western type of hero, while Dostoevsky's novels present a terrifying gallery of egotistical, self-centered, and murderous characters who equate autonomy, strength, and self-reliance with amoralism, demonism, crime, and emptiness. To account for this suspicion of heroism and self-assertion, the nineteenth-century critic, Apollon Grigor'ev, posited the dichotomy between meek (Russian) and predatory (inspired by the West) character types. Grigor'ev's dichotomy enabled another critic, Nikolai Strakhov, to announce in his review of *War and Peace:* "What is *War and Peace*—this vast and multicolored epic—if not the apotheosis of the meek Russian type" (1970, 150) and then to interpret Russian literature as engaged "in the intensive search for a purely Russian ideal" that demanded "the execution and dethroning of types with claims to heroism" (150).

This search for a "purely Russian ideal" that dominated the art and thought of major nineteenth-century Russian authors and critics created a situation in which the only possible form of heroism was that of self-renunciation. Cultural fixation on an otherworldly ideal enabled the Russian philosopher Georgii Fedotov to describe this spiritual tendency of Russian thought as "kenotic" (literally, "self-emptying"); that is, "the imitation of Christ in His kenosis, His self-humiliation and His voluntary, sacrificial death" (1975, xiii). Fedotov maintains: "kenoticism, in the sense of non-resistance, or voluntary suffering, remains forever the most precious and typical, even though not always the dominant motive of Russian Christianity" (xiii). This religious ideal might become fully secularized, as in the case of the radical intelligentsia—Sergei Bulgakov's essay, "Heroism and Sanctity" (*Geroism i podvizhnichestvo*) (1911) scrutinizes the process—yet its key components remain the same: promotion of self-sacrifice and self-renunciation at the expense of the liberating and creative potential contained in the self. Bulgakov (1993) observes: "the concepts of personal morality, of personal self-perfection, of the development of personality are extremely unpopular among the intelligentsia, and conversely, the word "communal" (*obshchestvennyi*) acquires a special, sacred character" (323). This impersonal orientation of Russian anthropology, this fear that one individual's gain is another's loss, is captured in the following observation of another Russian philosopher, Fedor Stepun (1936):

> The question is whether in its deepest soul a people is attracted more by the hero, glorious in his own right, or by the silent saint. . . . The whole meaning of saintliness is to have no individuality of one's own and to will no destiny of one's own, but to be only a window through which God looks into the world, and men look up to God. In the overcoming of the hero and the heroic pattern of life by the Saint, then, is to be sought the deepest meaning of all religious antipathy to form. (22–23)

Stepun suggests here that "the overcoming of the hero" implies obliteration of individuality, antipathy to form, and therefore to matter; refusal to be engaged in creating patterns or structures; and ultimately the embrace of silence.

Besides its obvious political and social implications, such an anthropology, with its tendency to reject heroism in favor of saintliness, creates a problem for aesthetics as well. The Slavophiles, who among the secular thinkers were the earliest to promote saintliness at the expense of heroism, clearly allowed ideology to muddle their aesthetic sensibility. Discussing the Slavophiles' failure to respond adequately to the Italian humanistic art in which "everything belongs to a human person," Vassily Botkin, one of their opponents in the Westernizer camp, observes:

> They [Slavophiles] got lost within their aesthetic dogmas. In order to be true to themselves they had to contemptuously reject all of the Italian school, yet beauty, unfortunately for them, influences even them, in spite of their views. . . . Because of that they constantly contradict themselves, lie, deceive, yet lack courage to turn themselves into true Russian Old-Believers; furthermore, various sciences have already corrupted them. (1984, 260)

Following a similar line of thinking, Dostoevsky (1972–90) once dismissed Pushkin's, Lermontov's, and Tolstoy's gentry characters as "representatives of petty ambition": "As heroes, those beginning with Sylvio and the Hero of our time down to Prince Bolkonsky and Levin represent nothing but petty self-love (*melkoe samoliubie*)" (16:329). Such wholesale dismissal fails to differentiate between Anatol' Kuragin and his sister on the one hand, and Andrei Bolkonsky and Natasha on the other. When applied to Lermontov, such an approach misses an important part of Lermontov's project: the constant juxtaposition of the heroic and nonheroic; that is, Pechorin and Grushnitsky, Kalashnikov and Kirebeevich, Arbenin and Prince Zvezdich.

In other words, if the critics' ideal of a hero is that of a monk, and if heroism implies the rejection of the world and the conquest of oneself through self-control and self-resignation, then it becomes difficult to judge dispassionately literary characters, most of whom operate in the world. Even if the presence of the kenotic ideal might account for the metamorphosis of, say, Tolstoy's Father Sergius, other characters of Russian literature, such as Pushkin's Tatyana or Grinev, Lermontov's Mtsyri or Pechorin, Tolstoy's Levin, Bolkonsky, or Bezukhov do not really fit into such a system of coordinates, or rather, when applied to them, it produces distorted results.

Equally inadequate is the traditional charge of "poshlost'" (banality) or "meshchanstvo" (petty middle-class concerns) with which Russian cultural tradition tends to dismiss decent characters, diligently working at maintaining social and material order.[2]

Chekhov (1974–83) reminded us that "between 'there is God' and 'there is no God' lies a huge field, which the truly wise man crosses with great effort. Yet, Russian man knows only one of those extremes, while the middle is of no interest to him" (17:224). To cross such a field requires a tremendous effort precisely because God is silent, and therefore the burden shifts to the individual; one has to rely solely on oneself in order to establish and maintain the individual commitments and relations that constitute one's life. In other words, there is a vast field of human activity—such as the production of artistic, intellectual, or material goods, or honorable and responsible behavior toward fellow men—that do not fit the strict dichotomy between material self-assertion and spiritual self-renunciation. It is this field that great literary texts, including those of Lermontov, strive to explore, as they are concerned with the study of actual human experience rather than the attempt to substitute some philosophical or moral scheme for it.

In her brilliant *Gentleman in Trollope: Individuality and Moral Conduct* (1982), Shirley Robin Letwin stresses the inadequacy of imposing abstract schemes upon the complexities of human character and experience:

> Any general or universal conclusions about the human world are necessarily abstractions from a reality that consists of distinctive individuals, of "characters," each of whom has to be known in himself and may always do something unexpected. Such abstractions may explain that reality by disengaging some aspect of it, but they are not an advance to a "higher truth" any more than a dressmaker's pattern is superior to the finished garment. (60)

Following the political philosopher Michael Oakeshott in his insistence on the inadequacy of applying the dichotomies used by science, philosophy, or religion to human individuality, Letwin (1982) observes:

> If all human experience is rational, a man is not a self-divided being, with "higher" and "lower" parts; he is not a "rational animal" born to one law and bound to another. He is all one, an intelligent being. . . . Human individuality is not due to passions escaping from the control of reason; nor is it the product of "alienation" or of adopting an independent standpoint; it is simply the inescapable quality of a rational being. One may choose . . . to regard individuality as an evil, to seek the uniformity of a commune. But short of destroying his rational faculties, a man cannot lose his individuality because he cannot cease to be the maker of his own experience. (59–60)

According to Letwin, serious authors approach their characters as "the makers of their own experience," constantly engaged in various relationships with fellow human beings; learning, modifying, and changing their conduct. Their nearsighted critics, however, resort to some external, a priori given system of values enabling them to simplify the choices, complexities, and tensions of human interaction. Letwin's own investigation of Trollope's gentlemen heroes reveals that a particular social and cultural situation—that of nineteenth-century England—has to be scrutinized from a perspective on human personality and human relatedness that goes beyond the usual dichotomies of "spiritual" versus "material," or "selfish" versus "altruistic." Complicated codes of honorable conduct typical of the aristocratic cultures of Europe, and England in particular, would not fit into these dichotomies.

In terms of Russian literature, Letwin's approach to fictional characters finds its parallel in William Mills Todd III's investigation of the aristocratic mastery of conventions, which enabled him to do justice to the accomplishment of Pushkin's Tatyana (1986, 106–37). Likewise, the theory of prosaics, articulated recently by Gary Saul Morson and Caryl Emerson (1990) can be interpreted as an attempt to consider the achievements or failures of various characters of Russian literature on the basis of the "prosaic," middle-class values, contained in the texts themselves, yet ignored by the critics. In a similar way I suggest that to evaluate Lermontov's exploration of heroism adequately one needs to consider it in the context of Lermontov's concern with the individualistic ethos of Romanticism. It was Lermontov who, long before Chekhov, set for himself and for his heroes a task of traveling through the huge field that lies "between 'there is God' and 'there is no God.'" The accomplishment of Lermontov and his protagonists should therefore be measured by the degree of their embodiment of the spirit of autonomy, dignity, and self-reliance, as well as by their refusal to side with those for whom the content of this vast field and the efforts one spends while crossing it is frequently "of no interest."

INDIVIDUALISM

It is clear that behind the culture's tendency to interpret certain actions or characters as heroic and misread others as trivial if not demonic lies the dominant expectations as to what constitutes human personality. In order to appreciate fully Russian views on the subject of human personality, a certain linguistic excursion is in order. The Russian language has various terms related to human being, three of which are essential. Russians differentiate between *individ* (an individual), *lichnost'* (which might mean both a person and personality), and *individual'nost'* or *samobytnost'* (uniqueness, individuality, personality). Pushkin, for example, provides the following gloss on the latter concept when in his 1830 story "The Squire's Daughter" (*Baryshnia-krestianka*) he refers to "the uniqueness of the character, its individuality (*osobennost' kharaktera, samobytnost'* [*individualité*]), without which, according to Jean-Paul, human greatness does not exist."

The majority of Russian thinkers view "individuality" as something positive; in fact, the argument that frequently unites the Slavophiles with Herzen, Kropotkin, and the Marxists is that Western individualism is the enemy of "individuality." Much more complicated, however, is the use of the concepts of "individ" and "lichnost'."

According to Veselitsky (1972), the cluster of words associated with the root "individ" began to be introduced into Russian philosophical and literary language in the late eighteenth century. They gradually replaced the set of words through which Russians attempted to provide a calque for the Latin root "individ": *nedelimyi, nerazdel'nyi, chastnyi, osoblivyi, osobyi, edinstvennyi, edinyi.* The process of replacement was not very peaceful, and conservatives voiced frequent complaints against the use of such obscure foreign terms as "individuum," or "individual'nyi." In a series of articles Belinsky defended the use of the terms, claiming that the complaints about the words reflected the refusal to come to terms with the very concepts that these words represented (Veselitsky 1964, 14–24). In fact, according to Veselitsky, it was Belinsky's frequent use of the term "individual'nost'" that was instrumental in its introduction into the Russian language. Pushkin, we recall, used a French spelling of the term for his tale.

Regardless of this initial reluctance, by midcentury the older concepts of *lichnost'/"lichnyi* (person/personal) began to be used interchangeably with the terms *individ/individual'nyi,* describing anything related to a human being: "in the first decades of the nineteenth century the words *individual'nyi, individuum* gravitated toward and, in fact, joined the range covered by words *lichnyi, lichnost', litso*" (Veselitsky 1972, 38, 159–60). It should be pointed out that the overlapping of semantic fields connected with these concepts continues today, as it does in English (see the recent discussion of these concepts by various Russian historians, sociologists, and psychologists in a 1990 issue of the Russian anthropology journal, *Odysseus: Man in History* (A. I. Gurevich 1990, 6–90).

However, at the beginning of the twentieth century, several Russian religious philosophers began once more to draw a sharp distinction between the concepts of *lichnost'* and *individ.* The texts of Berdiaev, Florensky, Bulgakov,[3] Vladimir Lossky, and many others elaborate or utilize a radical opposition between the terms, so that the term "individ" comes to mean a human being as that part of physical nature that cannot be further divided, while "lichnost" means a human being as reflecting the "image and likeness of God": it grows, is never identical to itself, and cannot be seen as a part because potentially it can encompass all.[4]

According to Vladimir Lossky, the road from an individual (*individ*) to a person (*lichnost'*) is paved by renunciation:

> A person who asserts himself as an individual, and shuts himself up in the limits of his particular nature, far from realizing himself fully becomes impoverished. It is only in renouncing its own possession and giving itself freely, in ceasing to exist for itself that the person finds full expression in the one nature common to all. In giving up its own special good, it expands infinitely, and is enriched by everything which belongs to all. (1976, 124)

The movement from one extreme to another is accomplished through asceticism: "The individual, i.e. that assertion of self in which person is confused with nature and loses its true liberty, must be broken. This is the root principle of asceticism" (Lossky 1976, 122). And it is also the root principle for becoming an ideal monk: "for that reason, F. Vagrius says that a perfect monk 'will after God, count all men as God Himself'" (122).

Although these concepts began to be articulated several decades after Lermontov, they are clearly grounded in a peculiar sensibility that was shaping Russian attitudes toward the individual back in the 1830s and 1840s. It is this sensibility that lies at the root of the frequent dismissals of anything related to *individ,* that is, of many self-evident Western individualistic values, such as religious, moral, legal, social, and economic autonomy, independence, and self-reliance. In order to clarify this sensibility and appreciate Lermontov's courageous challenge to it, let us explore the tortuous road traveled by the ideology of individualism within both Russia and the West.

During the first half of the nineteenth century Western Europe was a locus of profound cultural cataclysms and transformations. Religion ceased to exist as the organizing and unifying principle of society, culture, and personal conduct. In addition, historical and economic development resulted in particularization and alienation. "Things fall apart, the center cannot hold" (Yeats, "The Second Coming"): this passage sums up the point of view of the period. The nineteenth century gave birth to the concepts of alienation propounded by Hegel and Marx, to the pervasive pessimism of Schopenhauer, the religious existentialism of Kierkegaard, and to the literary expression of alienation and loss contained in the writings of numerous Romantic authors. Several key European events ushered in the collapse of existing social, political, and religious hierarchies, with an impact best summarized as the Miltonic "paradise lost." What Milton pronounced on observing the changes introduced by the Renaissance and Reformation became a fait accompli after the Enlightenment, the French Revolution, and industrialization.

Coincident with these losses, however, there appeared new patterns of heroic behavior that utilized the individual's inner resources, energy, and self-reliance. In other words, new realities resulted in the creation and articulation of new doctrines usually described under the general concept of "individualism." Commenting on this complicated term, Max Weber remarked: "the expression individualism includes the most heterogeneous things imaginable" (1958, 222). Indeed, according to Steven Lukes's evenhanded and informative study, *Individualism* (1973), the concept of "individualism" serves as an umbrella for various, sometimes distantly related, doctrines of economic, political, social, moral, and religious individualisms. While all these individualist doctrines began to appear at approximately the same time, and were caused by approximately the same historical events, such as the Renaissance, Reformation, and the emergence of capitalism, they are not logically or conceptually tied to each other. What connects them is their appeal to a system of core, individualistic ideas and values, such as "respect for human dignity, autonomy, privacy and self-development" (Lukes 1973, 125). Furthermore, regardless of the inconsistencies that these doctrines contain, and regardless of the artificial concept of the "abstract individual" central to the majority of them, the core values that inform these doctrines lie at the heart of two cardinal ideals of modern times: equality and liberty (Lukes 1973, 125–45).

Milton's portrayal of Satan captures the dynamics of the new trends. Satan finds himself on his own from the very beginning of the poem; he also articulates a rationale for dealing with new circumstances. Having lost the battle for supremacy over the outside world, he will rely on his inner strength: "What though the field be lost? All is not lost; the unconquerable will, and study of revenge, immortal hate, and courage never to submit or yield: And what is else not to be overcome?" (*Paradise Lost*, book 1, lines 105–8). Regardless of Milton's own intention to debunk his rebellious protagonist while promoting the cardinal Christian virtues of humility, obedience, and patience, Satan articulates and embodies new forms of heroism, such as energy, will, and refusal to submit. These features were to become the main traits of individualism, the core of its healthy ethos, so that unleashed individual energies helped the West to confront the numerous religious, economic, and social problems of the last two centuries. Religious/communal loss and disorientation was accompanied by the compensatory increase of individual heroism and self-reliance. In the West the death of God and the birth of the Superman historically go hand in hand. Hence the Romantic period was a period of great heroes such as Napoleon and Byron, as well as of hero worship, an attitude immortalized by Thomas Carlyle.[5]

This is not to say that the doctrines or values of individualism did not encounter resistance. Milton's Satan, we recall, always had both supporters and detractors. The same holds for individualistic doctrines and, paradoxically, for similar reasons. According to Ian Watt's *Myths of Modern Individualism* (1996), the cultural movement of the Counter-Reformation was, in part, an attack on the dangerous, individualist-oriented trends of the Renaissance and Reformation: this critique gave rise to the new myths of Don Quixote, Faust, and Don Juan. By producing "a hero who was an emblem of individualism which fails" (137) the initial creators of these myths highlighted the transgressive and destructive aspect of their protagonists. "The final emblematic punishment of all three protagonists can be seen as the unpalatable lesson which the Counter-Reformation attempted to teach to the individualism of the Renaissance" (ibid.). However, during the period of Romanticism the presentation of these characters became much more sympathetic, enabling Watt to characterize the later treatment of these mythic heroes as "romantic apotheosis of Renaissance myths" (193–228).

As they began to define themselves in opposition to the Enlightenment, however, various Romantic thinkers developed their own anti-individualistic program. Interpreting the excesses of the French Revolution as the direct result of the Enlightenment's rationalism, skepticism, and the glorification of the individual, these thinkers began to attack the allegedly dangerous doctrines of the philosophes. The most typical complaint was that of centrifugal, decentralizing tendencies inherent in individualism, tendencies bound to tear the state and society apart. A French conservative thinker, F. de Lamennais, prefiguring the endless complaints of other conservatives, be they Russian or Western, denounced "individualism which destroys the very idea of obedience and of duty, thereby destroying both power and law; and what then remains but a terrifying confusion of interests, passions and diverse opinions" (Lukes 1973, 6).

In other words, the anti-individualistic program ushered in by the Counter-Reformation received a second life in postrevolutionary Europe. As in the case of the Counter-Reformation, the most vocal critics were conservative Catholic thinkers, whose criticism, given Russia's recent emergence from medieval ways of thinking, exerted a lasting influence on the Russian outlook. One of the most extraordinary of these figures was Joseph de Maistre, who spent fifteen years in Russia serving as ambassador from the kingdom of Sardinia.[6] De Maistre's personal charm and powerful rhetoric had a lasting impact upon the Russian governing elite. In his 1811 note addressed to Count N. P. Rumiantsev, but clearly meant for Emperor Alexander I, de Maistre makes a powerful plea to Russia's ruling circles to save the country from the impact of Western education; according to him, Russia's institutions, including that of Orthodoxy, were too weak to confront the dangerous Western doctrines of freedom (Mestr 1937, 187–94). De Maistre's writings also influenced such diverse thinkers as Nikolai Karamzin, Petr Chaadaev, Mikhail Lunin, Aleksei Khomiakov, Feodor Tiutchev, and Vladimir Solov'ev. The latter wrote an entry on de Maistre in the *Brokgaus and Efron Encyclopedic Dictionary,* singling out his polemics with Bacon's empiricism, his critique of human rights that ignore the "organic solidarity of all creatures," and his interest in the "collective reason of humankind" (Solov'ev 1897, 349–52).

In fact, according to Isiah Berlin, it was this group of counterrevolutionaries who at the turn of the nineteenth century virtually invented the doctrine of "the western world as in some sense 'rotting,' as being in rapid decay" (1979, 64). This doctrine found its way to Germany and Russia, becoming a major tenet in the attitudes of numerous Russian thinkers, who were convinced (or rather, were reinforced in their convictions) that the West's new individualistic doctrines and values were dangerous and destructive, and that Russia had to be protected from them. Spurred by rivalry and insecurity, Russians, similar to Germans and other latecomers to modernity, have always been enthusiastic about various doctrines pronouncing the "decline of the West."

De Maistre, who never tired of attacking Protestantism, rationalism, and individualism, was adamant in his rejection of freedom and the autonomy of the individual. In fact, de Maistre was one of the first to use the term "individualism" in its modern sense, when in 1820 he spoke of "this deep and frightening division of minds, this infinite fragmentation of all doctrines, political protestantism carried to the most absolute individualism" (Lukes

1973, 4). In his *Etude sur la souveraineté,* De Maistre envisioned the following, clearly medieval, way of confronting this dangerous ideology:

> Government is a true religion. It has its dogmas, its mysteries, its priests. . . . Man's first need is that his growing reason be put under the double yoke [of church and state]. It should be annihilated, it should lose itself in the reason of the nation, so that it is transformed from its individual existence into another—communal—being, as a river that falls into the ocean does indeed persist in the midst of the waters, but without name or personal identity. (quoted in Berlin 1991, 125–26)

The conviction that individualism contained a destructive potential was shared by both left and right. Saint-Simon (an even more influential thinker in terms of emerging Russian views on the subject) attacked the eighteenth-century "defenders of individualism" for refusing to "go back to a source higher than individual conscience." He insisted that individualism with its two "sad deities . . . two creatures of reason—conscience and public opinion" led to "one political result: opposition to any attempt at organization from a center of direction for the moral interests of mankind, to hatred of power" (Lukes 1973, 7).[7]

Even the liberals, such as Alexis de Tocqueville, were if not downright critical of individualism, at least very much concerned with its inevitable outcome: selfishness, isolation, and a weakening of social bonds. Tocqueville clearly associated individualism with the spreading conditions of equality and democracy, yet warns of the price of this progress: "thus not only does democracy make every man forget his ancestors, but it hides his descendants and separates his contemporaries from him; it throws him back forever upon himself alone and threatens in the end to confine him entirely in the solitude of his own heart" (1945, 106). While distinguishing individualism, which he sees as a "calm and mature feeling of self-reliance," from egoism, he nevertheless maintains that "individualism, at first, only saps the virtues of public life, but in the long run it attacks and destroys all others and is at length absorbed in downright selfishness" (104).[8]

Individualism, as Tocqueville correctly foresaw, was destined to play a pivotal role in the history of the United States. In Russia, however, its march was much less triumphant, as Russia's historical development differed drastically from that of the West. The momentous development of the concept of the individual throughout the Renaissance and Reformation bypassed Russia entirely, while the teachings of the Enlightenment and French Revolution were often greeted with suspicion and misunderstanding.

In other words, the Counter-Reformation's critique of excessive individualism found a very receptive audience in Russia. It is hardly surprising that a country that never experienced the positive, liberating aspects of Renaissance and Reformation, but knew very well the dangers of disunity and civil strife, found the Counter-Reformation arguments against inevitable social and moral chaos very convincing.[9]

In Western Europe, cultural and spiritual losses occurred gradually and had prepared an individual strong or heroic enough to confront them. Not so in Russia, where the institutions of serfdom and autocracy, the system of ranks, the enforced Westernization of the previous century, the loss of religion among the ruling class, and a barely nascent middle class left the country with very few people ready to exercise and defend their individual rights and their autonomy. In her attempts to be on a par with Enlightenment Europe, Catherine the Great clearly encouraged the appearance of the new self. Catherine's reign, in spite of her later doubts, planted the seeds of individual dignity and individual importance, at least within the Russian nobility; it was further encouraged by Russia's victory over Napoleon. Yet barely had the Russian gentry began to enjoy its sense of independence and its pride in individual accomplishment than the Decembrist fiasco reversed the process, plunging the country into a trauma of resignation and alienation. As Herzen saw it, Russia's nobility had never recovered from the shock of suppression; "it withered away" (1954–66, 7:209). In the absence of historically grounded traditions, the emerging sense of self could not withstand the shock.

After the events of 1825, the Russian government increased the discouragement, if not outright suppression, of all political, social, and economic manifestations of individualism. This desire to stifle and submerge the individual in the hierarchies of state, religion, and community found expression in what became the government's guiding principle of cultural life in the 1830s and 1840s: "Autocracy, Orthodoxy, and Nationality." In a notorious 1848 statement to the teachers of military schools, a government official, Iakov Rostovtsev, relegated individual autonomy to the narrow confines of family life: "Conscience is needed only in family and private life; when it comes to matters of state and government service, its role is played by the authorities" (quoted in Ivanov-Razumnik 1911, 183). A. I. Bariatinsky, a prominent field marshal of the period, who also happened to have been a classmate of Lermontov at Saint Petersburg's Junker Academy, described Nicholas I's regime in the following terrifying image: "Nicholas saw the country as a billiard table, and did not like to see anything rise above the monotonous plane of the table surface" (quoted in Gershtein 1986, 211). Responding to the mood of the period, the popular court playwright, Nestor Kukol'nik, declared that "if they order me, tomorrow I'll become a midwife" (quoted in Ivanov-Razumnik 1911, 174). Indeed, Russian goverment seems to be very much concerned with appointing poets to the position of midwives, as one of the most thoughful people of the period, poet and critic Prince Viazemskii, acknowledges in his 1846 entry to his diary:

> Our government considers it is to be a weakness and example of dangerous permissiveness to take into account the natural abilities and inclination of the man who is being appointed to an office. Man is born to stand on his feet: that is precisely why he must be put on his hands and told "walk!" Otherwise, what is the meaning of power when it obeys the general order and flow of things? In addition, a certain apprehension plays its part here: man in his proper place acquires a certain strength, a certain individuality [*samobytnost'*] but the government wants mere tools, frequently crooked and unconfortable to use, but for that reason all the more dependent on its will. (Viazemsky 1992, 251)

These few examples taken at random indicate the reigning social and cultural attitude toward the values of individualism. Lermontov's contemporary, Alexander Herzen, commented on this essential difference between Russia and the West in a diary entry for 4 July 1843: "The rights of the free rational human being are accepted [in England] with the same certainty that they are entirely denied in our country" (1954–66, 2:292). In his memoirs, *My Past and Thoughts,* Herzen sees Russia's attitude toward human personality in a more tragic light: "Everywhere in Russia a man's personality is sacrificed without the slightest mercy and with no reward" (Herzen 1982, 149).

Subjected to the stern and repressive policy of the government, the Russian cultural elite found itself totally disoriented. Vissarion Belinsky, the most influential critic and key thinker of the period, gave voice to the post-Decembrist generation, complaining about resignation and tormenting "self-consciousness" (*refleksiia*). The recurrence of such images as "lost paradise" and "the wandering Jew" in his letters testifies to an emerging awareness of the individual's sense of loss and disorientation.[10] Unprepared to confront their losses by falling back upon inner resources, Russian intellectuals had to look for guidance to various philosophical, social, or religious systems. Belinsky's own furious and well-documented embrace of diverse doctrines, ranging from Hegelianism to Socialism, is a case in point. Setting the trend for future generations, Belinsky constantly searched for a master ideology, for what William Blake calls "mind-forged manacles," to guide him through the maze of unresolved moral questions.

As the Russian intellectual elite of the second quarter of the nineteenth century attempted to find a way out from its sense of disorientation and loss, it inevitably turned to the West. Therefore in Russia a comprehensive exploration of the theme of individualism began only with the advent of Romanticism. Many of the insights of Romanticism, insights that constitute only a chapter in the history of Western individualism, form an entire book in Russia.

Literature and the arts in general have frequently been the vehicle for introducing the Russian public to the equivalent of centuries of Western economic, legal, and cultural development. Romanticism, in this sense, was an enormously important cultural force. Its concern with the plight of the self, with rebellion, and even demonism provided Russian artists and ultimately the Russian public with an opportunity to rethink the makeup of the human personality, and to renegotiate its place within society and the universe. The symbolist poet and critic Viacheslav Ivanov acknowledged Russia's profound cultural indebtedness to Romanticism and its individualistic ethos in his essay, "Byronism as an Event in the Life of the Russian Spirit" (1916): "We, the Slavs, discovered the societal revelation of human personality in the depth of the English spirit. Such a revelation was Byronism" (1994, 269).[11]

Russians were certainly infected with European Romanticism's enthusiasm for individualism and its core values, yet they were also susceptible to its anti-Enlightenment program, with its attacks on the social contract, human rights, rationalism, and religious skepticism. As a result, many Russians could not fail to see individualism as an explosive, dangerous, and destructive force that disrupts the proper function of human society and culture. In fact, the negative qualities associated with individualism, namely, atomization, alienation, egotism, and the ensuing civil strife and disorder, were destined to alarm Russians, shaped as they were by the constant fear of invasion and civil strife. This fear of explosive individualistic doctrines was shared not only by the tsarist regime and the Church, but also by the majority of ordinary Russians. It is thus no surprise that appeals to confront this evil—if not by force, then by the means of religion, mystical doctrines of state and people, or by the calls for self-renunciation—became fundamental to the rhetoric of Russian opponents of individualism. Beginning with Karamzin, Russian intellectuals articulated Russian national identity precisely in terms of unity and social cohesion, as opposed to the Western fixation on individualism and its inevitable conflicts.

In other words, by the second quarter of the nineteenth century, the Russian cultural elite found itself confronted, on the one hand, by the Western Romantic ethos, with its revolutions, declarations of human rights, doctrines of individualism, and literary interest in self-analysis, biography, and confession; on the other, by post-Decembrist repression coupled with increased conservative attacks on individualism. The tension of this confrontation resulted in a lively debate on the nature of the human being and the limits of individual rights and responsibilities.

This debate was largely restricted to the literary journals of the day; these were practically the only forums in which public discussions of any question, whether cultural, social, or economic, could take place. The polemical texts of writers and journalists, both radical and conservative, Slavophiles and Westernizers, filled such periodicals as *Moskovskii Vestnik* (1827–30), *Moskovskii Telegraph* (1825–34), *Moskvitianin* (1841–56), *Sovremennik* (1836–66), and *Otechestvennye Zapiski* (1839–67). In fact, according to an authoritative student of Russian intellectual history, Andrzei Walicki, it was "the idea of personality" that fueled the polemic between Slavophiles and Westernizers (1979, 135). It was this polemic that was destined to shape all future Russian discussions on historical, philosophical, and religious issues.[12]

Westernizers embraced the Western type of personality and individualism, bemoaning its absence in Russia. In his seminal article "A Glance at the Legal Norms of Ancient Russia" (1847), the historian Konstantin Kavelin states that "an individual who realizes his eternal, unconditional dignity is a necessary condition for any spiritual development of a nation"; he stresses that it is the historical task of Russia "to create a personality" (*sozdat' lichnost'*) (Kavelin 1989, 22–23). In a letter to Kavelin, Belinsky sadly observes that "the concept of personality is only in its infancy among us" (1978, 9:682). In an earlier letter to his friend, V. P. Botkin, Belinsky maintains that "*the human personality* (*chelovecheskaia lichnost'*) is now more sacred to me than history, more sacred than society, more sacred than mankind. This is the idea and the thought of our age!" (9:403; emphasis in original). Herzen devotes an entire chapter in his collection *From Another Shore* (1850), entitled "Omnia Mea Mecum Porto," to a passionate defense of individualism against the traditional accusations of pride and egoism. "It is slaves who are the least selfish," remarks Herzen bitterly (1954–66, 6:130), adding that love, which moralists usually oppose to individualism, can be as "dirty, beastly, and narrow" as egoism. Another collection by Herzen, *Caprices and Meditation* (1862) which unites three of his essays written in the 1840s, argues that it is one's duty to discard existing intellectual authority and to strive for moral and philosophical independence and autonomy. Even the conservative Russian critic Stepan Shevyrev admitted in his essay "A Russian Looks at the Contemporary Education in Europe" that the question of human personality became central to both literature and criticism and acknowledged that Western education owed its success to Western individualism (1841, 219–96).

Regardless of such admissions, Shevyrev's lead article for the newly founded magazine, *The Muscovite* (*Moskvitianin*) (1841) also contained the term "the rotting West," which would serve as a battle cry for all future conservative attacks on the West. Shevyrev, not surprisingly, attributed the main source of Western "rot" to the excesses born of the overdeveloped ego of unrestrained individual freedom.

The thrust of conservative attacks can be seen in an exchange between Belinsky and a conservative critic, S. Burachok. Echoing the views of Kant, Belinsky once remarked that "the purpose of man is man." This relatively anodyne and hardly original remark produced the following bitter response from Burachok: "it is a lie . . . there is only one road that leads man toward happiness: cast yourself out, take up your cross and follow Christ" (1840, 78). Writing in a government-sponsored journal, Burachok not only hypocritically propounded the ideals of Christian self-renunciation but also took part in a very disturbing and long-standing practice of the Russian government: appropriating the nation's most cherished religious ideals for the sake of political expedience. Burachok is clearly unaware of what George Fedotov reminded us in his discussion of the first Russian monastic saint, Theodosius: "A true kenotic, in imitation of Christ, humbles himself before the lowly, not before the powerful" (Fedotov 1975, 13).

The calls for self-renunciation found further articulation in the writings of the Slavophiles. Their leading theoretician, Aleksei Khomiakov, insisted that human personality was the product of sin and evil, and one's task, therefore, was to renounce it and cease being a separate individual:

> God wanted man to rely on the strength of his faith, and his love of the Savior, in order to renounce his personality, the personality of sin and evil, and embrace the sanctity and perfection of his Savior. United in such a way with Christ, man is not what he used to be; he is not a separate person, he is a member of the Church. (1994, 93)

Khomiakov's rhetoric is telling as it underscores the dominant Slavophile oppositions: the human personality is deemed inherently malicious and sinful; this isolated and lonely personality is opposed to the man who renounces his personality and becomes a member of the Church.

Khomiakov's association of a separate personality with sin and evil is one of the most important features of Russian anthropology. Richard Gustafson (1995) points out that one of the most influential Russian philosophers, Vladimir Solov'ev, attributed the very existence of separate individuals to original sin: "Original sin is caused by the individual's separation from God and results in the individual's separation from other individuals" (177). We are obviously dealing here with a rather persistent paradigm that Gustafson traces back to the works of Origen: "With Origen, then, 'we are not fallen because we are men; on the contrary, we are men because we are fallen'" (172). In support of Gustafson's observations one can refer to Solov'ev's third public speech on Dostoevsky's death:

> While the dark foundation of our nature, evil in its absolute selfishness, and mad in its striving to satisfy its egoism, to *relate everything to the self and to define everything through oneself*—while this dark foundation is present, not yet transformed—while *this original sin* is not vanquished, we cannot accomplish anything real, and the question of what is to be done does not make any sense. (Solov'ev 1988, 311; my emphasis)

Solov'ev grounds the humanistic interest in the self in original sin and predictably insists that this self has to be vanquished. Furthermore, he sees individual human enterprise as the perpetuation of the fallen condition, and easily dismisses human achievements as illusory and irrational. Similar examples of the religious basis of Russian anti-individualism can be found not only in the texts of Khomiakov and Solov'ev, but in the majority of Russian texts that discuss the issue of human personality. Berdiaev (1939) observes: "*egocentrism is the original sin of man,* the violation of the true relationship between self and other" (111; my emphasis). Berdiaev defines individualism as "isolation of the part from the whole or the revolt of the part against the whole" (114) and then interprets it as a form of slavery: "the individualist is a slave of oneself" (115). Lossky (1976) underscores the theological foundation of these views of the separate self: "It was only as a consequence of sin that these two first human persons became two separate natures; two individuals, with external relationships between them. . . . After *original sin human nature became divided,* split up, broken into many individuals" (123; my emphasis). Echoing the Slavophiles, Lossky insists that the only way for human nature to be restored lies through the unity of the Church: "We find in the Church the unity of our nature perpetually being realized, for the Church is more united than a collective totality. . . . Only in the Church can they [human beings] realize themselves in their true diversity" (108).

The Slavophile attitude toward separation suggests that any interest in or insistence on autonomy and separation are bound to be viewed as sinful if not demonic. Indeed, Slavophile-inspired ideology demonizes Peter the Great for separating "the people" (*narod*) from the gentry; demonizes reason for separating itself from "integral knowledge"; demonizes law for separating people from the unity of love; Protestantism for separating people from the Church; and individualism for separating people from each other.[13]

By giving voice to subconscious cultural attitudes and shaping future religious and philosophical discourses, the Slavophiles left a lasting impact on Russian thought: unity, integrity (*tsel'nost'*), organicity, fullness (*polnota*), and brotherhood would be associated with positive and Orthodox values; autonomy, separation, property, self, rationality, law, and the impersonal collective with demonic and Western ones. If one considers the persuasiveness and resonance of Slavophiles dichotomies, it will become clear that individualism in Russia was damned before it even appeared.

Slavophiles are obviously correct in their basic premise of human interconnectedness; as Aristotle maintained in his *Politics,* one who lives outside the community is either a beast or a God. Yet the Slavophiles' fixation on this basic fact, their exaggerated interest in visions of the past and future harmonies at the expense of concrete individual experience, was bound to take a utopian and fantastic turn. Leo Tolstoy, no stranger to the idealization of the peasant commune and communal values himself, nevertheless insisted in 1895 that "in a heap, in a crowd, or gathering only evil can be accomplished. Good is done only by each single person separately" (1935–64, 53:7). Tolstoy was also appalled by the utopian, unfounded, and essentially irrelevant concepts of the Slavophiles. In his 1872 letter to Strakhov he writes:

> I hate all these chorus principles [*khorovye nachala*] and structurings of life [*stroi zhizni*] and communes and brother-Slavs, invented one way or another. I simply love things definite, clear, beautiful, and balanced, and I find them in peasant poetry, language and life, and I find the opposite in our way of life. (61:278)

Tolstoy, it should be noted, echoes here Lermontov's own response to the Slavophiles: his lyrical poem, "Motherland" (*Rodina*) (1841).

One thing can be said about the Slavophiles: they were consistent; they defended their ideals and fought the evil they perceived. "The autonomy of the individual, they [the Slavophiles] argued, leads to the disintegration of society and condemns human beings to isolation and loneliness" (Walicki 1989, 446). Slavophiles believed that the true freedom and development of an individual could only be achieved within the unity of believers (*sobornost'*). Yet, according to Walicki, "the freedom allowed by this type of unity is therefore a freedom prior to the stage of individuation: not freedom of the individual, but of the social collective" (199).

The Slavophile attitude is a clear example of what Louis Dumont in his study of individualism defines as "holism"; that is, "an ideology that valorizes the social whole and neglects or subordinates the human individual" (1986, 279). The opposite of "holism" is the ideology of individualism, which Dumont sees as "a major feature in the configurations of features that constitutes modern ideology" (279). In his *German Ideology,* Dumont interprets various German Romantic theories as typical "holistic" responses toward modern civilization, and stresses the inevitable similarities between German ideology and all later responses to modernity:

> All the cultures that later came under the impact of modern civilization were, like the German, essentially holistic, and therefore either had to operate similar responses to individualism, or find the German recipes ready at hand to help them. The success of the ethnic theory of the nation is thus no mystery nor, more specifically, is the reception of Herder among the Slavs of Central Europe, and the respective vogue of Schiller, Schelling, and Hegel in successive phases of Russian intellectual history in the nineteenth century. (1994, 26)[14]

Summarizing the polemics of the period, Walicki observes: "criticism of Western individualism—more primitive than that of the Slavophiles but founded on similar premises—was a cornerstone of all conservative doctrines during the reign of Nicholas." He then adds an observation that sheds light on Lermontov's predicament: "particular hostility—downright hatred at times—was shown to Lermontov, whose work was felt to embody individualism in its most arrogant and challenging form" (1989, 358).

By transforming the polemic over the duties and responsibilities of the individual into a discussion of the utopian harmony achieved by the human person within a peasant commune (*mir*) or religious community (*sobor-*

nost'), the Slavophiles neglected one of the burning issues of the day: the nature of everyday human behavior in contemporary society. Ginzburg (1977) puts it this way: "The Slavophile outlook included radical anti-individualism; therefore their circle could not spell out the problems of the contemporary reflexive personality" (39). Lermontov, however, was interested precisely in contemporary personality, as his novel *A Hero of Our Time* amply testifies. It is against the reigning attitudes toward the individual that one should consider Lermontov's position as articulated in *A Hero of Our Time:* "the history of a human soul, be it even the meanest soul, can hardly be less curious or less instructive, than the history of an entire nation—especially when it is the result of self-observation on the part of a mature mind" (63).

It is no coincidence that the Slavophiles were scandalized by Lermontov's antagonistic and self-asserting hero. One of the leading Slavophiles, Iuri Samarin, commented on Lermontov's death: "He owed a huge debt—his novel, *Hero of Our Time.* It had to be paid, and Lermontov, by going forward and abandoning his selfish self-reflection, would have paid and would have comforted many. Now nobody can repay it" (quoted in Gershtein 1941, 122). Obviously, by the debt, Samarin understood the damage done to Russian society by the presentation of a complex, contradictory, yet appealing protagonist, a man of autonomous and independent character, capable of both good and evil. Samarin's complaint was rather premature, however; if nothing else, Russian writers, including Dostoevsky, repaid Lermontov's debt in full, as they produced and dutifully condemned a whole gallery of autonomous, independent, and destructive individuals.

LERMONTOV AND HEROISM

Lermontov's work was immediately hailed by Belinsky as the expression of the dominant mood of the period because his lyric poetry provided the Russian public with a voice to express its sense of loss, despair, and disorientation. The greatest poem of Lermontov's early period, "Angel" (1831), describes an angel carrying a soul from heaven down into "the world of grief and tears" (*dlia mira pechali i slez*) (1:233). Although Lermontov started his career as a poet of loss, he did not remain an elegiac poet for long: his heroes do not merely contemplate or lament their losses, but confront them with energy and resoluteness. Indeed, already in his earliest prose text, the unfinished historical novel *Vadim,* Lermontov draws a clear opposition between active heroes and resigned observers: "Nowadays, the life of young people takes the form of thought, rather than action; there are no heroes, but there are too many observers" (4:180).

Lermontov's heroes refuse to remain observers. The actions through which they come to terms with their losses and with the universe that produces them defines the degree of their heroism. By the end of the century perceptive critics, like the populist N. M. Mikhailovsky in an essay on Lermontov aptly entitled "The Hero of Meaningless Time" (*Geroi bezvremen'ia,* 1891), recognized Lermontov's program of articulating a heroic personality for this period of repression and resignation: "If we start looking for the main motif in Lermontov's poetry, for that central point that preoccupied him most frequently and thoroughly, and to which the majority if not all of his texts can be directly or indirectly reduced, we'll find it in the realm of heroism" (1989, 414).

In his 1842 letter to Belinsky, Vassily Botkin, one of the few defenders of the middle class in Russia, makes the following estimation of Lermontov's impact upon Russian art, utilizing Shevyrev's connection of Western putrefaction to the advances of individualism: "It is through Lermontov that the spirit of 'European rot' appeared in Russian art for the first time. The essential inner unity of his art consists in the rejection of all patriarchy, authority, tradition, and existing societal conventions and connections" (Botkin 1984, 246). Botkin recognizes that Lermontov rejects "the spirit and worldview created in the Middle Ages; in other words, of the existing social organization" (246). It is curious that Botkin connects Lermontov's program with the attack upon the Russian Middle Ages, equating Lermontov's role with that played by the doctrines of individualism in the West. Lermontov, however, not only questioned traditional rules of conduct; he also explored new forms and principles of behavior based on the core values and ideals of individualism: autonomy, privacy, and self-development.

Early traumatic experiences (the death of his mother and separation from his father) left Lermontov vulnerable to images of evil, loss, alienation, and exile developed in Western Romanticism. The story of the fallen angel, or demon, who experienced the loss of paradise firsthand and is destined to be punished by God, was an important myth for Lermontov; it certainly supplied the poet with rich literary material. Lermontov opens his major narrative poem, "The Demon" (1838), on which he worked for almost a decade, with the theme of the Fall, with the Demon's exile and separation. Lermontov thus remains within the parameters set by Russian tradition, which sees separation and alienation as inexorably connected to the Fall. Yet, rather than bemoaning it or fantasizing ways of escape, the poet explores its inevitability. Paradise is doomed to remain lost for all of Lermontov's protagonists. How does one live in the present state of alienation and separation? How does one deal with other individuals? What choices does one make and on what grounds?

"The Demon" reveals the paradigmatic predicament of an individual: loneliness and anxiety caused by the memory of lost bliss is coupled with an awareness of the stifling confinement of the present. Both protagonists of the poem, the Demon and Tamara, feel stifled and frustrated in their worlds. Yet, similar to Lermontov's other protagonists, neither of them is willing to side with God as a means of overcoming their anxiety. Although she enters a convent, Tamara fails to find an escape from her inner tension, from her attraction to and fear of the Demon. It is only through a song that she finally expresses and overcomes her inner turmoil. The Demon, on the other hand, in his attempt to recover a "lost paradise," resorts to a tragic solution, echoed in other Lermontov texts as well: he strives to resolve his anxiety of loss and separation through love, in this case through possession of Tamara, but it leads only to her destruction. The poem is specific in its criticism of the hero's destructiveness, a destructiveness caused by the protagonist's investing erotic love with the potential for salvation. Lermontov's poem discloses the reasons behind the Demon's tragedy: the urgent need to recover lost bliss coupled with artistic fruitlessness. Lermontov underscores this fruitlessness by making the Demon compose a trite and primitive love song. The combination of aesthetic blindness with rebellion makes the Demon capable only of destruction.

Lermontov, as we see, is well aware of the potentially tragic consequences of blind self-assertion. Unlike the Enlighteners, Lermontov embraces the complex, contradictory, and precarious position of the individual, seeing his freedom as a tragic fate. Yet, he leaves it to other Russian writers to condemn the demonism, narcissism, and rebellion of an overdeveloped personality. The first major text that Lermontov published, "The Song of Tsar Ivan Vassilyevich, His Young Oprichnik, and the Stout-hearted Merchant Kalashnikov" (1837), constructs a self-reliant, independent hero and glorifies his defense of integrity, autonomy, and privacy.

In this poem Lermontov presents an emblematic heroic act: Kalashnikov challenges the external norms of society and religion on the basis of his own inner principles of honor and integrity. He challenges and kills the *oprichnik* Kirebeevich (who insulted his wife) and then refuses to disclose the motives for his action to the tsar.

By presenting a bourgeois character, who is noble and independent, Lermontov shows his true insight in the social, economic, and political dimensions of individualism. The merchant Kalashnikov is preoccupied with his property, yet he also guards his honor and integrity. The defense of property and the defense of self go hand in hand, suggests the poet, as opposed to numerous Russian opponents of private property.

Kalashnikov deliberately refuses to appeal to the two acknowledged authorities of Russian society: God and Tsar, rulers of heaven and earth. Without being a rebel against either of them, Kalashnikov disregards their commands. He posits personal truth as a legitimate contender among the truths of society and religion and asserts his right to live and act according to the laws of his own conscience. Having killed his enemy he responds to the tsar's inquiry: "I have killed him of my own free will; but why I did it, I shall not disclose to you, only to God" (*Ia ubil ego vol'noi voleiu, a za chto, pro chto ne skazhu tebe, a skazhu tol'ko Bogu edinomu*) (2:18). Even if Kalashnikov's words echo Christ's answer to the Pharisees, "Render therefore unto Caesar the things that are Caesar's; and unto God the things that are God's" (Matt. 22:21), Kalashnikov's independent actions and proud answer seem to add to Christ's maxim: "But I shall also render unto myself the things which are mine." Kalashnikov, who views his honor-driven actions as a fight for truth; who insists on the personal administration of justice and speaks truthfully with the tsar; and yet who refuses to explain the reasons behind his actions, is Lermontov's equivalent of the Declaration of Independence. The very suggestion that such reasons might lie outside the tsar's domain is surely a bold and almost unprecedented defense of the right to privacy in a country pervaded by "all-seeing eyes, and all-hearing ears" (1:76) and still shaken by the intrusive interrogations of the tsar and his committee and the rapid surrender of the Decembrists. Kalashnikov's actions, however, are rewarded only with a nameless grave. His claim to individuality is symbolically obliterated. However, the poem says that Kalashnikov's fate inspires the songs of wandering singers; that is, Lermontov's own song. The poet makes it his task to commemorate Kalashnikov's courageous actions, his heroic ability to preserve dignity and integrity, while navigating between all-out surrender and all-out rebellion.

Along with the depiction of heroic conduct, Lermontov attacks behavior that is blatantly nonheroic, that is, weak, impersonal, or irresponsible. Lermontov wrote at a time of almost universal fear, falsehood, and self-denial, occasioned by post-Decembrist repression and its subsequent social trauma. In his first major completed work, the drama *The Masquerade* (1835), Lermontov contrasts an independent powerful individual, Arbenin, to his society, that is, to a group of nonindividuals who flaunt their socially accepted masks and are incapable of expressing, let alone defending, their personality and their right to develop it.

The metaphor of masquerade that Lermontov constructs in this play is one of the governing metaphors of his art. Lermontov's hostility toward masks and role-playing is directly connected to his interest in the issues of heroism and individualism. The search for a hero and the attacks on masquerade are Lermontov's responses to a cultural conflict that seems to have become a permanent feature of Russian life: the conflict between "civilization and slavery" (Herzen 1954–66, 7:205), that is, between the values and ideology inspired by the West and the repressive reality of Russia. In the particular case of Lermontov's period, the liberating and individualistic values of Romanticism collided with post-Decembrist Russian oppression, creating a tension that was difficult to resolve. Trying to appear as free and progressive Europeans on the one hand, and obedient God- and tsar-loving Russians on the other, the educated Russian public resorted to an endless masquerade that encompassed not only social or political, but also intellectual spheres.

The Masquerade reveals Lermontov's two-pronged approach toward the representation of his society. The author includes several characters who make the concept of "our time" real and tangible, creating a background against which an independent, self-reliant, though violent protagonist becomes a hero. In other words, it is Arbenin's peers' involvement in lies and secret manipulations, their failure to question and modify what they are doing, that underscores Arbenin's heroism. However, Arbenin exemplifies an important paradox: while proudly rejecting the evil that he sees around him, he remains incapable of discerning any other force in the universe and so ends up embracing it. The play thus explores themes that were to remain central to Lermontov: mask-wearing and self-effacement, the resulting social ills on the one hand and the protagonist's "trial by evil" on the other.

Arbenin acknowledges evil's omnipresence: "I saw evil everywhere, yet, being proud, did not bow down to it" (3:39). According to him the world consists of ruthless and manipulative players (*igroki*) and their victims or playthings (*igrushki*). He tries to make his way through it by refusing to side with anyone. Likewise, Pechorin seeks a middle ground between master and slave, while Kalashnikov and the Demon navigate between the extremes of rebellion and surrender. Such a search for a middle ground points unequivocally to the relevance of Lermontov's thought; the articulation of such a middle ground of conduct is all the more important for a culture in which passion for the extreme is almost proverbial.

The Masquerade testified to the close connection between Lermontov's thought and the plight of contemporary society. Even though his view of it was rather pessimistic—"with sadness do I look at my generation," declared the speaker of the 1838 poem "Meditation" (*Duma*)—he was not ready to give up on it, at least not yet. *A Hero of Our Time* responds to a pressing problem of his day: how to exercise freedom and individuality in a society that has lost its traditional rules of conduct, yet is hostile to any manifestation of independence and personal choice.

In the chapter devoted to the longest tale of the novel, "Princess Mary," I examine the fundamental tragedy of Pechorin's time, epitomized by Pechorin's opponent, Grushnitsky: the refusal of post-Decembrist Russian society to confront its predicament with honesty and courage, hiding instead behind the masks and illusions of heroism and freedom created by epigones of Romantic literature (Alexander Marlinsky, in particular). I address the meteoric rise of Marlinsky and explore the cultural phenomenon of *marlinism;* that is, a mode of cultural behavior that supported and nourished blindness and pandered to immaturity, naive theatricality, and refusal to remain oneself. I demonstrate how Pechorin's attack on the human propensity to approach life with closed eyes, in the manner of Grushnitsky, finds its parallel in Lermontov's own attack on the cultural ills of his society.

Clearly I take seriously Lermontov's characterization of Pechorin as a "hero of our time" and try to bring Pechorin back to the critical discussion from which he has been too quickly dismissed by the moralizing tendencies of his many commentators: these include not only the Slavophiles and other religious thinkers but also the majority of the giants of Russian literature. Indeed, the readiness with which such authors as Turgenev (Luchinov in "Three Portraits" or Teglev in "Knock . . . Knock . . . Knock . . ."), Dostoevsky (the Underground Man and Stavrogin in *The Possessed*), Tolstoy (Dolokhov in *War and Peace*), or Anton Chekhov (Solyonyi in *The Three Sisters*) parody Pechorin's worst qualities without sufficiently analyzing the complexity of his character, or the message behind it, reveals in my view not so much the moral superiority of Pechorin's critics, but rather a blind spot in Russian culture.[15]

In the chapter devoted to the last tale of *A Hero of Our Time*, "The Fatalist," I explore the heroic dimension of Pechorin's conduct, his revolutionary combination of skepticism, sober evaluation of circumstances, resoluteness, and self-reliance. Pechorin risks his life not to test fate, but because he feels the need to prevent the execution of a dishonorable act against others: the slaughter of a son before his mother's eyes. Even though Lermontov condemns Pechorin's cruelty, and presents his plight as essentially tragic, as leading nowhere but to idle and cruel pursuits, he cannot help admiring his relentless self-scrutiny, his refusal to adapt to laws that go against his principles. Although skeptical about all traditional moral and religious doctrines, Pechorin nevertheless, acting on his own accord, chooses good and acknowledges his obligations toward others. That fact alone flies in the face of many pious condemnations of individualism, and its alleged connections to amoralism and selfishness.

Furthermore, I approach "The Fatalist" as a parable that contains Lermontov's warning against preoccupation with metaphysical or universal schemes, hopes, or illusions when confronted by concrete choices and concrete manifestations of evil. The tale's blindly courageous protagonist, Vulich, fails to notice a slaughtered pig and runs headlong to his death at the hands of a drunken Cossack destroying everything in his path. This was meant as a warning to Lermontov's contemporaries who refused to see what was under their nose, preferring to ignore the brutality and violence taking place in front of them yet who spent a considerable amount of energy studying and promoting Schellingism, Hegelianism, *sobornost'*, and other utopian schemes.

It should be noted here that the majority of Lermontov's protagonists fail in their proud desire not to bow down to evil but rather to find a way of avoiding the traditional extremes of victim and victimizer. Arbenin, Pechorin, and the Demon eventually surrender to evil, taking the aggressive side of the equation. Lermontov not only explains the reason for such a decision; more important he articulates the only possible way of confronting evil and resolving the hated extremes that all of his protagonists must face. I refer to the response of the lyrical persona in Lermontov's 1829 poem, "A Letter" (*Pis'mo*): "everything has betrayed me; poison is everywhere; only the sound of the lyre has been faithful to me" (*vse izmenilo mne, vezde otravy, lish liry zvuk mne neizmenen byl*) (1:101). Lermontov's characters inevitably find themselves in a world of evil. In the cases of Arbenin, Pechorin, or the Demon, it is pride and honor that they use as a bulwark against evil; in the case of the persona of "A Letter," it is "the sound of the lyre."

Analysis of Lermontov's oeuvre reveals that it is precisely the reality of harmonious sounds that constitutes a possibility of redemption, containing a secret knowledge of the world's lost harmony. Lermontov began to view art—that is, the awareness of and participation in the aesthetic dimension of existence—as the only tangible means of resolving inner turmoil and integrating the collapsed fabric of the universe.

Even though all of them strive to conduct themselves with integrity, self-reliance, and courage, Lermontov's heroes differ drastically in two separate yet related ways: their artistic sensibility, and their attitudes toward other individuals. They range from the likes of Arbenin and the Demon, who easily resort to evil and violence, to Mtsyri ("Mtsyri," 1839), who flatly rejects any imposition of himself upon others. The tragic denouements of Lermontov's major texts, whether *The Masquerade*, "The Demon," or *A Hero of Our Time*, reveal that pride, strength, and independence prove destructive if they are not moderated by aesthetic experience, by "the sound of the lyre." The orphan and exile Mtsyri yearns for his lost motherland and is tormented by the same anxieties as the Demon or Pechorin. Mtsyri, however, learns to accept his losses courageously and stoically and declines to try to recover them through external possession or aggression. Lermontov makes it clear that Mtsyri's stoicism and integrity are sustained by his artistic sensibility. Mtsyri's aesthetic experiences during his escape allow him temporarily to regain lost bliss, and thus give him strength and courage to persevere till the end.

Lermontov's ultimate hero, therefore, is Mtsyri, a character whose precarious balance between self-assertion and continuous rejection of evil is sustained by his artistic nature. Although many of Lermontov's heroes must face the same choices, only Mtsyri manages to achieve a balance as he both literally and figuratively travels the narrow path between extremes. In the figure of Mtsyri, Lermontov manages to solve the puzzle, to fuse his demand for heroic individuality with his poetic demand for nondestructiveness. Mtsyri's whole life is heroic (and that is why it is so short, one might add): he stoically and courageously confronts a cruel fate and manifests his heroism by combining activity and detachment, energy and nonviolence, lack of faith and transcendence.

Commenting on the terrifying and self-perpetuating symbiosis between tyranny and the suppression of individualism, Norbert Elias, a leading scholar on individualism, writes:

> Among the peculiarities of a dictatorial regime is the development of a specific social make-up in the individuals living under the regime. They are highly attuned to external control and often feel disorientated at first if this weakens or disappears. As personal initiative, the individual capacity to make decisions, is less socially rewarded in the framework of such a state, and perhaps disapproved of or even punished, such a regime often has a self-perpetuating character. The people living in this structure are often made more or less insecure, get into conflict with their consciences, when required in one way or another to show a greater degree of self-regulation. Their social make-up makes them tend involuntarily to re-establish the familiar external control, as by a strong leader. (1991, 181)

With this in mind, it would seem all the more necessary to heed those thinkers and writers who attempt to provide a groundwork for the healthy development of individualism; who refuse to appeal to any outside authority; who promote reliance upon inner resources and principles, thus contributing to a native tradition capable of putting an end to the self-perpetuating cycle described by Elias.[16] Seen from the perspective of Russia's persistent attempts to disregard the values of individualism, to promote the public over the private sphere, to reduce the individual to a function within the social hierarchy, or to concoct utopian schemes of universal happiness in the face of concrete abuse of the most basic human rights, Lermontov's own independence, his depiction of proud, autonomous, and self-reliant characters, is in itself heroic.

The paucity of legitimate models of behavior in a time of confusion, disorientation, and persecution makes Lermontov's contribution to Russian culture all the more significant. His literary representation of various heroes introduced the Russian public to the only models of behavior lying outside the usual paradigms of religious humility, resignation, or wholesale revolt. Lermontov seems to suggest that it is dangerous, futile, and dishonest for an individual—particularly within the Russian context—to fall back on ready-made formulas of obedience, service, and self-renunciation. On the other hand, the call for rebellion frequently denies the individual's responsibility toward others. Instead of such destructive extremes Lermontov advocates behavior based on individual choices, while insisting that such choices should be made on the grounds of inner principles of conscience and integrity. Just as Lermontov rose to the occasion and provided an immediate and brilliant poetic response to Russia's tragic loss of Alexander Pushkin ("Death of the

Poet" [*Smert' poeta*], 1837), so did he respond to his age's urgent need for heroes who embody and celebrate the values of individualism. Thus we can claim him to be not only Russia's greatest Romantic poet, or the father of Russian psychological prose, but also a courageous and consistent promoter and defender of the doctrine that for better or for worse defines modernity itself.

Chapter Two

"The Demon": How Not to Regain Paradise Lost

Мой юный ум бывало возмущал
Могучий образ! меж иных виденй,
Как царь, немой и гордый, он сиял
Такой волшебносладкой красотою,
Что было страшно. . . .
Но я, расставшись с прочими мечтами,
И от него отделался стихмаи!

(My youthful mind used to be excited by a powerful image! He stood out among other visions, like a tsar, silent and proud, and shone with such miraculously sweet beauty that it was frightening. . . . Yet, having parted with other dreams, I also got rid of him through poetry.)
—Lermontov, "Fairy Tale for Children" (1841)

LERMONTOV'S POEM AND LITERARY TRADITION

Fascination with demonism revived during the Romantic period. Many Romantic poets identified poetry with rebellion, exile, and loss, and, in turn, rebellion and exile with Satan.[1] Satan became a patron saint of poetry, and Blake seems to express the dominant attitude toward poetry in his evaluation of Milton: "The reason Milton wrote in fetters when he wrote of Angels and God, and at liberty when of Devils and Hell, is because he was a true Poet, and of the Devil's party without knowing it" ("Marriage of Heaven and Hell").

Lermontov was no exception to this. After he read Lermontov's celebrated narrative poem "The Demon," Grand Prince Michael Romanov noted: "Before we had the Italian Beelzebub, the English Lucifer, the German Mephistopheles, now the Russian Demon has appeared. Well, there is increase in the forces of evil." He adds, with a rather surprising malice, "one thing is unclear to me, who was invented by whom: the Spirit of Evil by Lermontov or Lermontov by the Spirit of Evil" (quoted in Gershtein 1986, 73).

For all its negativity, the Grand Prince's statement proved somewhat prophetic: it foreshadowed two strands of criticism of the poem. Most work on "The Demon" is primarily concerned with placing the poem among European diabolic fiction, or with addressing the origins of Lermontov's own demonism. Curiously, the charge that Lermontov is a demonic creature is echoed even by such illustrious writers as Dostoevsky and Vladimir Solov'ev.[2]

Lermontov clearly operates within the culture of his period. His most frequently cited Western precursors include Milton's *Paradise Lost,* Goethe's *Faust,* Thomas Moore's "The Loves of the Angels," Byron's "Cain," and Alfred de Vigny's "Eloa." His debt to the Western tradition of literary demonism has been extensively explored in Russian and Soviet scholarship.[3] Merely cataloguing the myriad connections of Lermontov's poem with these works does little to elucidate the design and execution of Lermontov's poem, or the relevance of "The Demon" to Lermontov's thought and art.

As if to signal that "The Demon" differs from its more philosophical precursors, preoccupied with theology and metaphysics, Lermontov drastically narrows the focus of his poem. Its plot is a love story, with the subtitle "An Oriental Tale"; thus the exotic and erotic dimensions of "The Demon" are underlined, echoing both Byron's Orientalist love stories and the traditional Russian Romantic poem, which usually centers on a love conflict. In "The Demon" this conflict is characterized by the presence of two centers, the Demon and Tamara, each with a specfic role and agenda. The tension between these two characters, their mutual attraction, and their peculiar ways of responding to such an attraction, give the poem its unique character.[4]

Both Byron and Alfred de Vigny subtitled their poems "Cain" and "Eloa" "mysteries," thus referring to the medieval literary genre using oppositions—God and Devil, good and evil—in order to externalize and dramatize the problem of human choice. By contrast, in Lermontov's poem, the conflict is internalized. The Demon is placed in a murky domain confounding traditional oppositions:

То не был ангел небожитель,
Её божественный хранитель. . . .
То не был ада дух ужасный,
Порочный мученик—о нет!
Он был похож на вечер ясный:
Ни день, ни ночь,—ни мрак, ни свет!
(2:55)

(He was not an angel, a guardian from above who lives in heaven. Nor was he a terrible spirit of hell, a sinful sufferer—Oh, no! He resembled a transparent evening: neither a day nor night; neither darkness, nor light.)

The Demon is presented both as victim and victimizer, enabling Lermontov to explore psychological tensions and scrutinize individual choices that one makes among contradictory drives, desires, and values that confound the traditional division between good and evil, spiritual and material.[5]

The creative history of Lermontov's poem testifies that his stress was on the explosive interplay of good and evil within the Demon himself. In that sense, it is revealing to contrast Lermontov's poem with Alfred de Vigny's "Eloa" (1822), as it is to this poem that Lermontov himself compared his creation. De Vigny's Satan does not undergo any changes in the poem; its main focus is on Eloa and her infinite compassion and the fall that results from it. Lermontov, on the other hand, does not make Tamara the main protagonist of his poem, even though Tamara clearly grows in prominence as Lermontov's work on the poem progresses.

Lermontov's contemporaries were perhaps more attuned than we are to this focus on the Demon's inner struggle, the oscillation of his mood, and its tragic outcome. For instance, Lermontov's friend Shan-Girei objected to the presence of the angel in the poem and the implication that it was the angel's hasty interference that prevented the Demon from turning to good:

> I suggested another plan: to deny the Demon any intention of repentance and resurrection, to let him act directly with the purpose of destroying the soul of the sacred hermit [Tamara]. "Your plan," said Lermontov, "is not bad, but it sounds too much like *Eloa, Soeur des anges* by Alfred de Vigny. Anyway, let's think about it. We'll hold off with publishing 'The Demon' for now." (1989, 47)

Lermontov has a point. Without the Demon's emotional oscillations the poem would be, indeed, like "Eloa."

It is thus difficult to see "The Demon" as a manifestation of Lermontov's so-called "wrestling with God" (*bogoborchestvo*), as critics who approach Lermontov from a religious perspective usually claim. These critics, among whom Solov'ev is prominent, seem to attack the demons of the Christian tradition rather than the Demon of Lermontov's making. Lermontov's Demon is less concerned with God and his creation than he is with Tamara, with the angel, or with himself. His falling out with God took place in the past, outside the scope of the poem; this enmity does not define the Demon's existence, as, say, Satan's enmity toward God defines his subversive activity in Milton's *Paradise Lost.* Lermontov's protagonists are not concerned with arguing about the origins of the world's evil, as are Lucifer and Cain in Byron's "Cain." Censorship, ecclesiastic censorship in particular, would surely put a stop to it; however, for Lermontov and his protagonists an evil universe seems to be the point of departure rather than the final result of an argument. Rather than debating whether God's universe is indeed evil and why, Lermontov focuses on concrete questions of existence in such a world. In other words the focus of the poem is the exploration of an inner psychological conflict rather than cosmic and metaphysical ones.[6] Lermontov's poem scrutinizes the manifestations of such internal conflict and explores various ways of resolving it.

Even less convincing than a metaphysical reading is a social one, which casts the Demon as a revolutionary opposed to the tyranny of the tsar.[7] Both readings, are, in fact, closely related, and often appear together, as both interpret the Demon as a rebel against some sort of external ruler. Surely, the Demon by his very nature presupposes rebellion, but the theme of rebellion is neither stressed nor developed in the poem. Infrequent references to knowledge, doubt, and negation seem almost perfunctory. They present a tribute to the tradition rather than a sustained argument. It is difficult to see any veiled condemnation of the stifling atmosphere of Russia under Nicholas I in this psychologically charged love story. Lermontov could be explicit and direct in his criticism of Russia's political and social situation, as many of his other works attest.

Thus, instead of reiterating Lermontov's indebtedness to his cultural environment, I propose to concentrate on certain salient features of "The Demon" and to explain them in the context of Lermontov's psychic and philosophical makeup. The Demon, tormented by the memory of an irrevocably lost paradisiacal bliss, exists in a world in which he is doomed to suffer. Lermontov's poem is a unique and provocative study of life dominated by a pervasive sense of loss. It explores not only the causes but also the manifestations of this powerful emotion: malice, anxiety, eroticism, and creativity. The Demon views his universe as the desert, a place of misery and exile: "being exiled long ago, he wandered in the desert of the world without a refuge" (*davno otverzhennyi bluzhdal v pustyne mira bez priiuta*) (2:45). Both he and Tamara find themselves in a typical individualistic predicament—in psychological and physical exile, alienated from traditional systems of values and looking for some new guiding principles. Their conduct contains the paradigmatic choices that would be echoed by Lermontov's other heroes.

Lermontov explores two drastically different ways of confronting one's sense of alienation and loss. A creative and artistic response, at least temporarily, transcends a painful existence and provides spiritual nourishment and encouragement. That seems to be Tamara's solution. The Demon's solution, however, is different: he hopes to regain the state of former bliss through erotic possession. This solution is futile, also destructive, but nonetheless, very appealing: Arbenin, Pechorin, and numerous heroes of Lermontov's lyric poetry tend to resort to it. In other words, "The Demon" contains an insight explored in all of Lermontov's mature works: that people, depending on personality, and particularly on aesthetic sensibility, act differently even if they share similar losses, anxieties, and pessimistic outlooks.

DEMONIC TRANSFORMATIONS

Even though Lermontov worked on "The Demon" for almost a decade, expanding it, changing the setting, and switching from poetry to prose and back, the plot remained the same.[8] The Demon falls in love with a woman and is ready to declare his love, renounce his old ways, and embrace the good again, but on his way to the woman's room, he encounters her guardian angel. The encounter angers him so much that he decides to seduce and destroy the heroine. The confrontation with the angel and its disastrous consequences are a central part of the plot.

Regardless of Romanticism's tendency to reverse traditional associations of good with God and evil with Satan, demonic malice remains an attribute of Lermontov's Demon, as it had been through the centuries of Christianity. Malice and anger, awakened by the encounter with the angel, are present in all variants of the poem. Rather than exposing the Demon's evil, as required by the Christian tradition, or redefining it as good, as suggested by the Romantic one, Lermontov explores how and why the Demon's malice is awakened by his encounter with good.

It is curious that Lermontov's friend A. Shan-Girei vehemently denies that it is the appearance of the angel that sets the Demon off, and claims that Lermontov could not have even entertained such an idea:

> The idea turned out to be one that—it is ridiculous to say—the author did not even entertain. Indeed, let's recall the stanza:
>
> And he enters, ready to love,
> With his soul open to good . . . etc.
>
> Isn't it true that on such an occasion the Prince de Talleyrand would have had to repeat to the heavenly police his: "*surtout pas trop de zèle, Messieurs!*" The messenger of paradise picked the wrong time to defend Tamara from a danger that did not exist, and by that faux pas he prevented the Demon's resurrection. . . . Lermontov could not have entertained such an immoral idea. (1989, 47)

Shan-Girei's denial suggests, in fact, that he grasps the problem of the poem better than many critics, who fail to pay attention to the momentous and fatal interference of the angel. Why is the angel present in all the variants of the poem? What aspects of the Demon does this encounter reveal?

Malice is not the Demon's dominant feature. His usual state is one of boredom. When the Demon is first introduced, Lermontov stresses emptiness and indifference rather than active evil and hostility. The Demon himself realizes that he cannot be defined by evil. He complains that he is doomed "to try to hate everything, but to despise everything instead" (*starat'sia vse voznenavidet', i vse na svete prezirat'*" (2:62). Like Arbenin or Pechorin, the Demon becomes bored in the absence of worthy competition: "while ruling the petty earth, he planted evil without any joy. He did not encounter any resistance to his skills, and thus evil became boring to him" (*nichtozhnoi vlastvuia zemlei, on seial zlo bez naslazhdenia. Nigde iskusstvu svoemu on ne vstrechal soprotivlenia—i zlo naskuchilo emu*) (2:45).[9]

Such perennial boredom, however, must be interrupted, and this gives "The Demon" its initial impetus. Paradoxically, and in spite of Shan-Girei's protests, the Demon's malice is awakened only after his exposure to goodness. Transported by Tamara's song, the Demon feels an upsurge of love for her. On his way to her room, however, the Demon sees her guardian angel. Rivalry with the angel awakens in the Demon what in the text is called "an ancient hatred" (*starinnaia nenavist'*) (2:60), so that he decides to destroy Tamara and succeeds in doing so. Thus, the encounter with the angel brings to the surface the Demon's hatred and aggression; it also reveals the origin of these feelings and their connection with the most noble strivings and passions.

When Dostoevsky's Underground Man, incapable of overcoming his aggressive, hostile impulses, declares that "they don't let . . . I cannot be . . . good!" (1972–90, 5:175), he seems to be complaining of the predicament familiar to Lermontov's Demon. Dostoevsky was only partially correct when he claims: "Only I alone presented the tragedy of the underground that consists in torment, self-punishment, and striving toward something better, yet an inability to achieve it" (16:329). Lermontov had explored the psychological dynamics of underground malice long before Dostoevsky and clearly influenced him.

As if to underscore the Demon's paradoxical transformation of good into evil, Lermontov echoes it on two other occasions in his poem. When the Demon first sees Tamara, he is transformed by her dance. The next few sections, however, prefigure the fatal confrontation with the angel. Tamara has a bridegroom, and the Demon sets up a fight between him and robbers, who kill him. The poem ends with one more encounter with the angel. The angel takes Tamara's soul to heaven but the Demon appears and claims her: "And proudly, in his mad daring he says: 'She is mine'" (*I gordo v derzosti bezumnoi on govorit: "Ona moia!*) (2:71). The Demon's enmity and malice fix his face, which becomes immobile. At this moment his oscillation between good and evil ends:

Но, Боже!—Кто б его узнал?
Каким смотрел он злобным взглядом,
Как полон был смертельным ядом
Вражды, не знающей конца,—
И веяло могильным хладом
От неподвижного лица

(2:71)

(But, heavens, who would have recognized him? How malicious was his gaze, how full of the deadly poison of animosity that knows no end. And a gravelike cold wafted from his immobile face.)

Thus the final version of the poem features three transformations of the Demon, all of which follow the same pattern: a resurgence of love and goodness is reversed by an encounter with a rival. All the variants of the poem include a confrontation with the angel. In the very first unfinished version, which dates from 1829, the Demon's recollections of his happy state are interrupted by the following prose statement: "The Demon finds that the angel loves a mortal girl. The Demon learns about it and seduces her, so that she leaves the angel" (2:416). What is peculiar in this scenario is that the Demon becomes interested in the girl only after learning that the angel is interested in her. But on the next page of the same draft, the conflict takes its final form: the Demon falls in love with a mortal girl, then, just prior to his declaration of love "the Demon sees her guardian angel and decides to destroy her because of his envy and hatred" (2:417). From that variant onward the shape of the conflict does not change.[10]

It is thus a paradoxical reaction to good rather than a consistent evil that constitutes Lermontov's Demon. In that respect, Lermontov's Demon is closer to the demons of the Christian tradition than to those of Milton and Romanticism. The famous episode at Gerasenes, when Christ encounters a man possessed by "an unclean spirit" who manifests an aggressive and violent reaction toward Jesus (Mark 5:2) typifies the demonic response to goodness in that tradition. Lermontov presents the Demon's encounter with the angel in the same biblical terms: "and the ray of heavenly light suddenly illuminated *the unclean gaze*" (*i luch bozhestvennogo sveta vdrug osvetil nechistyi vzor*) (2:60; my emphasis).

THE DEMON AND LOSS

The tension and complexity of Lermontov's poem depends on the mystery of the Demon's transformation. What is it that causes the Demon, ready to love, whose feelings of goodness were awakened (*i vnov' postignul on sviatyniu liubvi, dobra i krasoty*) (2:49) to turn into a Satanic creature?

The contest with the angel foregrounds the source of evil in the Demon. The angel warns: "Do not set your criminal trail to my love, to my holy one" (*k moei liubvi, k moei sviatyne ne prolagai prestupnyi sled*) (2:60) and provokes the following reaction:

Зарделся ревностию взгляд;
И вновь в душе его проснулся
Старинной ненависти яд.
Она моя!—сказал он громко.
Оставь ее, она моя. . . .
Здесь больше нет твоей святыни,
Здесь я владею и люблю.

(2:60)

(Jealousy set his gaze on fire, and the poison of ancient hatred reawakened in his soul. She is mine—he declared loudly. Leave her, she is mine. . . . There is no place here for your veneration; here, I possess and love.)

The Demon's "here, I possess" stresses his painful awareness that there are other domains where he does not possess. The angel awakens in the Demon "the poison of ancient hatred." The ancient character of his enmity suggests that it has roots deeper than a competition for a beautiful woman. It puts the Demon's rivalry with the angel in terms of their first struggle; that is, the struggle for paradise.

As if to clarify the origins of "the ancient hatred," the Demon refers later to his "ancient wound." He declares to Tamara that ever since he saw her "grief stirred at the bottom of an ancient wound like a snake" (*i grust' na dne starinnoi rany zashevelilasia kak zmei*) (2:61). The image of a disturbed and potentially dangerous snake suggests the rhythm of the Demon's emotions: love and beauty cause sadness, awaken the wound, and result in aggression.[11] What is this "ancient wound" underlying the Demon's contradictory drives and emotions, that turns love into aggression?

The word "ancient" (*starinnyi*) describes both the Demon's hatred and his wound. If "ancient hatred" is indeed the reference to the first battle between the Demon and the angel, then it is clear that the "ancient wound" refers to its tragic outcome, to the loss of paradise. The Demon is afflicted with an incurable wound of loss, exile, and alienation. This experience is the Demon's dominant quality. The first line of the poem describes the Demon as "the spirit of exile" (*dukh izgnania*) (2:45), and this line remained unchanged throughout the ten years of Lermontov's work on the poem. The wording is significant: the Demon is not an exiled spirit, as we might expect, but "the spirit of exile"; that is, he symbolizes exile, and thus embodies and reveals its predicament. In the space of the first four stanzas he is called "an exile" three times.[12]

The imagery of loss dominates the opening of the poem:

Печальный Демон, дух изгнанья
Летал над грешною землей,
И лучших дней воспоминанья
Пред ним теснилися толпой
Тех дней, когда в жилище света
Блистал он чистый херувим. . . .
Когда сквозь вечные туманы,
Познанья жадный он следил
Кочующие караваны
В пространство брошенных светил;
Когда он верил и любил
Счастливый первенец творенья!
Не знал ни злобы ни сомненья,
И не грозил уму его
Веков бесплодных ряд унылый. . . .
Давно отверженный блуждал
В пустыне мира без приюта

(2:45)

(The sad Demon, a spirit of exile, flew over the sinful earth; and the memories of his best days crowded around him, of the days when he, a pure cherub, shone in the dwelling of light. . . . when he, eager for knowledge, would trace the wandering caravans of heavenly bodies thrown into space; when he, the universe's first-born, loved and had faith, and his mind was not threatened by the mournful sequence of fruitless centuries. . . . Long ostracized he wandered in the desert of the world without shelter.)

The sense of loss reverberates through the concepts of "wandering," "an exile," "abandoned planets," "ostracized," "without shelter." The rhyme that opens the poem immediately reveals the cause of the Demon's torment: Lermontov rhymes *izgnaniia* (exile) with *vospominaniia* (memories). The Demon's torment consists in the gnawing awareness of loss and exile coupled with the impossibility of forgetting former bliss. Painful as such a memory is, the Demon refuses to forget it: "God did not grant him oblivion, and he would not have taken it, anyway" (*zabvenia ne dal Bog, da on i ne vzial by zabvenia*) (2:49).

The first stanza introduces the opposition between what was and what is, between what is lost and what is left: "ostracized" versus "first born"; "without shelter" versus "the dwelling of light." The Demon loses more than a physical home; he also loses an internal state of bliss. The blissful state of being loved and of loving is replaced now by aimless wandering in the desert of the universe and a vain search for shelter. Furthermore, the Demon has lost not just heaven, but his ability to respond to and enjoy the earth: "nature's warm embraces have forever become cold for me . . . like Eden, the world became silent and empty" (2:62–63). The wilderness in which the Demon is wandering has penetrated his soul; his emotional state is characterized as a "silent desert" (*nemaia pustynia*). The external loss is described mostly in order to convey the sense of his spiritual emptiness coupled with his inability to respond to beauty.[13]

In this poem Lermontov brings the causes of the Demon's hostility to the surface and reveals that it is the deep-seated sense of loss that informs the Demon's contradictory behavior. To be more precise, it is not just loss, but the awareness of loss coupled with the memory of former bliss, that defines Lermontov's Demon and makes him unique among other literary demons. In his lyric poem "My Demon" (1831) Lermontov concludes a description of the demon that torments the speaker:

И гордый демон не отстанет,
Пока живу я, от меня,
И ум мой озарять он станет
Лучом чудесного огня;
Покажет образ совершенства
И вдруг отнимет навсегда

И, дав предчувствия блаженства,
Не даст мне счастья никогда.
(1:202)

(And the proud demon won't leave me as long as I live, and he will illuminate my mind with the rays of a miraculous fire; he will show me the image of perfection and take it away for good; and while giving a foretaste of bliss, never give me happiness.)

These lines present Lermontov's demon as a kind of cosmic tease: he inflicts on his victims a dual experience, both of perfection and of its inaccessibility. This ever-present, bittersweet, and simultaneous awareness of bliss and of its irredeemable loss constitutes demonic possession in Lermontov's world.

In the narrative poem the Demon plays similar tricks on others: the bridegroom is killed while imagining marital bliss with Tamara, Tamara is tormented by the miraculous but fleeting image of the Demon. More significant, however, it is the Demon himself who suffers from the affliction with which he torments his victims: the "foretaste of bliss" with Tamara is denied, and so is paradise itself. Moreover, the syndrome of vanishing bliss is a permanent feature of the Demon's psychological makeup, informing his vision of the world: "paradise lost" seems to be a single unit in the Demon's thought. The Demon endows the world with a certain structural rhythm: bliss–loss. The Demon's oath is a good example of this outlook:

Клянусь я первым днем творенья
Клянусь его последним днем,
Клянусь позором преступленья
И вечной правды торжеством.
Клянусь паденья горькой мукой,
Победы краткою мечтой;
Клянусь свиданием с тобой
И вновь грозящею разлукой.
(2:65)

(I swear by the first day of creation and by its last; I swear by the shame of crime and by the triumph of eternal truth. I swear by the bitter torment of fall, and by the short dream of victory; swear by our meeting and by the separation which threatens us again.)

The oath, which critics view as a rhetorical or mechanical play with oppositions (Eikhenbaum 1987, 222; Udodov 1973, 445–48), is much more than that. "Victory," "triumph," "meeting" with Tamara are inevitably connected in the Demon's mind with "loss," "shame of crime," and "separation."

Furthermore, in his confession to Tamara the Demon posits loss, even when he describes his presence in paradise. It turns out that even in paradise the Demon was troubled by a certain absence:

В душе моей с начала мира,
Твой образ был напечатлен,
Передо мной носился он
В пустынях вечного эфира. . . .
Давно тревожа мысль мою,
Мне имя сладкое звучало;
Во дни блаженства мне в раю
Одной тебя не доставало.
(2:62)

(In my soul your image had been imprinted from the beginning of the world. It was fleeting in front of me in the deserts of eternal ether. . . . Tormenting my thought, your sweet name has resounded for a long time; during the days of bliss in paradise you were the only one I missed.)

This is the very core of the Demon's (and ultimately Lermontov's) paradox: the Demon's sense of loss is so powerful that he posits loss even within paradise and manages to see paradise as a "desert." If, according to Milton's *Paradise Lost,* "mind is its own place, and in itself can make a Heav'n of Hell, and Hell of Heaven," then the mind of Lermontov's Demon makes a "paradise lost" of any experience. Thus, the Demon's love for Tamara is inseparable from his ubiquitous sense of grief: "he became aquainted with a new grief; he looked at her with such love, with such grief; his grief stirred . . . like a snake" (*on s novoi grustiu stal znakom; vzor ego s takoi liuboviu, tak grustno na nee smotrel; grust' . . . zashevelilasia kak zmei*) (2:49, 55, and 61).

Lermontov, like his Demon, suffers from the "ancient wound," from cosmic anxiety, that he never tires of exploring. The most famous declaration of this occurs in his lyric masterpiece "Alone I Walk Out on a Road" (*Vykhozhu odin ia na dorogu*) (1841): "Heaven is solemn and marvelous, the earth sleeps in blue mist, why do I feel so much pain and uneasiness?" (*V nebesakh torzhestvenno i chudno, spit zemlia v tumane golubom, chto ze mne tak bol'no i tak trudno?*) (1:85). Along similar lines is the blatantly autobiographical character in Lermontov's 1831 play *A Strange Man* whom "some kind of a deep grief has tormented . . . since childhood. God knows what was the cause of it" (3:347).

The poet does not explain the causes of this grief.[14] What matters is that the grief, or the wound, is there. Throughout his work Lermontov explores various types of loss, associating anxiety and pain with all of them. In his archetypal poem "The Angel" (1831) he describes loss both in religious terms (the soul's descent from heaven) and in psychological and physical ones (the soul's inability to forget the tender embrace and the song of the angel). Similarly, "The Demon" balances cosmic and personal losses.

It is tempting, and probably partially correct, to attribute Lermontov's deeply felt grief and anxiety to his early loss of his mother, who died when he was less than three years old. In 1830 Lermontov wrote: "When I was three years old there was a song that made me cry. I cannot recall it now, but I am sure that if I heard it again, it would have the same effect. My late mother used to sing it to me" (4:352). It is easy to understand the tears shed in the present, the tears caused by the song that reminds the poet of his mother. Lermontov, however, states that the song made him cry even before, in the presence of his mother. Like the Demon, who suffers from loss even in paradise, Lermontov experiences a sense of loss, even during a blissful moment. "Paradise lost" haunts the poet as it does his characters.[15]

Lermontov's characters themselves describe the simultaneous sensation of bliss and loss, the experience of "paradise lost" as demonic possession. This psychic dilemma is never fully resolved. The memory of bliss incites Lermontov's characters to strive to regain it, yet their constant sense of loss informs them that their attempts have failed. As Lermontov puts it elsewhere: "one cannot be saved from one's soul even in happiness itself" (*No ot svoei dushi spaseniia i v samom schastii net*) (1:251).

The Demon, in fact, chooses a destructive, if typical, way to come to terms with his loss: he tries to recover it through possession, or to be more precise, through erotic conquest. Contesting Tamara's fate with the angel, the Demon declares: "I love and possess here" (*Zdes' ia vladeiu i liubliu*) (2:60). The sense of possession is reiterated when the Demon twice refers to Tamara mainly in terms of property: "she is mine." Symbolically, the Demon substitutes for the Angel's word *sviatynia* (something holy or sacred) the notion of "possession," by changing the angel's formula of "my love, my holy one" into: "your holy one is gone, I love and possess here" (*zdes' bol'she net tvoei sviatyni, zdes' ia vladeiu i liubliu*) (2:60). To the Demon, the Angel wants to repossess what the Demon perceives as rightfully his.[16] The pain of loss makes the Demon see the world solely in terms of possession, with an aggressiveness typical of a bereaved person, an aggressiveness that blinds him to the fact that Tamara has a bridegroom or a guardian angel.

Insistence on special rights of possession marks many of Lermontov's characters. The desire to defend what is one's own, and to fight for it against usurpers usually seems commendable. Kalashnikov acts heroically when he stands up for his wife against the intruder, especially when the intruder has the tsar and the empire behind him. The situation becomes more blurred in the case of Arbenin, who, while insisting on his special rights, kills his own wife. Pechorin goes further and claims possession of a woman who might be attracted to him, but who is in no way "his." Maksim Maksimych recalls how Pechorin expresses his attitude toward Bela: "'she is mine, for she won't belong to anybody but me,' he added, hitting the table with his fist" (24). Likewise, the Demon twice reiterates "she is mine" and is ready to fight for Tamara with the angel and the whole heavenly empire. Both the Demon and Pechorin demonstrate courage, nobility, tenderness, but also murderous resoluteness in the way they dominate their loved ones. As the deaths of both heroines attest, such aggressive possessiveness is ultimately destructive. In "The Demon" Lermontov makes the interplay between the Demon's "ancient wound" and destructive eroticism the subject of thorough analysis.

RECOVERING LOSS: THE DEMON AND EROTICISM

In "The Demon" Tamara is introduced in the following manner: "Ever since paradise on earth was lost, I swear such beauty has never grown under the southern sun" (*s tekh por, kak mir lishilsia raia, klianus' krasavitsa takaia, pod solntsem iuga ne tsvela*) (2:48). The narrator deliberately connects the beauty of Tamara with lost paradise. This tribute connects her beauty with the loss of paradise and implies that they are of the same order; therefore paradise can be regained through Tamara's beauty. The identification of Tamara with paradise sets the stage for the Demon's exploits.

In Lermontov's world women are often viewed as a means to regain lost paradise; erotic possession is equated with the recovery of a lost state of bliss. Lermontov never tires of exploring the promise of erotic love in his work, through the figures of Arbenin, Pechorin, and the Demon among others. In "The Demon" Lermontov explores, problematizes, and ultimately condemns such an equation. The Demon's reaction to beauty is tragic; he cannot offer any response to it other than the drive to possess. Dostoevsky's novel *The Idiot,* with its triangle of the beautiful Nastasia Filippovna, the angelic Myshkin, and the demonic Rogozhin, as well as Rogozhin's murderous reaction toward beauty, clearly comes to mind here.

The Demon's conflict and subsequent tragedy consist of his failure or refusal to differentiate between the state of bliss, which he tries to regain, and the possession of Tamara, who has inspired the dream of bliss in the first place. When the Demon declares his passion for Tamara, she interrupts him and questions his motives: "Why do you love me?" The Demon's answer is telling:

> Зачем, красавица? Увы,
> Не знаю! Полон жизни новой,
> С моей преступной головы
> Я гордо снял венец терновый,
> Я все былое бросил в прах:
> Мой рай, мой ад в твоих очах.
> (2:62)

> (Why, my beauty? Alas, I don't know! I am now filled with new life, and I have proudly taken the thorny wreath off my criminal head. I cast all my past into dust; my paradise and my hell are in your eyes.)

The Demon does not know why he loves Tamara, except that heaven and hell are concentrated for him in her eyes. The Demon hopes that Tamara's love will guarantee recovery of a state of bliss:

"The Demon"

Меня добру и небесам
Ты возвратить могла бы словом.
Твоей любви святым покровом
Одетый я предстал бы там,
Как новый ангел в блеске новом
(2:61)

(With one word you could have returned me to heaven and goodness. Under the sacred cover of your love I could have reappeared there, like a new angel in new radiance.)

The Demon's confusion, the tension between the desire for a state of bliss and for an object of love, his tragic tendency to destroy through love and attraction, is most clearly seen in his dialogue with Tamara. The very beginning illuminates the Demon's confusion. When questioned about his identity and intentions he can only acknowledge Tamara's beauty: "O! Who are you, your speech is dangerous! Were you sent by hell or heaven? What do you want?—You are beautiful" (*O! Kto ty? rech' tvoia opasna! Tebia poslal mne ad il' rai? Chego ty khochesh'?—Ty prekrasna!*) (2:60). The Demon glosses over what he wants or who he is, but he is quick to acknowledge that Tamara is beautiful. Whether consciously or unconsciously the Demon sidesteps the question of his identity. It is no coincidence that the word "beautiful" (*prekrasna*) rhymes with "dangerous" (*opasna*). Such avoidance is dangerous. The Demon's confession reveals both his desire to relieve the pain of loss, and also the desire to seduce. The tragedy of the Demon is that he strives for the former, but his efforts result in the latter. Many other Lermontov characters, like the Demon, describe their pain and suffering in order to relieve their pain through female sympathy, but then abuse this sympathy. Pechorin's confession to Mary is linked to the Demon's confession to Tamara.[17]

The revealing early poem "I've Seen the Shadow of Bliss" (*Ia videl ten' blazhenstva*) (1831), states:

Есть рай небесный, звезды говорят,
Но где он—*вот вопрос и в нем весь яд.*
Он сделал так, что в женском сердце я
Хотел сыскать отраду бытия.
(1:231; my emphasis)

(There is a paradise in heaven, the stars keep on telling me, but where is it? *That is a question, and it holds all the poison.* He made it so, that I wanted to find the joy of existence in a woman's heart.)

These lines suggest that "poison" (*iad*) does not lie only in enmity and hatred. The poet calls "poison" the desire to find paradise, to locate it inside a woman's heart.[18] Significantly, the phrase "that is the question" (*vot vopros*) echoes the famous existential musings of Hamlet ("to be or not to be: that is the question"). To the poet the search for paradise lost is equivalent to the fundamental question of being.

In Lermontov's interpretation the poison lies precisely in the tendency to equate the regaining of lost paradise with the possession of the woman's heart. As the poison quickly makes health into sickness, living into death, so the vision of beauty causes the beholder to shift from angelic contemplation to a demonic desire to possess, to the statement "she is mine," pronounced with a distorted face. It is not surprising that a kiss, so easily translating an elevated desire for bliss into a desire for physical possession, is often called "poisonous" in Lermontov. As if to underline the ambiguous nature of the kiss, the Demon's kiss kills Tamara. The moment of possession coincides with the moment of loss.[19]

In one of his earliest poems Lermontov declares, "everything has betrayed me, poison is everywhere, only the sound of lyre has been faithful to me" (*vse izmenilo mne, krugom otravy, lish' liry zvuk mne neizmenen byl*) (1:101). Poison provides the illusion that possession is bliss, and according to Lermontov everything but poetry contains such poison. Nevertheless, even though Lermontov suspected from an early age that desires fail, that they turn poisonous, and produce nothing but despair and destruction, he constantly returns in his work to the exploration of this tendency of human desire to destroy while searching for paradise.

When the Demon first sees Tamara dancing he is transfigured. At that moment he is incapable of even trying to seduce her; he experiences the bliss of renewed feelings and even sheds a tear. But then the desire to possess comes into play. It is precisely at this moment that the angel appears and brings the destructive dimension of the Demon's eroticism to the surface.

In the figure of the Demon Lermontov explores the universal human desire to find a place in the universe, to regain paradise lost. In paradise the Demon lacked the beloved; with the beloved on earth, he misses paradise. He hovers between heaven and earth in his fruitless flight, trying to fill the void of his loss with the promise of erotic bliss. The Demon's predicament, in fact, highlights and clarifies the plight of Lermontov's other demonic characters. Like the Demon, Arbenin and Pechorin invest eroticism and possession with salvational values and experience the same tragic dynamics: constant search for bliss, identification of bliss with an object of love, and then temporary possession followed by new loss. None of these characters does evil for its own sake; they all want to recover the state of love and bliss.

Furthermore, Lermontov provides here a clear diagnosis of many modern predicaments, and explains various attempts to recover spiritual loss through material possessions, whether property, love objects, or so on. This confusion of a state with an object appears to be the blueprint for many of the conflicts of the nineteenth century. Ever since the Enlightenment, the atrocities of the French Revolution, and gradual loss of religion, people have been haunted by a sense of paradise lost, yet its recovery is often reduced to the recovery not of a state, but of objects. Pushkin explored this phenomenon brilliantly in his portrayal of the Baron in "The Covetous Knight." The Baron strives to satisfy his spiritual needs through gold and treats his money as if it were a divinity: witness the "black mass" that he offers to his gold in the cellar. Another way to recover lost bliss is not through gold but through eroticism: Pushkin's Don Juan is a good example ("The Store Guest").

The rejection of what is given and the hope of recovering what has been lost through eroticism is a feature typical of both Lermontov's protagonists and the Romantic hero generally. The association of a nihilistic demonic character with eroticism is one of the reasons why demonic characters were such powerful sex symbols at the time. (Mario Praz's well-known study *The Romantic Agony* [1933] concerns the erotic dimension of demonism.) Practically all of Byron's demonic characters experience tragic love and passion, as "Manfred" or the Oriental tales reveal. Gothic novels also attest to the popularity of erotic demonism. Erotic love becomes for demonic and nihilistic heroes a vantage point from which to negate or scorn the rest of the world while preserving something positive or tangible. Curiously, negation continues to go hand in hand with the erotic in modern and especially French thought; from Baudelaire's *Les fleurs du mal* to Bataille's *Eroticisme*, French artists and thinkers seem unable to disconnect the two forces and thus to escape the shadow of the so-called divine Marquis, probably the first writer in modern literature to offer a seductive amalgam of eroticism and negation.

In the world of Lermontov nothing except art is capable of truly relieving and suspending the pain of loss. The state of bliss is recovered only through another state, that of aesthetic experience. The magical domain of sound produces in some of Lermontov's characters a trancelike state in which they reexperience lost bliss:

> Я б хотел забыться и заснуть . . .
> Чтоб всю ночь, весь день мои слух лелея,
> О любви мне сладкий голос пел,
> Надо мной, чтоб вечно зеленея,
> Темный дуб качался и шумел.
>
> (1:86)

> (I would like to forget everything and fall asleep . . . so that a sweet voice would sing about love, day and night caressing my ears, and the dark oak, forever blossoming, would shake and rustle above me.) ("Alone I Walk Out on a Road")

The speaker knows that the sweet song about love provides such a lasting and transcendent experience as love itself cannot. The poetic state of transcendence is transient, and the speaker of the poem associates this state with a dream. What is important, however, is that during this aesthetic experience nothing is destroyed. Paradise is doomed to remain lost for all of Lermontov's protagonists; as they attempt to recover it, Lermontov's poets create rather than destroy.

ARTISTIC SENSIBILITY IN THE POEM: TAMARA

Lermontov often returns to the connection between loss and art; nevertheless, this connection remains largely unexplored in the criticism. "The Demon" is Lermontov's metapoetic statement; in this poem he expresses his views on the origins and the role of the creative process. The Russian poet Alexander Blok has pointed to the metapoetic character of Lermontov's "Demon" and foregrounded Lermontov's connection between poetry and the experience of confinement and loss. In his article "On Lyric Poetry" (1907) Blok claims that in "The Demon" Lermontov creates the modern myth of lyric poetry: "This man, the fallen angel-demon, is the first lyrical poet. The cursed song-legend about him was created by Lermontov" (Blok 1962, 130). Inspired by Lermontov's poem, Blok stresses that art arises as a response to beauty experienced in the state of confinement and exile:

> The lyric poet is the one who is buried alive in the magnificent grave. . . . He is beating against the walls of this grave, against the green earth and blue firmament, as if against alien elements. The universe is alien to him, but rich and magnificent is his reception of this universe. There is slavery in confinement, but in magnificence there is freedom. (Blok 1962, 134)

The complexity of studying the poetic dimension of "The Demon" lies in the fact that the Demon himself is not a creator; I disagree with Blok's assessment of him as a lyric poet. Lermontov deliberately draws our attention to the barren, noncreative nature of his protagonist. The Demon is very much like Pechorin: strong, courageous, but ultimately barren: "the brightness of nature inspired in the fruitless breast of the exile neither new emotions nor new strength" (*prirody blesk ne vozbudil v grudi izgnannika besplodnoi ni novykh chuvstv, ni novykh sil*) (2:47). In fact, the word "fruitless" occurs several times in connection with the Demon; in one particular case we learn that he is doomed to live through "fruitless centuries" (2:45). The fate and actions of the Demon reveal the ultimate sterility of his rebellion; neither earth nor heaven is perfect, and the Demon has reason to feel confined in his environment and suffer in exile. Nevertheless, the Demon challenges God, who, at least, is a creator, and a magnificent one at that:

> И дик и чуден был вокруг
> Весь Божий мир; но гордый дух
> Презрительным окинул оком
> Творенье Бога своего,

> И на челе его высоком
> *Не отразилось ничего*
> (2:46; my emphasis)

> (And God's world around him was wild and fantastic, but the proud spirit looked around his God's creation with contempt, and his high brow *reflected nothing.*)

The actual poet in the poem, its narrator, describes God's creation with admiration, while the Demon can only despise it.

Like the Demon, Tamara is tormented by her confinement and loss. However, Lermontov stresses the connection between Tamara's premonitions of a new enslavement and her outbursts of creativity. She resorts to artistic expression, be it singing or dancing, instead of futile pursuits or destructive rebellion:

> В последний раз она плясала,
> Увы! заутра ожидала
> Её, наследницу Гудала,
> Свободы резвую дитя,
> Судьба печальная рабыни,
> Отчизна, чуждая поныне,
> И незнакомая семья.
> И часто тайное сомненье
> Темнило светлые черты;
> И были все её движенья
> Так стройны, полны выраженья,
> Так полны милой простоты.
> (2:49)

> (She was dancing for the last time. Alas, in the morning the sad fate of a slave, a land unknown until now, and a strange family awaited her, the heir to Gudal and the vivacious daughter of freedom. And frequently, a secret doubt would darken her fair features, and all her movements were so harmonious, so expressive, so full of sweet simplicity.)

The description of Tamara's dance in the penultimate version of the poem discloses that through dancing Tamara transcends her earthly confinement: "being carried away by her fiery dance she forgot the earthly world" (*uvlechena letuchei pliaskoi ona zabyla mir zemnoi*) (2:463).

Tamara's artistic activity is even more emphasized in the final version of the poem. Moreover, this activity acquires a clear symbolic meaning—though one that has so far eluded critics. Throughout the variants Tamara sings a song and the Demon reacts to it and falls in love. The two most mature versions differ, however. Tamara first dances and attracts the Demon's attention; he in turn charms her with his own "unearthly beauty" and "miraculous voice." Then, while enclosed in her nun's cell, at a moment of conflict between her sense of confinement and striving for the beloved, Tamara composes her song of heavenly perfection. In other words, her attraction to the Demon (that is, "demonism" par excellence) does not always result in destruction; in Tamara's case it results in art:

И звуки песни раздались
И звуки те лились, лились,
Как слезы, мерно друг за другом;
И эта песнь была нежна,
Как будто для земли она
Была на небе сложена.
Не ангел ли с забытым другом
Вновь повидаться захотел,
Сюда украдкою слетел
И о былом ему пропел,
Чтоб усладить его мученье?
(2:59)

(And the sounds of song began to be heard, and these sounds kept on pouring, like tears, one after another. And that song was as tender as if it had been composed in heaven for the sake of earth. Could it be that an angel flew secretly to earth to see again a forgotten friend, and sing to him of the past, in order to assuage his pain?)

The last lines are revealing: only a song can provide relief from the torment of exile and loss.

Through Tamara's art Lermontov defines, or at least clarifies, his own artistic response to the torment of the demonic predicament. Both Tamara and the Demon are frustrated with earth and earthly "imprisonment," both are afflicted with the desire for bliss. Nonetheless, even though there are obvious similarities between the two, Tamara's fascination with the Demon finds expression in the heavenly song that she composes and not in murder or destruction.[20] Lermontov frequently returns to the connection between inner turmoil and artistic expression. In his unfinished novel, known by the editor's title as *Vadim* (1833–34) Lermontov describes the dance of another tormented heroine and compares it to the process of writing poetry:

soon she lost her inhibitions and let her inner torment show freely; similar to a poet, who in the moment of inspired suffering casts divine verses upon the paper, neither feeling nor remembering them, she did not know what she was doing, she was not concerned with the propriety of her movements, and that is why they enchanted her audience. (4:165–66)

To underscore the importance of Tamara's artistic nature, Lermontov allows the angel to declare that Tamara is saved because "the Creator has woven the living strings [of her soul] out of the best ether" (*Tvorets iz luchshego efira sotkal zhivye struny ikh*) (2:72). The angel's announcement of God's decision associates redemption with an artistic nature.

Lermontov does not, however, primarily envision Tamara as an artist. In fact, Lermontov appears to be confused about her role, as the variants to the poem testify. Tamara's character, fate, and actions change throughout the variants, in contrast to those of Demon. Lermontov does make the Demon's rhetoric and invectives more colorful, but his actions and motives, though ambivalent, seem to run an already charted course. Tamara, on the other hand, turns into an evil spirit in the first version, and is saved in the final one, whereas in the intermediate versions she simply dies and nothing is known of her afterlife. Moreover, while in the later versions Tamara falls in love with the Demon, in earlier versions she was in love with the angel, and even composed a song about this love. Such a range suggests Lermontov's uncertainty concerning the fate and the role of Tamara and explains why he was not in a hurry to publish his poem, even when there seemed to be a possibility of doing so. What the poem lacks in conclusiveness, it gains in complexity and ambiguity as Lermontov directs his sympathy toward both the Demon and Tamara.

Tamara visibly grows in stature as Lermontov's work on his poem progresses. She is no longer simply a foil for the Demon. Even in the final version, though, she is still too passive and reactive to take on the Demon and overshadow him. Lermontov was unwilling to turn Tamara into his main protagonist, not only because of his fascination with the Demon, but mostly because the structure of the poem would probably not sustain such a drastic change of focus. Similar tensions between design and execution seem to operate within Pushkin's *Eugene Onegin*. The two poets spent the major parts of their creative lives on these texts (approximately seven years each), and during this time each shifted the center of gravity toward the heroine, yet neither in the end broke away from the original focus on the male protagonist.

Oscillations in Tamara's fate occur because the poem assigns to her two functions that are not only disjointed but even opposed to each other. On the one hand Tamara is a beautiful woman; she inspires in the Demon hope and love, but inevitably lets him down. When the Demon reappears to claim her she hides from him behind the angel. In her role as the object of the Demon's love, Tamara does not transcend the usual role of women in Lermontov's work: beautiful but eventually disappointing. Tamara's role and fate vis-à-vis the demonic protagonist is reminiscent of Nina in *The Masquerade*, whom Arbenin characterized as "a weak creature but an angel of beauty" (*sozdan'e slaboe, no angel krasoty*) (3:39). On the other hand Tamara is a poetic soul bored with earthly songs: she does reject earthly happiness and all the men who pursue her. She strives for the image of perfection, which she envisioned in the Demon, and which she cannot renounce even in the seclusion of the convent. These two opposing Tamaras are the main reason for the unresolved nature of the poem. It is only in Lermontov's final narrative poem, "Mtsyri," in a hero who manifests the poetry of Tamara without her passivity and weaknesses, that Lermontov successfully integrated heroic strength with artistic and nonviolent means of transcending a sense of confinement and loss.

ARTISTIC SENSIBILITY IN THE POEM: THE DEMON

The Demon, even though he inspires Tamara's artistic expression, is not creative himself. Like Pechorin and Arbenin, he can register beauty and poetry but is incapable of producing them. In the early variants, descriptions of the Demon include images of a dark wave or a stormcloud briefly illuminated by the light from a star, but then returning to its previous darkness. The Demon is presented like the black hole of astronomy, which devours light without being changed by it. The noncreative, deadening aspect of the Demon manifests itself most clearly in his song to Tamara. Except for the two final variants of 1838, the Demon does not sing in the poem, yet it is this very song that condemns him most. The song reveals the Demon's real tragedy: a fruitless soul failing to transcend the sense of loss.

Surprisingly, critics have lavished praise on the Demon's song. William Edward Brown calls it "a wonderful song about the beauty and tranquillity of the natural world" (1986, 206); Irina Rodnianskaia hears in it nothing less than "the music of the spheres" (1981, 150); while Robert Reid goes so far as to claim that "the Demon in the poem is not so much a good being as one capable of great aesthetic experience and expression" (1982, 209). The Demon might be capable of limited aesthetic experience—he is moved by Tamara's dance and song—but aesthetic expression remains beyond his reach.

While Tamara's song is an act of pure art that assumes no listener to please or impress, the Demon's song has a pragmatic and cynical purpose to it. It is a song with words; its purpose is to promote an argument, to convince Tamara to be indifferent toward her bridegroom, whom the Demon has just killed. Thus art is supposed to justify murder, and Lermontov shows how it fails.

Significantly, the words of Tamara's angelic song are not given. Similarly, the soul in "Angel" remembers the sound of the angel's song, but not the words: "and the sounds of his song have remained in the young soul—without words, but alive" (*i zvuk ego pesni v dushe molodoi ostalsia bez slov, no zhivoi*) (1:233). The opposition between melody and words is, indeed, a marked one in Lermontov, as he underscores vividly in poem "There are Speeches" (*Est' rechi*) (1839): "There are certain words the meaning of which is either obscure or insignificant, but it is impossible to listen to them without agitation" (*est' rechi, znachenie temno i nichtozhno, no im bez volnenia vnimat' nevozmozhno*) (1:47). The words of the Demon's song, unlike Tamara's, are provided:

На воздушном океане,
Без руля и без ветрил,
Тихо плавают в тумане
Хоры стройные светил;
Средь полей необозримых
В небе ходят без следа
Облаков неуловимых
Волокнистые стада.
Час разлуки, час свиданья—
Им ни радость, ни печаль,
Им в грядущем нет желанья
И прошедшего не жаль.
В день томительный несчастья
Ты об них лишь вспомяни;
Будь к земному без участья
И беспечна, как они!
(2:53–54)

(On an ocean of ether, without rudder or sail, the orderly choirs of planets float quietly in the fog. Among the limitless fields of heaven the woolly flocks of fleeting clouds move without leaving a trace. An hour of separation, an hour of meeting, brings them neither sadness nor joy. They do not desire anything in the future, nor do they pity anything in the past. On a painful day of misery just recall them, and be as indifferent toward Earth and as carefree as they are.)

Eleven of the sixteen lines of the song stress lack or negation and reveal the thrust of the Demon's argument. The clouds and planets are characterized by lack, by absence, by indifference; they do not experience separation, they do not look forward to anything, nor do they regret anything.

Nothing is happening in this poem; clouds and planets move in the fog leaving no trace and following an orderly course created by an external entity. The present tense of the imperfective verbs of motion underlines the recurring movement depicted in the song. The clouds are described as "stada" (herds); they are not just indifferent but also faceless, as are the planets. The tediously repetitive mass movement is conveyed through numerous parallel constructions: (*bez rulia—bez vetril; na vozdushnom okeane—sred' polei neobozrimykh; tikho plavaiut v tumane—v nebe khodiat bez sleda; khory stroinye svetil—voloknistye stada; chas razluki—chas svidania; ni radost'—ni pechal'*). The rhyming pattern is equally unimaginative. While the rest of the poem employs all the possibilities of rhyme that involve four or more lines, each of the song's quatrains rhyme *abab* throughout. The words that rhyme are equally trite: *svidania—zhelania; pechal'—zhal'* (rendezvous—desire; sorrow—to be sorry).

It is telling that the Demon returns to the imagery of clouds, planets, and sailing later on in the poem, when he complains about his miserable life after the fall:

> Мир для меня стал глух и нем.
> По вольной прихоти теченья
> Так поврежденная ладья
> Без парусов и без руля
> Плывет, не зная назначенья,
> Так ранней утренней порой
> Отрывок тучи громовой,
> В лазурной вышине чернея,
> Один, нигде пристать не смея,
> Летит, *без цели и следа,*
> Бог весть откуда и куда!
> (2:63; my emphasis)

> (The world became for me mute and deaf, in the same way a broken boat sails without a sail or wheel, unaware of its destination, following the unrestrained will of a current. In the same way at dawn a torn piece of cloud darkens the azure heights, alone, not daring to anchor anywhere, flying without purpose or trace, God knows whence and where.)

This passage reveals that what the Demon has described to Tamara as a scene of tranquillity and peace is, in fact, a picture of hell, of mindless, traceless, purposeless movement.

Significantly, the bliss that the Demon has lost is a state of activity and involvement: "when he loved and believed, when the flying comet would exchange greeting smiles with him" (*kogda on veril i liubil; kogda begushchaia kometa, ulybkoi laskovoi priveta liubila pomeniat'sia s nim*) (2:45). The present, on the other hand, is characterized by monotonous stasis: "sad succession of fruitless centuries" (*vekov besplodnykh riad unylyi*) (2:45). The Demon suffers from the fruitlessness and indifference that he preaches to Tamara.

Following the example of clouds that leave no trace is an inhuman prospect. The song is a typical demonic seduction in exhorting indifference toward the earth. Lucifer in Byron's "Cain" instills similar feelings of indifference toward the earth in his victim: "Think not the earth, which is thine outward cov'ring, is existence—it will cease, and thou wilt be no less than thou art now." If the Demon really means what he says about the indifference of clouds, then neither Tamara nor the Demon himself should have fallen in love. As if to teach the Demon how to write poetry about indifferent clouds, Lermontov wrote his own meditative poem "Clouds" (1840), in which clouds are presented as cold and indifferent and thus unable to convey the human predicament of loss and exile. Similarly, when in "Alone I Walk Out on a Road" (1841) Lermontov describes his own indifference toward the past and the future, this indifference is presented as a sign of resignation and hopelessness, not as a solution to pain and loss: "I do not expect anything from my life, and I do not miss anything in the past" (*Uzh ne zhdu ot zhizni nichego ia i ne zhal' mne proshlogo nichut'*) (1:85).

The flaws of the Demon's poem are also conveyed on a nonsemantic level. His song, in trochaic tetrameter rather than the iambic tetrameter of the rest of the poem, creates a jarring effect on the listener. It stands out, as a blatant lie should. By contrast, the comforting song of the goldfish in "Mtsyri" preserves the meter of the main narrative.[21]

None of Lermontov's mature poems use trochaic tetrameter, except the 1837 "To the Prisoner" (*Uzniku*) and the 1839 "Gifts of Terek" (*Dary Tereka*). "To the Prisoner," significantly, concludes with a description of the monotonous, endless movement of a prison guard who fails to respond to a prisoner:

Одинок я, нет отрады. . . .
Только слышно за дверями
Звучно мерными шагами
Ходит в тишине ночной
Безответный часовой.
(1:27)

(I am lonely; there is no joy. . . . I can only hear how behind the doors, an unresponsive guard walks in the silence of night with his measured and resounding steps.)

The same meter connects the indifferent movements of the clouds, described in the Demon's song, with the indifferent and monotonous shuffle of the prison guard's steps. The similarity reveals that the Demon preaches to Tamara not the orderly beauty of nature, but the orderly terror of confinement.

According to M. L. Gasparov (1984) trochaic tetrameter was very popular in the eighteenth century and was later reserved for songs, ranging from anacreontic verse such as Baratynsky's "Enjoy Your Life; Everything Passes By" (*Naslazhdaisia, vse prokhodit*) (1835) and Pushkin's "If Life Would Deceive You" (*Esli zhizn' tebia obmanet*) (1825), to folk stylizations or religious songs (113–15). Similarly, Boris Unbegaun (1977) observes that trochaic tetrameter was replaced during the first half of the nineteenth century by iambic tetrameter, and it took refuge in popular songs and verse tales; "it became the rule in the imitation of folk-poetry" (28). In the nineteenth century it became the meter of Pushkin's fairy tales, such as "A Fairy Tale About the Tsar Saltan" (*Skazka o tsare Saltane*) (1831) and "A Drowned Man" (*Utoplennik*) (1828), and A. I. Podolinsky's verse tale "Peri and Div" (1827).

Lermontov utilizes the metrical scheme of popular songs, old-fashioned poetry, or poetic imitations of folklore, to show that regardless of all his intensity and beauty the Demon has problems with art: his song is by no means wonderful or majestic, but almost a Mephistopheles-like parody of an anacreontic theme familiar from the verses of Pushkin or Baratynsky: carpe diem.

Furthermore, it appears that the Demon's song is Lermontov's poetic gesture pointing toward Pushkin's narrative poem "The Gypsies." Lermontov knew Pushkin's poem well; he wrote a libretto based on it. As in "The Demon," the iambic pentameter of the main narrative is interrupted by the trochaic pentameter of the song, which summarizes Aleko's experience with the Gypsies: "God's bird knows neither labor nor worries" (*Ptichka Bozhiia ne znaet ni zaboty, ni truda*). Pushkin's song is an important antecedent to the Demon's song, in its three quatrains, rhyming scheme, and content (indifference toward earthly worries). The similarities between the songs suggest that the glorious and mysterious figure of the Demon has its Romantic antecedent, a more familiar Byronic type, Aleko. Both characters, disillusioned about the ways of the world, aspire to resolve their alienation, anxiety, and unhappiness through love affairs. Once their erotic possessions are threatened, both resort to violent and murderous behavior toward their rivals, as well as toward the loved ones. In juxtaposing the fruitless Demon and artistic Tamara, Lermontov follows Pushkin's poem, which contrasts Aleko to his counterpart: an exiled poet, Ovid, who confronts the anxiety of exile and loss with his art.

Chapter Three

The Hero and the Masquerade: Temptations of a Gnostic Outlook

Пускай глядит он без упрека
На ложный блеск и ложный мира шум.

(Let him look without reproach
At the world's false glitter and false noise)
—Lermontov, "Upon The Birthday of a Dear Child" (1839)

Беден, кто, судьбы в ненастье
Все надежды испытав,
Наконец находит счастье,
Чувство счастья потеряв.

(Poor is the one who at fate's malevolent hour,
has exhausted all his hopes,
And who finally finds happiness,
Having lost the feeling for it)
—Lermontov, "Advice" (1830)

LERMONTOV DID NOT SEE his play *The Masquerade* performed or even published. It was eleven years after his death before selected scenes of this drama were first staged. Even though the rest of Lermontov's plays, as well as the majority of his early poetry, were not published during the poet's lifetime, *The Masquerade* deserves special attention as it was the first text that he actively sought to make public. In fact, Lermontov was so concerned with getting the play out that he undertook two drastic revisions, all in vain. Such confidence in a young author is noteworthy. A lyric poet, customarily accused of Byronic monologism, Lermontov nevertheless wanted to start his literary career with a play, that is, with the genre that by definition represents the interaction of various states of consciousness. Even if the rest of the characters are meant to reflect on the play's protagonist, Arbenin, and are clearly overshadowed by him, Lermontov also uses these characters to explore different sensitivities, outlooks, and agendas.[1]

Lermontov's texts, including his plays, feature one dominant heroic figure. However, to concentrate only on this hero, whether Arbenin, the Demon, or Pechorin, and to interpret this hero as the embodiment of Lermontov's artistic or personal concerns, is simplistic and nearsighted. Even Lermontov's early plays, *Strange Man* (1831), *Two Brothers* (1832–35), or *Menschen und Leidenschaften* (1830), manifest how skillfully Lermontov confronts different characters with a similar predicament or how skillfully he invests them with the ideas or traits important to him.

Because the identification of Lermontov with a dominant character of his texts became, unfortunately, a permanent feature of Lermontov criticism ever since Belinsky, it is important to stress that Lermontov is neither awestruck nor blinded by his heroes. He never focuses his attention solely upon them. Lermontov dramas are the ground where he tries out various personas or masks, and explores various modes of behavior and their outcomes. There seem to be no absolutes in Lermontov's outlook except, perhaps, the value of poetry; hence, each mode of behavior, each system of values, becomes a subject for exploration and reevaluation.

Disappointed with his reception, Lermontov did not return to theater after *The Masquerade;* yet his theatrical apprenticeship, during which he completed five plays, was a great imaginative school for creating longer artistic texts. It enabled him to master the challenging art of creating various characters in all the complexity of their interaction. Insights acquired during the composition of his dramas came to fruition in the complex narratives of "The Demon" and *A Hero of Our Time.* Pushkin was a well-established poet long before venturing into drama, yet he realized that he had "developed to his full potential" only upon the completion of his *Boris Godunov* (1825).[2]

ARBENIN AND HIS DOUBLES

Let us briefly summarize the events of Lermontov's play. Arbenin, the protagonist, meets Prince Zvezdich in a gambling house, after the latter has already lost a great deal of money. A former gambler, Arbenin decides to play on behalf of the Prince, and easily recoups his losses. Upon this happy resolution both men go to the masquerade. Baroness Strahl uses the anonymity of the masquerade as an opportunity to seduce Prince Zvezdich. She becomes alarmed by his rash desire to transform their fling into a serious love affair, and decides to shield herself at the expense of Arbenin's wife, Nina. The Baroness, helped by the unsavory Shprikh, spreads rumors that it is Arbenin's wife, Nina, who is having an affair with the Prince. Deceived by the Baroness, Zvezdich begins to pursue Arbenin's wife, which in turn leads to Arbenin's jealousy, the cruel punishment of Zvezdich, the murder of the innocent Nina, and Arbenin's madness.

The play opens without Arbenin. We are first introduced to the characters that the protagonist must deal with, to the world of deception and manipulation. Such an opening becomes a frequent structural device of Lermontov's: both *A Hero of Our Time* and "The Song of the Tsar Ivan Vasilievich" employ a similar strategy of first presenting the environment within which the protagonists have to function. The reader is encouraged to consider a protagonist against the background of more typical representatives of his time, who reflect, reveal, and highlight the heroic features of the main character. This method of presentation is developed further not just in Lermontov's texts, but in such classic works of Russian literature as *Crime and Punishment.*

The opening scene takes place in a gambling house, which is not only symbolic, but also historically accurate. Lermontov addresses the concrete cultural situation of his time: the 1830s in Russia witnessed a revival, if not an explosion, of several activities already popular in the 1820s, such as gambling, masquerades, and the consumption of ultraromantic tales of exotic adventures. A provincial nobleman, N. I. Vtorov, complains, for example, that the Kazan of the 1840s is "empty, heartless and dead," since he "likes neither cards, nor silent dinners, nor proper, artificial, mechanical balls" (*Russkii Arkhiv* 2 [1877], 160). The titles of numerous popular texts of the period testify to the increased interest in card games. The 1827 melodrama *Thirty Years or the Life of a Gambler* (*Trente ans; ou, La vie d'un joueur*) by the French playwright Victor Ducange (1783–1833) immediately appeared in two different translations for the theaters of Moscow and Saint Petersburg and was staged there in 1828. In the same year Alexander Shakhovskoi published excerpts from his unfinished comedy *The Gamblers.* There were also, of course, Pushkin's "Queen of Spades" and Gogol's *The Gamblers,* both written in the 1830s. Lermontov's own texts, including "The Wife of a Tambov Tax-Collector" (*Tambovskaia kaznacheisha,* 1837–38), "The Fatalist," and his unpublished tale known as "Faro" (*Shtoss,* 1840–41), utilize cards for plot development.[3] A curious testimony to the gambling mania of the period is provided by Osip Senkovsky's sketch "Arithmetic" (1833), in which the narrator bemoans the amount of paper and labor that goes into the production of cards. He refers to a factory that produces 1.8 million decks of cards a year, and wonders about the number of useful books that could have been printed on that paper.

The world of gambling entered in *The Masquerade* is of a rather peculiar kind, however: what looks like an honest cardgame turns out to be a setup by a group of players intending to cheat Prince Zvezdich. Instead of epitomizing the world of chance, gambling becomes a symbol of manipulation.[4] Something similar, in fact, happens in Lermontov's later description of a masquerade: what is expected to be a domain of anonymous chance encounters turns out to be a place of calculated, well-planned actions against the ingenuous Zvezdich.

The opening scene projects the governing principles of the universe that Arbenin enters: he will not only have to face manipulation and dishonesty, but also surrender. One of the key metaphors of the play, utilized by Lermontov on three occasions, is introduced at the outset. Referring to the betting process signaled by the bending of a card, one of the gamblers quips: "Listen, dear friend, nowadays, if you don't bend, you don't get anywhere" (*Poslushai, milyi drug, kto nyneche ne gnetsia, ni do chego tot ne dob'etsia*) (3:8). Lermontov's pun on the verb "bend" (*gnut'*)—which means both "to bet on a card" (by bending it) and in its reflexive form "to bow down"—is clearly meant to be read emblematically. In the world of *The Masquerade* success depends less on betting (taking chances) than on bending; furthermore, by fusing the two images Lermontov suggests that the daredevil attitude of gamblers conceals, in fact, their bending spines, their readiness to surrender.

The metaphorical use of the word *gnut'*—utilized also by Pushkin in "From Pindemonti" (*Iz Pindemonti*, 1834), "for the sake of power or courtier's uniform to bend neither conscience, nor thoughts, nor neck"—is associated, in fact, with Alexander Griboedov's celebrated play, *Woe from Wit* (*Gore ot uma*, 1824). A direct antecedent to Lermontov's drama, Griboedov's play contains an exchange between two ideological opponents, Famusov and Chatsky, in which the former refers approvingly to a haughty courtier, who "in order to obtain a favor from a superior would bend over backwards" (*Kogda zhe nado podsluzhit'sia, i on sgibalsia vperegib*). Chatsky dismisses this story as belonging to the distant past when "glory would go to the one whose neck would bend more frequently" (*kak tot i slavilsia, ch'ia chashche gnulas' sheia*) (Griboedov 1987, 77).

It is precisely Arbenin's refusal to bow down that distinguishes him from the rest of the characters: "I've seen evil everywhere and, being proud, nowhere did I bow to it" (*Vezde ia videl zlo i, gordyi, pered nim nigde ne preklonilsia*) (3:39). Similarly, refusing to go along with the social pressure of his peers, Arbenin asserts: "Oh, I am not their servant; it is too late for me to bow down to them" (*No ia ne ikh sluga, mne pozdno pered nimi gnut'sia*) (3:66). This theme of resistance to evil, as well as the particular image of bending down to it, has a long history in Lermontov's oeuvre. In 1831, in the epistolary poem "Enough Excuses for Corruption" (*O polno izviniat' razvrat*), the main achievement of the poem's addressee is his refusal to bend in the face of evil: "you saw evil, yet your proud brow did not bow down to it" (*ty videl zlo i pered zlom ty gordym ne ponik chelom*) (1:179). The patronymic ("Paramonovich") of the merchant Kalashnikov, another of Lermontov's stern and courageous heroes, comes from a Greek root that means "decisive, unbending." Arbenin simply voices the proud conviction of Lermontov himself. The events of the play point out, however, that Arbenin's proud and stern disposition results in his failure to be merciful. He kills his innocent wife, refusing to listen to her pleas. In an ironic way Arbenin fulfills the prophesy of a gambler: his proud refusal to bend gets him nowhere.

It is Arbenin's former partner in card games, Kazarin, who best epitomizes the universe of gambling in the play. Kazarin is a cynical and unscrupulous gambler whose every action or word is manipulative and self-serving.

Having heard from Kazarin unflattering characteristics of those present in the gambling house, Arbenin ironically comments: "Oh, you are very picky about the company you keep" (*Da, vy razborchivy na novye znakomstva*) (3:12). Kazarin is clever and witty, yet he uses his talents and experience of gambling to articulate a rather peculiar philosophy. Believing only in the reality of evil, Kazarin deliberately drags anything not crudely material through the mud. Kazarin is the embodiment of the demon described by Lermontov in his early poem "My Demon" (1831): "He mocks the words of sympathy, as he mocks anyone who has faith; he is a stranger to love and pity; he lives by earthly food" (*emu smeshny slova priveta i vsiakii veriashchii smeshon; on chuzhd liubvi i sozhalen'a, zhivet on pishcheiu zemnoi*) (1:201).

Kazarin does not direct his cynicism to his own material pursuits, which he promotes with the help of fixed cardgames. Arbenin, on the other hand, even if he shares a skeptical outlook with Kazarin, has given up on cards. Unlike Kazarin and the other gamblers, Arbenin does not like to play when he is certain of his victory: "I see through it all. . . . I know all their tricks, and that is why I don't play nowadays" (*Ia vizhu vsio naskvoz'. . . . vse tonkosti ikh znaiu, i vot zachem ia nynche ne igraiu*) (3:17). The Demon displays a similar attitude: "He did not encounter any resistance to his skills, and thus evil became boring to him" (2:45). Having mastered the rules of his world, Arbenin becomes bored with it, while the rest of the characters are all avid to be engaged in manipulations or betrayals.

If Arbenin's former friend and partner, Kazarin, represents the world of gambling, articulates its governing principles, and confirms Arbenin's worst fears about his society, Shprikh functions as the grotesque parody of Arbenin's personality. Shprikh is a theatrical villain, an almost comic character whose egoism and lack of scruples are so constant that they are easily utilized by others, such as the baroness, to promote their own secret agendas. Kazarin, the authority on evil within the play, discerns similarities between Arbenin and Shprikh. Addressing Shprikh, he compares him to Arbenin: "and you, my friend, might be a child in comparison, yet, you also have a little devil inside" (*I ty, moj drug, khot' pered nim rebenok, a i v tebe sidit chertenok*) (3:16). However, this similarity is of a specific type; they are similar as two opposites are, like all and nothing, like Jekyll and Hyde. Kazarin characterizes Shprikh as a mirror: no individuality or principles of his own, but an ever-changing mask:

> Был бит не раз, с безбожником—безбожник,
> С святошей—езуит, меж нами—злой картежник,
> А с честными людьми—пречестный человек.
> (3:11)

(He was beaten on numerous occasions; he is an atheist among atheists, and a Jesuit among the pious; among us he is an all-out gambler, but with honest people—the most honorable one.)

Shprikh is the reverse image of Arbenin, a powerful, overbearing personality who does not wear a mask even when he attends the masquerade. Shprikh bends in any direction; Arbenin refuses to bend altogether. Arbenin's hostility toward Shprikh, which seems unprovoked at first, is quite similar to the hostility of Pechorin toward Grushnitsky, the hostility of a real thing to its shadow. In fact, with his tendency to appear everywhere, Shprikh physically shadows Arbenin.

Shprikh's ubiquitousness underscores his representative nature. Being only a reflection, Shprikh poses no threat and no challenge in this society of role-playing and mask-wearing; he is thus welcomed everywhere: "He knows everyone, he has business everywhere" (*so vsemi on znakom, vezde emu est' delo*) (3:11). For Lermontov, to be fully integrated into the social domain is to have no personality of one's own.

While the first scene presents the world of gambling, the second scene introduces the world of the masquerade. The masquerade has its own master, Baroness Strahl, the same two participants, Arbenin and Shprikh, and the same victim, Prince Zvezdich, who is being taken advantage of in both settings. The Prince remains a gullible fool throughout the play, failing to recognize that he is used first by the group of gamblers, then by the Baroness and Shprikh, and finally by Arbenin.

The Baroness, in contrast to Kazarin, has some aspirations and scruples: she reads George Sand and is unhappy with society's hypocrisy; like Arbenin, she rails at its injustice, yet quickly surrenders to it. It is the Baroness who provides the most thorough description of Prince Zvezdich and accuses him of weakness, yet, manifesting an even greater weakness, she falls in love with him. Describing Prince Zvezdich, the Baroness maintains that his combination of weakness and lack of principles reflects the dominant attributes of her age:

> Бесхарактерный, безнравственный, безбожный,
> Самолюбивый, злой, но слабый человек;
> В тебе одном весь отразился век,
> Век нынешний, блестящий, но ничтожный.
> Наполнить хочешь жизнь, а бегаешь страстей.
> Все хочешь ты иметь, а жертвовать не знаешь,
> Людей без гордости и сердца презираешь,
> А сам игрушка тех людей
>
> (3:22)

> (You are a person without character, morals or God; you are ambitious, spiteful, yet a weak man. The whole century is reflected in you, the current century, glittery yet petty. You want to fill your life, but avoid passions; you want to have it all, but do not know how to sacrifice; you despise people without heart or pride, but you yourself are a plaything of these people.)

The Baroness's subsequent behavior reveals, however, that her condemnation can be applied to herself, as well. Like Zvezdich, she remains a compliant toy of her society. She recognizes evil, but cannot resist it. When Zvezdich's active pursuit threatens her reputation, she is quite ready to sacrifice Nina: "But I will save myself . . . even at the expense of another" (*no ia sebia spasu . . . khotia b za schet drugoi*) (3:51).

Echoing the Baroness's noble aspirations, Prince Zvezdich frequently invokes the concept of "honor." He gives his word of honor not to pursue his masquerade acquaintance, yet immediately violates it. He pursues Nina against her protestations; having learned of Arbenin's jealousy, he prefers to make light of it. It never occurs to him to apologize to the man who had previously saved his fortune. The Prince might complain of losing his honor after Arbenin has skillfully insulted him, yet he does not manifest honorable behavior to begin with. It is just a mask that he has learned to wear. By flaunting their masks of honor and nobility the Prince and the Baroness only mimic and parody the essential aspects of Arbenin's personality.

The reason for Lermontov's relentless attacks on human weakness, on the propensity to "bend," is revealed in the Baroness's speech: weak people might detest villains, such as Shprikh or Kazarin, yet they eventually become their playthings (*a sam igrushka tex liudei*). The actions of the Baroness and the Prince fully support the truth of this ethical maxim.

The concept of *igrushka* (toy, puppet) occurs frequently in *The Masquerade* and acquires a symbolic meaning comparable to that of "bending" (*gnut'sia*). Arbenin describes Zvezdich as "the plaything of a masquerade" (*igrushka maskarada*) (3:40). The Baroness realizes that she herself is a toy when she muses upon the plight of women in society: "What is a woman, nowadays? A creature without will, a plaything for the passions and whims of others" (*Chto nyne zhenshchina? Sozdanie bez voli, igrushka dlia strastei il' prikhotei drugikh*) (3:43). Both the Prince and the Baroness are indeed "the playthings of a masquerade." It is only fitting that their love adventure as well as their eventual downfall originates there. It seems that the participants of Lermontov's drama are divided into "igroki" (players) and "igrushki" (playthings); that is, into the cynical and manipulative people like Kazarin, and their victims, those they play with.

Due to their strength and independence Lermontov's heroes cannot be anybody's toys. In his paradigmatic poem "Poet" (1838), Lermontov compares a contemporary poet to a harmless "plaything" (*igrushka*), a once-deadly dagger now hanging on a wall, and contrasts that ignoble plight to the poet's former glorious role of hero's companion:

Теперь родных ножон, избитых на войне,
Лишен *героя* спутник бедный,
Игрушкой золотой он блещет на стене—
Увы, бесславный и безвредный!

(1:37)

(Now, the hero's unfortunate companion is devoid of its former war-weathered sheath. Like a golden toy it shines on the wall, alas, inglorious and harmless.)

Similarly, Pechorin, having overheard a plan to orchestrate a duel with only one loaded gun, declares: "Take care, Mr. Grushnitsky. I am not to be trifled with like that. . . . I am not a *plaything* for you" (*Ia vam ne igrushka*) (147). Also, the name of Pechorin's rival, the foolish and naive Grushnitsky, practically echoes the word "*igrushka*" (a plaything).

The polarities of the gambling world (*igrok* versus *igrushka*) represent the two extremes of social possibilities between which Arbenin tries to mediate. What makes Arbenin the play's hero is that he strives to avoid the immoral dichotomy between players and playthings. He refuses to let others play with him, yet he hardly sees the point of playing with others. In a similar vein, Pechorin strives to be neither a master nor a slave. One of the tragedies of the play is the fact that Arbenin eventually sides with the victimizers. When asked by the humiliated and outplayed Prince whether he is a demon or a human being, Arbenin declares: "I am a gambler" (*Ia igrok*) (3:81).

Arbenin's words might resemble those of the Baroness or the Prince, as his actions resemble those of Kazarin or Shprikh, yet this resemblance is superficial. Arbenin is, in fact, drastically different from the doubles of the cardtable and masquerade. Manipulation for the sake of material gain, petty demonism, mask-wearing, or surrender to the necessity of evil are foreign concepts to him. It is his insistence on fair play that precludes Arbenin from murdering his rival, Prince Zvezdich. Arbenin, in fact, rushes to the Prince intending to kill him, yet, finding him asleep—that is, completely in his power—he does not kill him. Rather than slaying his helpless rival, as Pushkin's Aleko ("The Gypsies") does, or giving up on the very idea of retribution at the first check, as would many self-conscious yet weak characters of Russian literature, Arbenin finds a way to punish the Prince in an open confrontation and in a very elegant and appropriate manner. Arbenin is not bragging when he maintains that he has always stood up to evil. Nor is he bragging when he declares that he relies only on himself to achieve his goals. Arbenin is a person of integrity; he keeps the promises that he gives to himself and others, in contrast to the Prince or the Baroness, who fail to synchronize their words and actions.

Why is Lermontov more hostile to the Prince or the Baroness than to the murderous Arbenin, let alone the actual villains, such as Kazarin or Shprikh? Instead of dividing the world into a traditional mythical dichotomy of heroes and villains, Lermontov describes a modern phenomenon: that of a mass culture. For Lermontov the opposite of a heroic personality is not a villain, but a weak person. Lermontov never tires of presenting situations in which weak and gullible people become the playthings of evil, and thus extremely dangerous. By flaunting their masks of nobility and respectability they provide evil with what it needs the most: the appearance of good. (Lermontov's profound ethical insight that weakness inevitably becomes a servant of evil finds further development in Chekhov's work. Chekhov's numerous works, including *The Three Sisters* or "Ward No. 6," are closely associated with the issue. It is hardly a coincidence that Chekhov was one of Lermontov's greatest admirers.)

Having learned from the Baroness that she loves him and that he was pursuing the wrong woman, Zvezdich does nothing, failing to take either Nina or the Baroness seriously. The Prince might be less conniving than the rest of the characters, yet he remains a weapon in their hands. Characters like Zvezdich or Strahl point prophetically to the miseries of the next century, to the "banality of evil," which manifests itself not through a single villain, but through the masses of good-natured yet compliant individuals. Lermontov modeled the dynamics of the Baroness's and Prince's behavior, their involvement in literal and figurative masquerades, on his particular historical situation: the 1825 Decembrist uprising and its cultural aftermath. It is the events of this period that Lermontov's play captures in the vivid and encompassing metaphor of the masquerade.

MASQUERADES AND FREEDOM

Hard as he tried, Lermontov failed to get his play on stage. He encountered a power of censorship that was even more paranoid in the domain of theater than in that of belles-lettres (Kholodov et al. 1978, 28–31). *The Masquerade*'s censor E. Ol'dekop wrote in his report on Lermontov's play:

> Dramatic terrors have ended in France; do we really want to resurrect them here? Do we want to introduce poison into families? . . . Do we want to mimic dramatic ugliness that repulses even Paris? This is more than terrible, this simply does not have a name for itself. I am not sure whether the play can be allowed even after changes. . . . I cannot understand how the author dares to challenge ball-masquerades organized by Engelgardt. (quoted in Lermontov 1954–57, 5:741)

Oldekop's righteous indignation at "dramatic terrors" is all the more surprising when one considers the repertoire of Russian theater at the time: mostly frivolous vaudevilles and translated melodrama featuring incessant murder and violence.[5] One of the characters of A. F. Koni's vaudeville *Passion for Writing, or Here is a Robber for You* (*Strast' sochiniat' ili vot razboinik*) provides the following description of the situation on the Russian stage:

> Кинжалы и яды—
> Вот наши отрады!
> Все виды смертей:
> Удары мечей
> И казнь палачей
> И когти чертей.

Жалеть не должны мы,
Пусть будут казнимы,
Душимы, давимы
Все лица тотчас!
Чем больше у нас
Погибнет народа,
Чем больше потеха,
Тем больше успеха,
Тем больше дохода.
(quoted in Kholodov et al. 1978, 67)

(Daggers and poison—these are our joy, [and so are] all kinds of death: the blow of a sword, execution, or devils' claws. We should not feel pity; let everyone be immediately executed, strangled or crushed. The more people perish, the more fun, the more success, the more profit.)

Tsar Nicholas I, on whose behalf Oldekop was defending the purity of the Russian stage, is known to have asked his favorite actor Karatygin, "How many times have you strangled or stabbed your wife on stage this year?" (refering to Karatygin's wife, the well-known actress Kolosova, who frequently played opposite Karatygin).

If violence is not the reason, perhaps Lermontov's "romantic drama" contains other elements that would explain the censor's zealous outrage. Theatrical productions of the period, whether historical drama, melodrama, or vaudeville, rarely deal with events of contemporary Russia. Lermontov's play, on the other hand, while containing elements of romantic melodrama, presents a rather unflattering picture of high society. Five out of the play's ten scenes depict gambling, masquerades, affairs, gossip, and other favorite pastimes of Saint Petersburg's beau monde. The censor preferred to allow one more play of Gothic terror than a play subjecting contemporary Russian society to unflattering scrutiny. It is indicative that Oldekop focuses on masquerades and is scandalized by the way they are presented in the play. Furthermore, after having read the revised version of the play, Oldekop voiced the same complaint: "In the new version we find the same indecent attacks on Engelhardt's ball-masquerades . . . and the same insolence toward the noble ladies of high society" (quoted in Lermontov 1954–57, 5:742). Is the censor simply barking up the wrong tree, or does Lermontov's interpretation of masquerades indeed constitute "a challenge" to the institution of masquerades, and thus to the autocratic system that patronizes them?

By now it has become almost canonical to view masquerades as a realm of sexual freedom. This scholarly dogma owes much to the carnivalesque utopia of Bakhtin, and was further developed by scholars in search of some kind of alternative to the hierarchical and oppressive systems they found objectionable. Terry Castle's *Masquerade and Civilization* (1986) is a noteworthy example of such endeavor. Clearly, sexuality plays an important role in masquerades, these "promiscuous gatherings" as they were called in eighteenth-century England. Lermontov could not but acknowledge the erotic and liberating dimension of masquerades. Nevertheless, even if sexual intrigue forms the basis of the play, Lermontov's interests lie elsewhere. Lermontov's play describes a popular pastime of Russian nobility, suggests the reasons for the masquerade's popularity, and warns of its dangers. What follows explores how Lermontov criticizes the institution of masquerades for providing only a simulacrum of freedom and liberation.

Arbenin, who gives up on cardgames (*igra*) and other games his society enjoys, comes to the masquerade without a mask. He is thus instantly recognized and insulted by someone who hides behind the anonymity of a mask. In a society where mask-wearing becomes the norm, where success depends only on one's ability to wear masks that fit dominant cultural expectations, Arbenin's bare face creates a scandal and arouses hostility. Nevertheless, it is precisely the lack of a mask, the ability to bare one's face in a society where playacting and hypocrisy have become the norm, that qualifies Arbenin for the title of hero. He might make mistakes, but at least they are his own; they are the product of his own personality and his own "proud mind."

By contrast, the anonymity of the mask allows the Baroness to assume any identity that fits the occasion. In terms of Lermontov's play she can be "a Diana in society and a Venus at the masquerade" (*Diana v obshchestve, Venera v maskarade*) (3:20). The Baroness moves freely between the unrestrained freedom of the masquerade and the oppressive structures of her society. Her manipulative association with social norms exposes the repressive rather than liberating role of masquerades. Lermontov's interpretation of the masquerade hardly fits Bakhtin's utopian vision of the carnivalesque. Bakhtin (1968) viewed the masquerade under the general rubric of a carnival: "The Romantic mask still retains something of its popular carnival nature" (39–40).

As though following Lermontov's exposure of the dual role of the Baroness, several critics of Bakhtin have observed that the carnival itself is deeply implicated in the hierarchical structure of society. As Linda Hutcheon (1989) notes: "the motivation and the form of the carnivalesque are both derived from authority: the second life of the carnival has meaning only in relation to the official first life. . . . The medieval church may have tolerated, legalized, perhaps even preserved or created, the carnivalesque forms, but it did so only for a permitted length of time" (99).

Lermontov is clearly aware of the subversive or even liberating aspects of masquerade. Yet the events of the play suggest that Lermontov refuses to acknowledge genuinely liberating effects behind such a moment of abandon. Masquerades encourage or even presuppose anonymity, and thus have nothing to do with individual courage and responsibility. It is hardly a coincidence that Arbenin accuses the person who insulted him while hiding behind the mask of dishonorable conduct: "Take off your mask—and now, you act dishonorably" (*snimite masku—i seichas! Vy postupaete beschestno*) (3:24). For Lermontov the theatrical and impersonal simulation of freedom is not a substitute for genuine liberty.

For Bakhtin, by contrast, carnivals, regardless of their license and impunity, possess "inner freedom," an assertion that puzzles many of his readers. Bakhtin maintains: "Exterior freedom and impunity are inseparable from the inner positive meaning of [the carnival]. . . . The exterior freedom of popular-festive forms was inseparable from their inner freedom" (1968, 270–71). Bakhtin's eulogizing of the carnival is bound to confuse, especially when on the same page that he asserts the inner freedom of the carnival, he interprets the sadistic actions of Ivan the Terrible in terms of Ivan's appropriation of carnivalesque methods (270–71). Commenting on these passages Morson and Emerson (1990) are justifiably puzzled: "The extent and kind of double-voicing operative in such passages is exceedingly difficult to determine" (447–48). It is a rather benevolent evaluation: it grants Bakhtin his favorite "loophole" (*lazeika*) to avoid responsibility for his book, which, regardless of its anthropological insights, appears to be a rather consistent embrace and justification of all possible communal abuses.

In fact, the freedom of the masquerade was glorified in Russian society long before Bakhtin, and precisely for the same utopian reasons. Here are a few lines from a poem entitled "Why I Love Masquerades" (*Zachem ia liubliu maskarady*) (1850), written by one of Lermontov's contemporaries, Evdokia Rostopchina (1986):

> Измучась жизнию действительной, вседневной,
> Я жизни призрачной наружный блеск ловлю,
> И даже суету, и даже ложь терплю
> Чтоб только мне спастись от истины плачевной. . . .
> Да, точно я люблю *свободу маскарада;*
> Так не замечена, *не знаема никем,*
> *Я правду говорю и всякому и всем;*
> Я, *жертва общества, раба его,*—я рада,
> Что посмеяться раз могу в глаза над ним.
> (228; my emphasis)

> (Having been tormented by real, everyday life, I try to capture the external glitter of the imaginary life, and tolerate anxiety and even lies, only to be saved from the tragic truth. . . . Indeed I love *the freedom of the masquerade,* when *unnoticed and unknown I tell the truth to everyone and to all; I, the victim and slave of society*—I am glad I can look into its eyes and laugh.)

Rostopchina honestly admits that she finds redeeming the very aspects of the masquerade that Lermontov condemns: its lies, its avoidance of painful realities, its license to pronounce anonymous truths, while hiding behind a mask. Rostopchina, though, is courageous enough to realize that the freedom of the masquerade is the freedom of a slave, the last resort of victims sticking out their tongues at those who enslave them. Rostopchina finds such impersonal reenacting of freedom satisfying, while Lermontov clearly shows that the theatrical simulation of freedom is, in fact, a contradiction in terms. Complaints about the repressive role of society were, in fact, a part of social and literary discourse. Writings from Griboedov to numerous society tales, whether by Vladimir Sollogub or Odoevsky, amply testify to this. Lermontov mocks such clichéd condemnations when he reveals that the Baroness's diatribe is inspired by her reading of George Sand, another fashionable author of the period. The Baroness, as usual, follows fashions and plays by the rules, and her references to George Sand and complaint of repression are simply a fashionable mask.

MASQUERADES AND POST-DECEMBRIST RUSSIA

The scope and sharpness of Lermontov's attack on masquerades and on the general "masqueradization" of his society become even more impressive when the cultural atmosphere of the period is considered. Scholars of the period do not completely neglect the period's propensity for role-playing and mask-wearing. Inspired by Iuri Lotman's work on theatricality in the early nineteenth century, scholars frequently employ theatrical concepts in discussing fictional characters of that period, including Lermontov's characters. It is a rare essay on *A Hero of Our Time* that does not make reference to Pechorin's mask-wearing.[6] It is clear, though, that the earlier *Masquerade* rather than *A Hero of Our Time* is a more logical place to begin analysis of Lermontov's preoccupation with mask-wearing. However, scholars who explore Lermontov's treatment of theatricality only rarely give Lermontov's play the attention it deserves.[7]

Lermontov's hostility toward mask-wearing is well attested both in his life and in his texts. He refused to take a pen name when it was very fashionable to do so; his protagonists reject mask-wearing, and such poems as "Surrounded by a Colorful Crowd, How Frequently . . ." (*Kak chasto pestroiu tolpoiu okruzhen*, 1840) contain outbursts of anger about masked balls. In fact, Lermontov is known to have insulted the masked members of the royal family at one of the masquerade balls of 1840. It is my contention that Lermontov's hostility toward masks and role-playing is directly connected to his preoccupation with the issues of heroism and individualism; that is, with the expression of individual courage, dignity, and responsibility. The search for a hero and the attacks on masquerades are Lermontov's responses to the cultural conflict of his period, when some of the liberating, individual-centered values of Romanticism were exposed to post-Decembrist Russian oppression, resulting in a conflict that was all but impossible to resolve, unless one was willing to tolerate inner disunity, falsehood, and mask-wearing.

Pushkin (1937–59) reflects on his society's increased preoccupation with mask-wearing in his sarcastic description of Evgenii Onegin:

> Скажите: чем он возвратится?
> Что нам представит он пока?
> Чем ныне явится? Мельмотом,
> Космополитом, патриотом,
> Гарольдом, квакером, ханжой,
> Иль маской щегольнет иной.
> (6:168)

> (Tell me, who would he be upon his return, what will he present to us, how would he appear? As Melmoth, a cosmopolite, a patriot, Childe Harold, a Quaker, a prude, or would he flaunt another mask?)

The popularity of mask-wearing when Pushkin composed these lines can be discerned from a curious fact. The late 1830s in Russia was a time of odd pen names, name-masks that were fashionable among the great and not-so-great Russian writers: Belkin (Pushkin), Rudyi Pan'ko (Gogol), Gomozeika (Vladimir Odoevsky), Baron Brambeus (Senkovsky), Kazak Lugansky (Dahl), and so on. This fashion, like many other Russian fashions, had been popularized by Alexander Bestuzhev, who under his pen name, Marlinsky, virtually dominated the Russian literary scene of the 1830s. Lermontov, it should be stressed, remained aloof from such literary trends.

The post-Decembrist period saw the increased popularity of actual masquerades among Russia's high society (see Gershtein 1986, 41–55). Like masquerades in other countries, Russian masquerades, at least judging from their representation in fiction, were rather democratic. According to one observer, masquerades "democratically united the highs and lows of Saint Petersburg—everyone appeared there, from haughty princesses to flighty seekers of fleeting pleasures" (quoted in Ashukin 1941, 225). Everyone who could pay the price of the ticket and who wore a costume was admitted. An author of a tale appropriately titled "Masquerade" and published in the popular magazine *Library for Reading* (*Biblioteka dlia chteniia*) observed that participants addressed each other in familiar terms, "na ty," and that women pursued men, so that "men would frequently blush" (Neverin 1839, 41). The most popular masquerades were organized by one Engelhardt (both Lermontov's play and the censor Oldekop refer to him), who had secured from the government the right to conduct them. Engelhardt's masquerades, which were a regular feature of Saint Petersburg life from 1829 to 1835, were a popular if expensive entertainment. He, in fact, had to reduce the entrance fee from ten to five rubles in order to make it affordable for more people.

Russian literature reflected the increased popularity of masquerades. Marlinsky's society tale "The Trial" (1830), for example, features the usual combination of masquerades, sexual intrigues, impending duels, and even a character named Zvezdich. That fact alone should alert us to the polemical nature of Lermontov's play. There are also stories such as "Masquerade" (1834) by Nikolai Pavlov, or the already quoted "Masquerade" (1839) written by one G. Neverin. The latter tale features no other than Alexander Pushkin, who uses all his wit and mastery of masquerade rules to help an industrious woman get the man she pursues. Such stories vividly attest to the increased popularity of masquerades in fiction, and ultimately in real life.

The proliferation of actual masquerades, as well as the texts devoted to them, are clearly connected to the figurative masquerade in which the general public was engaged: the post-Decembrist masquerade of pretension and self-deception. The post-Decembrist period was by far the most traumatic period of the Russian nineteenth century. The belief in individual possibilities that resulted from victory over Napoleon were abruptly replaced by brutal investigations, the secret police, and fear. The faith in its own strength that the nobility had only begun to acquire after the reigns of Catherine and Paul was shattered by the reign of Nicholas I.

A brief passage in Goncharov's memoirs vividly describes the masqueradization of social life, the process that Lermontov and his contemporaries had to witness, if not participate in:

> All terrorized masons, nonmasons, and erstwhile liberals, as a result of the harsh government measures, calmed down, effaced themselves, and quickly turned into archconservatives, even chauvinists—some sincerely, some put on masks (*nadeli maski*). But they would use any opportunity, even when it was not called for, to declare their devotion to the "throne and fatherland." . . . Everyone got himself a uniform; former atheists began attending holiday church services and would then visit and congratulate the governor. They would take off their hats before any high-ranking visiting official, and then pay visits to him. (1986, 152)

Goncharov, in fact, describes the period of 1834–35, precisely the years when Lermontov's play was written. Goncharov conveys the atmosphere of fear that had paralyzed even the most noble and courageous members of the gentry. Events in Russia during the next century would probably dwarf post-Decembrist anxiety and hypocrisy, yet the scare was real, as were its effects on human behavior. Describing the conduct of one courageous navy officer, Goncharov writes: "Like many others, he was terrorized by the alarm that 14 December produced in all of Russian society. The tail of that alarm kept on wiggling not only in the provinces but even in the capitals" (1986, 150). The government's violence and bullying led not to the expression of outrage, but to the internalization of fear and guilt: "Everyone who was summoned and interrogated got so scared that for a long time afterward they were afraid to discuss it even among themselves, even in a whisper" (152). Goncharov illustrates this assertion by describing how Simbirsk residents would resort to whispering when referring to the secret torture of an innocent member of a local mason lodge (152).

A famous Russian historian, Sergei Solov'ev, characterizes Nicholas I and his reign in the following manner: "a despot by nature . . . he was an incarnated 'shut up and listen.' . . . The military parade became the purpose of social and national life. Everything was done for the sake of showing off, for the sake of making sure that the sovereign would arrive, examine, and pronounce: 'good, everything is in order'" (quoted in Ashukin 1941, 211–12). Solov'ev clearly connects the reigning terror with the masqueradization of all national and social institutions.

The reigning hypocrisy was quite shocking for foreigners. The marquis de Custine, who had visited Russia in the late 1830s with the stated purpose of finding a haven from the abuses of democracy, was in fact scandalized by the incessant Russian need to pretend, to be engaged in a perennial masquerade: "With the Russians, appearance is everything, and among them appearance deceives more than it does among others. . . . Social life in that country is a permanent conspiracy against the truth" (1989, 615). He continues his attacks on lies and hypocrisy: "The strength of despotism lies in the mask of the despot. When the sovereign can no longer lie, the people are free; thus I see no other evil in this world except that of falsehood" (603). As if echoing Kazarin's assessment of his society, de Custine observes: "In Russia, whatever be the appearance of things, violence and arbitrary rule are at the bottom of them all" (611). In light of such statements the observation of Lermontov's early translator and biographer, Friedrich Bodenstedt, acquires new urgency: "Having been raised in a society where hypocrisy and deception are considered the sign of bon ton, Lermontov remained a stranger to all lies and pretenses till his last sigh" (Vatsuro and Gei 1989, 365).

The Decembrist uprising was surrounded by silence throughout the reign of Nicholas I. Censors, for example, were forbidden to allow in print even references to the Decembrists' names; a formidable task, no doubt, since the Decembrists were among the most prominent people of the period, well known to anyone on the cultural scene. The trauma of the events—from the failed and disorganized attempt at revolt, to the denunciations and treachery of the investigation, to the ruthless punishment—was too great even to acknowledge. Applying the insights of psychoanalysis to the cultural life of society, one might conclude that this traumatic experience resulted in arresting Russia's cultural development, or even in reversing its development. Thus, the resurgence in the 1830s of a certain type of 1820s behavior was not coincidental. It was a reaction, at least in part, to the events of the Decembrist uprising.[8]

In a series of articles Iury Lotman has addressed the theatricality of everyday behavior in the early nineteenth century. Commenting on the theatrical behavior of the Decembrists, Lotman praises its liberating effect and writes: "It was precisely the model of theatrical behavior that, by turning a person into a character in a play, liberated him from the automatic sway of group behavior and of custom" (Lotman and Uspenskii 1984, 160). In fact, becoming a "character in a play" is as enslaving as any other mode of group behavior or custom. As if sensing that he is on the same shaky ground as Bakhtin, Lotman adds a proviso: "A little time would pass and the literalness and theatricality of the real-life imitators of Marlinsky's or Schiller's heroes would itself become a group norm that hindered the individual expression of the personality" (Lotman and Uspenskii 1984, 160).

Lotman never explains why one theatricality liberates "the individual expression of the personality" while the other hinders it. It seems that theatricality and affected behavior provided the Decembrists with the surrogate freedom of a masquerade. In fact, Lotman quotes Marlinsky's brother, Nikolai Bestuzhev, who called Kondraty Ryleev's plan of going to the Senate Square on 14 December in peasant clothes "a masquerade" (Lotman and Uspenskii 1984, 150).

It is my contention that the theatricalities of the 1820s and 1830s in large part mirror each other. In both decades theatricality represents a self-deluding attempt to come to terms with a lack of basic freedoms. There is an important difference between the two, however. The theatricality of the 1820s was irresponsible and childish, yet organic, so that the youthful and naive dreamers genuinely aspired to achieve freedom by taking their masquerade tactics to the Senate Square. In the next decade, the already frightened public attempted to relive its childhood aspirations and cautiously limited its search for freedom to artificial constructs, such as literary fantasies, or fashionable masquerades. In other words, while the masquerade of the 1820s was spontaneous, the latter one was institutionalized and directed from above. Lermontov's Zvezdich, who does not know when to stop his masquerade love affair, captures the mood of the 1820s, while the more careful and cynical Baroness Strahl is a perfect representative of the post-Decembrist decade.

Masquerades, however, are a bad school for responsibility. It is not surprising that the Decembrists' naïveté, lack of experience, and reliance on romantic slogans left them helpless in the cellars of the Peter and Paul Fortress, prey to treachery, denunciations, and cowardice. Serious students of Decembrism have been scandalized by the ready capitulation of some of the noblest and bravest of Russian men. Shchegolev (1926) writes:

> Having been subjected to investigation the plotters failed to show any strength, and with surprising abandon rushed to inform their judges of all their secret actions, all words dropped with or without intention in a mindless chatter. . . . They rushed to mention more and more names, knowing well that every such

reference would lead to an arrest. They sometimes did not even pause before an obvious libel and went on with their endless expressions of remorse. . . . Had they not been so eloquent and verbose, had they thought more about the result of their denunciations, undoubtedly there would have been fewer victims and less suffering. (138)

Lermontov himself, although acquainted with many Decembrists, remained notably hostile to their naive enthusiasm. The Decembrist M. A. Nazimov, for example, recalls: "We did not understand each other well. . . . He would appear frequently as the realist, glued to earth, without inspiration; while in his poetry, he was flying high on his powerful wings. . . . He mocked government's decisions with which we fully sympathized and about which we dreamed in our unfortunate youth" (quoted in Viskovatov 1987, 272). The reason for Lermontov's hostility is clear. Aware of the events surrounding the Decembrist uprising and its aftermath, and hostile to the human weakness that easily becomes a plaything of evil (a dynamic vividly demonstrated by numerous Decembrists), Lermontov could not take their aspirations seriously. Lermontov knew a Prince Zvezdich when he saw one.

This survey of the historical situation enables us to appreciate fully the thrust of Lermontov's play. Some rather traditional preoccupations of gentry society, such as cardgames, masked balls, and dueling experienced a sudden and powerful revival in the 1830s. Lermontov's play scrutinizes these popular activities of his society and approaches their revival with caution, if not with criticism. These three activities, separate and different as they are, have certain things in common. From a psychological perspective they express the need to surrender to the unknown, to chance, so as to avoid the total domination of the tsar and his ministers, to escape the social and cultural control that had become intolerable. Lermontov's celebrated poem "Farewell, Unwashed Russia" (1840) expresses a desire to avoid "the all-seeing eyes and all-hearing ears" of the Russian tsars. The Russian nobility, crushed by punishment and unable to manifest its individuality or dignity in a straightforward way, had to resort to a rather strained manifestation of these qualities. Cards, duels, or masquerades testify not so much to the corruption of ruling classes, as to a desperate search for independence, anonymity, and escape from totalitarian control. It is thus hardly a coincidence that Bakhtin articulated his theories of the carnival precisely at a time of increased Stalinist tyranny. It seems that not only carnivalization, but also its theoretical or artistic explorations, are encouraged by repressive hierarchy.

Lermontov knows that the proper evaluation of such activities as masquerades, gambling, or dueling demands an understanding of the circumstances that give rise to them. However, despite his understanding, he does not find these manifestations of the human spirit heroic, not because they are "sinful," but because they still avoid individual choice and responsibility. As his presentation of Arbenin makes clear, Lermontov is aware that such activities provide only a poor substitute for freedom and happiness; they remain as restricting and limiting as the society that embraces them. Arbenin masters these activities, understands their inner mechanisms, and concludes that "happiness is not to be found there" (*schastiia zdes' net*) (3:14). Returning to the governing metaphor of the text, that of "bending," it might be concluded that the play exposes and condemns a "bending spine," whether it belongs to those who bend a card, or those who resort to masquerades in a futile search for dignity and freedom.

ARBENIN: WOE FROM WIT

Even if Lermontov elaborates upon the complex metaphor of masquerade, and creates secondary characters to articulate what he thinks about post-Decembrist Russia, he is also concerned with the construction of a hero of that time. The character of the play's protagonist, Arbenin, is the first serious attempt on the part of Lermontov to come to terms with a Byronic hero. Arbenin exhibits the whole range of such generic features as boredom and disillusionment, search for love and revenge, strength and integrity.[9] Lermontov's hero, nonetheless, exhibits several rather singular features. One that I shall explore in the remainder of the chapter is Arbenin's involvement with issues that were to haunt several of Lermontov's heroes: namely, his attempt to come to terms with such fundamental aspects of human existence as happiness and knowledge, as well as their complex interaction. The dynamic of this interaction became a subject of scrutiny for Lermontov's contemporaries as well, as the very title of Griboedov's famous comedy *Woe From Wit* underscores.

Lermontov's play, subtitled a "romantic drama," contains elements of several previous texts that range from the Romantic theater of Schiller and Hugo, to French melodrama, to Shakespeare's *Othello*, Pushkin's "Gypsies," and Griboedov's *Woe from Wit*. While the similarities to most of these texts can be grouped under the heading of learning the craft, the dialogue with Griboedov's play appears to be an integral part of Lermontov's design. Lermontov's earlier play *A Strange Man* (1834) already showed the thematic and linguistic imprint of Griboedov's masterpiece. In *The Masquerade*, however, Lermontov's writing is mature enough to engage Griboedov's text in order to advance his own artistic and philosophical agenda.[10]

Similarities between the plays point unequivocally to *Woe from Wit* as the formal, thematic, and even philosophical antecedent of Lermontov's play. Both are four-act plays written in the same metrical scheme (rhymed iambic verse with varying numbers of feet per line); both contain witty and biting characterizations of members of contemporary society; both feature a female heroine, who tries to extricate herself from a compromising situation by utilizing the mechanism of society gossip. The plays also include immoral male characters who serve as vehicles for transmitting such gossip (Shprikh and Zagoretsky). In both plays, the attempts of intellectually brilliant protagonists to secure happiness within their societies are thwarted, whether by the actual loss of sanity (Arbenin), or by the accusation of madness (Chatsky). *The Masquerade* addresses directly Griboedov's theme of intelligence and its relationship to success and happiness. In fact, Lermontov's play ends with a line that points directly to the title of Griboedov's play *Gore ot uma.* Commenting on Arbenin's madness, one of the characters declares: "He is happy without his wits" (*On bez uma . . . schastliv*) (3:114).

However, it is the differences between the two plays that reveal the originality and thrust of Lermontov's creation. Griboedov dramatizes a clear-cut conflict, already familiar to the readers of *Don Quixote:* between the crude materialism of society and the idealism of the protagonist. Lermontov preserves the structure of the conflict and utilizes Griboedov's satirical methods to criticize contemporary society. But he also explores moral and philosophical issues that remain out of Griboedov's reach and creates a much more complex and dynamic picture of his protagonist. Chatsky's conflict with Russian society is externalized: he remains a stranger to his Moscow hosts; he comes from abroad and then rushes away. Arbenin, on the other hand, is closely tied to his society, socially, morally, and philosophically. Striving to overcome and transcend these ties Arbenin struggles mostly with himself.

Some of the differences between the protagonists can be attributed to the zeitgeist, to the fact that *Woe From Wit* and *The Masquerade* belong respectively to the early and later stages of Romanticism.[11] Having lost his very first confrontation with evil, Chatsky rushes away, expressing his indignation at the fact that the world belongs to mediocre conformists like Molchalin, yet doing nothing about such a state of affairs. As a true Byronic hero, Arbenin, on the other hand, insists on active counterattack and revenge. Chatsky suffers from excessive idealism (which gave Pushkin and others an opportunity to accuse Chatsky of foolishness); regardless of numerous things that he observes, Chatsky refuses to think ill of Sophia. It is precisely the lack of idealism that ruins Arbenin, who views his wife as an archvillain upon the slightest suspicion. If an early Romantic hero was more idealistic than his society (Goethe's Werther, for example) the later one scandalizes his society with cynicism and skepticism even if he himself suffers from such an outlook. Griboedov presents Chatsky's wisdom as a kind of light, engulfed by the darkness of society. Internalizing the play's conflict, Lermontov presents Arbenin's wisdom—that is, his experience, skepticism, and skills—not only as light, but also as a darkness that ultimately fails to come to terms with light. Arbenin's cynical, pessimistic outlook is as much the cause of his fall as are the intrigues of a hostile society.

It seems that Lermontov explores a more profound and pertinent question than does Griboedov when he contrasts his idealistic protagonist to a cynical society. Given that reality, and particularly Russian reality, has a swift and brutal way of curing excessive idealism, what is one to do with an excessive awareness of evil? How does one respond to a universe already perceived as evil? Life would hardly prove anyone wrong who expects the worst of it. To hope that nature will take its course and cure excessive pessimism is rather naive, if not irresponsible; it would only lead to the opposite effect. It is my contention that Lermontov—through such characters as Arbenin, Pechorin, Kalashnikov, or Mtsyri—thoroughly addressed the issues of theodicy, and examined various lines of reasoning and modes of behavior that result in and help to vanquish encroaching gloom and pessimism.

The title *Woe from Wit* suggests a certain causal relationship between happiness/misery and wisdom/ignorance: wisdom and woe go together. It is clear that such an evaluation of this relationship is as old as the first bite of the biblical apple. The famous verse from Ecclesiastes echoes this sentiment: "for in much wisdom is much grief, and he that increaseth knowledge, increaseth sorrow" (1:18). That maxim has achieved the status of a proverb in the Russian language, and it is clear that both Griboedov and Lermontov respond to it. Griboedov's play shares the outlook of the biblical text, yet it does not deny the possibility of happiness at least for the ignorant. The universe of the play condones or even rewards obscurantism, vulgar materialism, and ignorance, while punishing the disinterested search for knowledge. Famusov, in fact, explicitly views conformism and social climbing as intelligence. Referring to a notorious practitioner of these pursuits, he states: "according to our standards, he is clever"; while Famusov's daughter Sophia dismisses the impractical mind of Chatsky: "but can such a mind provide happiness for his family?" Sophia is wise enough to know that happiness and intelligence occupy two opposite poles of human existence.

Lermontov, who was truly haunted by the theme of evasive happiness, makes happiness the subject of his most penetrating scrutiny in the play. *The Masquerade* does not dispute the biblical equation, yet Arbenin goes even further in denying the possibility of happiness. He is convinced that happiness is out of reach of both the wise and ignorant.

One of the first lines that Arbenin utters stresses the unattainable nature of happiness. When the Prince expresses the hope of getting lucky at the cardtable, Arbenin remarks: "Oh, happiness is not to be found here." He knows that success in gambling, as it is practiced in his circle, has nothing to do with luck. However, if taken on a more symbolic level, the remark prophetically points to the absence of happiness in this world. Happiness surely eludes the gullible victims of deception and manipulation, yet it equally eludes those who win. Gamblers in Lermontov's play rely on certainty rather than on chance; they thus lack openness to the unexpected, an essential element of happiness. That is one of the reasons behind Arbenin's relinquishing gambling. Having recouped the Prince's loss Arbenin comments: "I see through it all . . . know all their tricks, and that is why I do not gamble now" (*Ia vizhu vsio naskvoz' . . . vse tonkosti ikh znaiu, i vot zachem ia nynche ne igraiu*) (3:17). Arbenin's knowledge and skills are such that he could not have lost, yet happiness cannot be gained in the absence of chance and true competition.

Describing the days when he could, in fact, lose as "blessed days," Arbenin acknowledges that the experience of bliss is connected with accepting limits to one's own knowledge, with being open to uncertainty and chance; that is, with being at least partly ignorant. Arbenin returns to this connection between chance and happiness in the next scene as well. During the masquerade ball the Prince comments on his adventure with an unknown mask: "But happiness descended all by itself" (*no schast'e naletelo samo soboi*); to which Arbenin responds: "Yes, happiness always does that" (*da, schast'e—vechno tak*) (3:29). Happiness is thus directly connected with the unexpected, with the uncertain. Nonetheless Arbenin refuses to accept such a shaky foundation for his happiness; he is convinced that even if happiness and ignorance might feed off each other, they inevitably self-destruct:

Видал я много юношей, надежд
И чувства полных, счастливых невежд
В науке жизни . . . пламенных душою,
Которых прежде цель была одна любовь . . .
Они погибли быстро предо мною

(3:13)

(I've seen many young men, full of hopes and emotions, happy ignoramuses in the science of life . . . with a burning soul, whose only goal was love . . . yet, they all perished in front of my eyes).

Describing ignorant people as "happy" and rhyming "hopes" with "ignoramuses" (*nadezhd/nevezhd*) Arbenin acknowledges the strong ties between ignorance on the one hand and happiness, hope, and love on the other. However, ignorance in "the science of life" leaves one vulnerable, unprotected, and bound to be destroyed. Happiness does not last; woe from foolishness is as inevitable as woe from wit.

Arbenin finds himself in a paradoxical situation. He is aware that knowledge is detrimental to happiness because it eliminates chance and uncertainty. Yet it is that very uncertainty that Arbenin perceives as a threat to his happiness. He reveals this in one of his monologues. Claiming to be bored with his wisdom and knowledge, he admits to being terrified by the uncertainty brought to him by his love for Nina:

Романа не начав, я знал уже развязку. . . .
И тяжко стало мне и скучно жить. . . .
Как агнец божий на закланье,
Мной к алтарю она приведена. . . .

И вдруг во мне забытый звук проснулся:
Я в душу мертвую свою взглянул. . . .
И увидал, что я ее люблю;
И стыдно молвить . . . ужаснулся! . . .
Опять мечты, опять любовь. . . .
Изломанный челнок, я снова брошен в море:
Вернусь ли к пристани я вновь?

(3:32)

(Before starting the affair, I already knew the outcome. . . . And life became hard and boring for me. . . . Like a sacrificial lamb she was taken by me to the altar, and suddenly a forgotten sound awoke in me. I looked into my dead soul and saw that I loved her, and I am ashamed to say it. . . . I got terrified! Again the dreams, again love. . . . A broken boat, I am cast into the sea again: will I return to safe haven this time?)

The image of a broken boat cast into a sea reveals Arbenin's fears. He expresses a normal human desire to return to a safe haven; but this haven, in terms of his life, can only be the former world of gambling, that is, of knowledge, certainty, boredom, and misery.

Arbenin recovers his happiness after he marries Nina. In his speeches he frequently connects happiness and Nina: "I am happy, happy. . . . When I am away from the envious and evil crowd, I am happy . . . I am with you! We are talking about my happiness here" (*ia schastliv, schastliv. . . . Daleko ot tolpy zavistlivoi i zloi, ia schastliv . . . ia s toboi; O schastii moem tut rech' idet*) (3:36–37). But the arbitrariness and uncertainty of love scandalize him; they put his happiness on the same shaky foundation as the bliss of the naive fools whom he despises. Arbenin is thus in a dilemma: in striving for happiness he rejects the randomness and unpredictability that accompany it. This situation is rather common in the world of Lermontov: in one of his 1830 poems, "Advice," he bemoans the plight of someone "who finds happiness, having lost the feeling for happiness" (1:134). In other words, anything that constitutes happiness becomes meaningless for someone who is no longer open to the unknown and unexpected.

That is why love becomes such a stumbling block in Lermontov's world. All his characters seek love with inexhaustible ardor and energy, yet they rarely become happier even when they find it. Love for another human being presupposes the freedom of love's object, and therefore the possibility of losing it. When the Demon falls in love with Tamara, he experiences "the fear of the unknown" (*strakh neizvestnosti*) (2:59). The acceptance of the unknown is the price for the possibility of happiness, yet neither Arbenin nor the Demon is willing to pay it. Totality of knowledge seems to be their main goal, for which they sacrifice their happiness. They would rather know evil than take chances with goodness. As the play progresses Arbenin feels an increasing need to control the freedom and uncertainty that accompany love; he insists on knowledge and certainty even if such insistence takes him back to the world of gambling and away from love.

THE PHILOSOPHY OF A DECK OF CARDS

Trying to attract Arbenin back to his gambling world, Kazarin insists that the microcosm of gambling should be seen as an emblem of the macrocosm. Kazarin introduces his outlook with the following words: "I'm going to disclose the mystery of earthly wisdom" (*otkroiu tainstvo premudrosti zemnoi*). We are dealing with ultimate philosophical issues:

Что ни толкуй Вольтер или Декарт
Мир для меня—колода карт,
Жизнь банк; рок мечет, я играю,
И правила игры я к людям применяю.
(3:61)

(No matter what Voltaire or Descartes says, the world is a deck of cards for me. Life is a bank; fate deals, I play, and I apply to people the rules of the game.)

Arbenin, we should remember, enters the play not as a gambler, but as a happy family man. Gambling was a thing of his past, something that he would rather forget. Yet, even if he easily gives up the thrill of victory or the material gains that might be associated with gambling, it proves more difficult to resist the intellectual temptation of extrapolating the "rules of the game to people" and develop another outlook than that of a gambler (*igrok*). Spurred by the events surrounding the loss of Nina's bracelet, and tempted by the words of the play's demon, Kazarin, Arbenin eventually returns to his former outlook and identity as a gambler. In a symbolic exchange at the end of the play, Zvezdich asks Arbenin: "Are you a demon or a human being?" (*demon vy il' chelovek?*); to which Arbenin responds: "I am a gambler" (*ia igrok*) (3:81). The circle is complete. Arbenin, who first destroys the gamblers' plan to take advantage of their plaything, Prince Zvezdich, is now being welcomed back to the brotherhood of gamblers. Kazarin understands this when he remarks: "now he is mine" (*teper' on moi*) (3:65).

What are the rules of the gambling world that Kazarin insists on applying to people? Arbenin, who like Kazarin sees gambling as some kind of philosophical enterprise, articulates these rules in his own speech on gambling.[12] Discussing gambling in such unusual terms as knowledge, wisdom, and experience, Arbenin connects the victory at the cardtable with ruthless self-analysis, with philosophical inquiry based on skepticism, and with contempt for all external laws:

Но чтобы здесь выигрывать решиться,
Вам надо кинуть всё: родных, друзей и честь,

Вам надо испытать, ощупать беспристрастно
Свои способности и душу: по частям
Их разобрать; привыкнуть ясно
Читать на лицах, чуть знакомых вам,
Все побужденья, мысли; годы
Употребить на упражненья рук,
Всё презирать: закон людей, закон природы,
День думать, ночь играть, от мук не знать свободы,
И чтоб никто не понял ваших мук.
Не трепетать, когда близ вас искусством равный,
Удачи каждый миг постыдный ждать конец
И не краснеть, когда вам скажут явно:
"Подлец!"

(3:13)

(But if you decide to win here, you'll have to abandon it all: relatives, friends, honor; you'll have to subject your soul and your abilities to a passionless scrutiny; to learn to dissect them. Get used to reading clearly in the faces of others, who are hardly familiar to you, all their inspirations and thoughts. Spend years exercising your hands; learn to despise everything: the laws of people, the laws of nature; think all day long, and gamble at night; do not know freedom from pain, and yet hide your suffering from others. Do not tremble when dealing with someone equal to you in skills, expect any minute the shameful end of your luck, and never blush, when being openly called "a scoundrel.")

Arbenin describes here the process of intense philosophical inquiry that his terminology reveals: "try, experiment, think, decipher, take apart, analyze, the laws of people, the laws of nature." The ultimate result of this quest is total intellectual clarity and certainty: "to read clearly in the faces of others . . . all their inspirations and thoughts." Yet, by learning to read *all* the thoughts and intentions of his rivals, and to respond to them immediately, Arbenin dooms himself to an existence in the predictable world of skills and certainty, where nothing unusual can happen; where every sign, as every card, means something. Arbenin is aware of the price that such wisdom and success demand: separation from everything, whether oneself, others, traditions, values, or happiness. Arbenin views the mastery of the world of gambling as epistemological success, but as a human failure.

It is this comfort of certainty and knowledge that Arbenin gives up when he falls in love with Nina. Conversely, Arbenin's downfall, his retreat from love, is directly connected to his search for the totality of knowledge and control. Arbenin's intellectual prowess clearly deserves praise, since even in such a chance-ridden universe as that of gambling, he manages to acquire the skills, mastery, and experience needed to eliminate chance. Yet, when he tries to "apply the rules of the game to people" he inevitably encounters a setback. Abstraction and synthesis are the first steps of any intellectual pursuit, yet blind reliance on such intellectual instruments is hardly sufficient for advancement in human affairs. Such notions as "all," "everybody," "everything is like that," "everyone acts like that" are as helpful as they are misleading. Therefore it is symptomatic that when Arbenin articulates the need to challenge laws, he immediately asserts new ones. Depicting the universe of gambling, Arbenin describes a world of universal rules, rather than of particular incidents. His speech is dominated by such words as "everything, all, everyone" (*vse, vsio, vsekh*). Even before Lermontov, this wholesale intellectual approach was brilliantly analyzed and condemned by Pushkin in "A Scene from Faust" (1826). In this text Mephistopheles tempts Faust to approach the world, people, his own experiences in a similar wholesale manner, until Faust finally succumbs and pronounces his terrifying "drown them all" (*vsekh utopit'*) about a distant ship full of people. Both Pushkin and Lermontov make explicit the fact that approaching the world only in terms of universals, like *vse*, results in boredom, misery, and destruction. Pushkin's Faust complains of boredom from the outset of his conversation with Mephistopheles. Both Pushkin and Lermontov reveal that Romantic ennui has its own philosophical/epistemological roots, just as it has social and cultural ones.

Arbenin, nevertheless, persistently describes and evaluates the world in terms of knowledge/ignorance, and makes knowledge the domain of those who can make universal claims. Addressing Nina, Arbenin proudly declares:

> Ни сердца своего, ни моего не зная,
> Ты отдалася мне—и любишь, верю я. . . .
> Но я люблю иначе, я всё видел,
> Всё перечувствовал, всё понял, всё узнал. . . .
> Так прежде я тебе цены не знал, несчастный!
> (3:34)

> (Knowing neither mine nor your own heart you gave yourself to me, and, I believe, you love me. . . . But I love differently; I've seen everything, felt everything, understood everything, learned everything. . . . I was miserable before, when I did not know your true value.)

Not only does Arbenin claim to know and experience all; the conviction of his intellectual power leads him to conclude that he now "knows" Nina's value. Lack of intellectual humility intoxicates Arbenin until it poisons him and others. Hence, his choice of a murder weapon. Another of Lermontov's "know-it-all" heroes, the Demon, also kills Tamara with a poisonous kiss, while his speeches are characterized as "poison" (*otrava*) in the text.[13]

Arbenin might understand Nina better than most, but the knowledge of human value can never be a complete one. Upon his surrender to Kazarin's temptation, Arbenin begins to apply the rules of gambling to Nina and to view her as if she were one of his gambling opponents whose mind he has learned to read. As the events of the play reveal, Arbenin's confidence in the power of his understanding results not just in boredom, but (as is the case of Pushkin's Faust) also in crime. Since he already knows it all, he feels justified in his refusal to listen to Nina's pleas of innocence:

> Но ты, мои рай,
> Небесный и земной . . . прощай! . . .
> Прощай, я знаю всё. . . .
> Наизусть
> Я знаю всё, что скажешь ты. . . .
> Вот женщина! . . . о, знаю я давно
> Вас всех, все ваши ласки и улреки,
> Но жалкое познанье мне дано.
> (3:40–42)

(But you, my paradise both heavenly and earthly . . . farewell! Farewell, I know it all. . . . I know by heart all that you are going to tell me. . . . O, woman! I have known you all for a long time, all your caresses and reproaches, but what a pathetic knowledge is given to me.)

Arbenin's approach to life in terms of knowledge and his reliance on his own all-embracing wisdom clearly leads to his tragic fall. Arbenin loses his mind after a confrontation with the character called "Unknown" (*Neizvestnyi*). This character convinces Arbenin of Nina's innocence, and discloses the limits of Arbenin's knowledge. Tortured by guilt, realizing how much he has failed to know, Arbenin loses his mind. Because of his failure to incorporate the unknown into his outlook, Arbenin is punished by Unknown. This message was so important to Lermontov, that in order to convey it he was willing to violate generic norms by introducing a symbolic figure that seems to belong to a mystery play rather than to a romantic drama.

The certainty and universality of knowledge to which Arbenin clings with such energy is, paradoxically, the knowledge of evil's omnipotence. In both his early "I saw evil everywhere" (*vezde ia videl zlo*) (3:39) or the later "evil and deception are everywhere" (*povsiudu zlo, vezde obman*) (3:61), Arbenin articulates this conviction, which might be useful when dealing with gambling opponents, yet hardly adequate to the complexity of human relationships.

It is the fate of such a pessimistic outlook that constitutes the ideological center of the play and that Lermontov explores with unparalleled originality and insight. Lermontov fuses the issues of knowledge and happiness into a religious, moral, and philosophical problem of theodicy and allows his characters to formulate their own solutions. Lermontov's characters, including his lyrical persona, seem to agree that if one possesses a sufficient amount of knowledge, one realizes that one lives in an evil, hostile world, where happiness belongs only to the naive or ignorant. Such an attitude leads to a view of the world that is essentially gnostic, acknowledging that "the world is enthralled by evil" (*mir vo zle lezhit*). It is this gnostic outlook that becomes a powerful if not insurmountable temptation for Lermontov's heroes, as well as the object of Lermontov's own scrutiny.

Gnosticism offers an answer to the question of theodicy, an answer that is rather appealing to the religious mind: God, responsible for such an unfair world, is evil. Lermontov's cruel universe where its ruler, in the Demon's words, "can forgive, but will not" (*prostit' on mozhet, khot' osudit*) (2:64) does fit gnostic interpretation, though the positing of an evil or unfair God is not a uniquely gnostic phenomenon. Camus (1956) analyzes such a view and calls it "metaphysical rebellion." Yet gnosticism, as it is now recognized by scholars of Romanticism, is the concept that describes the metaphysical outlook of Romanticism more adequately.[14] The moral subjectivism manifested by Arbenin is another important feature that Romantic ethics shares with gnosticism. Many a Romantic hero is ready to challenge the whole world order on the grounds of personal convictions. This subjectivism points to a key aspect of gnosticism; that is, to the belief in the salvational value of personal knowledge (gnosis) of certain secrets that some souls acquire or retain regardless of their degradation in this world. Such a belief found proponents in the majority of Romantic poets, including Lermontov.[15]

While articulating Arbenin's metaphysical outlook Lermontov seems to rely on two intellectual traditions. He was clearly influenced by Byron and other English Romantic poets interested in gnosticism.[16] There is also a Russian tradition of religious rebellion that Berdiaev (1971) frequently calls "marcionism." According to Berdiaev, gnostic belief in an evil creator is caused by the inability to solve the problem of theodicy. He writes: "Russians are prone to a peculiar form of marcionism; the creator of this world cannot be kind, since the world is filled with suffering, an innocent suffering" (81). Berdiaev's example of Russian "marcionism" is the rebellion of Ivan Karamazov, who prefers to denounce God and his world rather than negate God's existence. In his final speech Arbenin addresses God and also reproaches him: "I was telling you that you were cruel" (*Ia govoril tebe, chto ty zhestok*) (3:114).

In his fixation on evil Arbenin becomes susceptible to the philosophy of the play's demon, Kazarin, which consists of discovering evil at the bottom of everything. That is how Kazarin explains Arbenin's interference in the card game, an action brought about by Arbenin's desire to help the prince:

Не выдержал, зажглося ретивое. . . .
Глядит ягненочком, а право, тот же *зверь*.
Мне скажут, можно отучиться,
Натуру победить—*дурак* кто говорит;
Пусть ангелом и *притворится*,
Да черт-то все в душе сидит.
(3:16; my emphasis)

(He could not resist, and here he is again. . . . He *looks like a lamb,* but he is the same *beast* he used to be. They say that one can unlearn, and conquer one's nature—the one who says so is *a fool.* Let him to *pretend* to be an angel, yet the devil still sits within his soul.)

For Kazarin, only fools believe in the possibility of change, let alone goodness. Kazarin's creed is simple and leaves no room for uncertainty: humans are nothing but demons who put on the masks of angels. Kazarin responds to Arbenin's grief over Nina's death with his usual cynicism:

Да полно *брат, личину* ты сними,
Не опускай так важно взоры.
Ведь это хорошо с людьми,
Для публики,—а мы с тобой *актеры*. . . .
О, старый плут.
(3:101; my emphasis)

(Oh, *brother,* that is enough. Take off your *mask;* don't lower your eyes so solemnly. It is fine for other people, for an audience, but we are both *actors*. . . . Oh you old cheat.)

His terminology is self-explanatory: "mask," "actor," "pretend." Furthermore, Kazarin calls Arbenin "a brother," sinisterly underscoring their similarity.

By the end of the play, Arbenin will come to share Kazarin's outlook. His wife, whom he calls "an angel" on several occasions, eventually becomes for him a demon. Likewise, the mystery of life ceases to be a problem for Arbenin. Life is a lie, a long-known series of deceptions:

Что жизнь? Давно известная шарада
Для упражнения детей;
Где первое—рожденье! где второе—
Ужасный ряд забот и муки тайных ран,
Где смерть—последнее, а целое—обман!
(3:94)

(What is life? A tedious charade for a children's play. Where first there is birth, then comes a terrible sequence of worries and the pain of secret wounds, where death is last, and the whole thing is a deception.)

The vision of life as a masquerade, as a malicious deception, is here stated explicitly. Arbenin might be unhappy about his knowledge—on one occasion he calls knowledge "pitiful" (3:42)—yet he persists in it.

Kazarin's view of the world as a morality play, as a ritual in which evil puts on the mask of good, is supported by the events of the play. Arbenin is manipulated by the intrigues of Kazarin, the Baroness, or Shprikh. Success at gambling does not depend on chance, but rather on the collusion of some of the players. Similarly, the seemingly random events of the masquerade, such as Zvezdich's sexual encounter, or Nina's misfortune, are controlled by the Baroness. In the same way, Arbenin is a plaything in the hand of Unknown. Even the duel that is supposed to be a contest in which uncertainty plays an important role is skillfully avoided by Arbenin, who achieves his revenge not through a duel, but through a masterly manipulation of the Prince and the rules of society. In other words, the world around Arbenin conforms to his worst projections.

Even if such events are evil, they are evil in a rather different way than Kazarin describes or Arbenin imagines. Arbenin is so eager to embrace the gnostic outlook, to confirm the universality of evil, that he fails to see that Zvezdich might be having an affair with another woman, or that Nina has simply lost her bracelet. Furthermore, even if evil seems to be the guiding force behind the actions of many characters, neither Nina nor Arbenin really fits that scheme. In fact, even the manipulative Baroness changes, tormented by remorse. Arbenin is proud and independent enough not to wear masks for his own advantage, yet he is convinced that everybody else is masked. Pervasive as the metaphor of the masquerade is, it proves to be inadequate as an emblem for the world of the play; it points rather to Arbenin's moral and philosophical mistake, to his philosophical hamartia. The universe of *The Masquerade* turns out to be too complex and uncertain for its main protagonist. Arbenin's embrace of the omnipotence of evil proves ultimately as simplistic as the optimism and benevolence of Chatsky. Like the gnostics before him, Arbenin fails to acknowledge the inexorable connection of good and evil, the fundamental fact that, in Milton's inimitable phrase, "It was out of the rind of one apple tasted that the knowledge of good and evil as two twins cleaving together leapt forth into the World" (*Areopagitica*). In contrast to the simplifying polarities of Arbenin, the seventeen-year-old Lermontov already knew that "only in people does sacred meet sinful, and all human miseries stem from that" (*Lish' v cheloveke vstretit'sia moglo sviashchennnoe s porochnym. Vse ego muchenia proiskhodiat ottogo*) (1:208).

Nina's deathbed scene with her nurse invites a comparison with Shakespeare's *Othello*. Arbenin echoes Othello's rash conviction to attribute evil acts to his beloved Desdemona, while failing to see villainy behind Iago's actions. Othello's belated recognition that he loved "not wisely, but too well" seems to summarize Arbenin's own predicament. Regardless of all his claims to wisdom and knowledge, Arbenin certainly fails to love wisely.

Arbenin is so certain of the omnipotence of evil that when Nina's bracelet is not found, he solemnly declares: "I knew it" (*ia eto znal*) (3:38). By imagining a world which obeys the semiotic certainty of a dishonest card game, where every move or gesture of a partner or opponent means something and should be counterattacked immediately, Arbenin remains a gambler with disastrous consequences for himself and others. As such a gambler, he refuses to admit the accidental nature of a lost bracelet; it must be a sign of Nina's guilt. Uncertainty, which according to Wittgenstein lies at the core of any serious philosophical issue, surely accompanies such complex emotions as love or such global moral categories as good and evil. However, an encounter with uncertainty only scandalizes and confuses Arbenin. If we recall Arbenin's image of a bark yearning for safe haven, the resolution of his confusion is not surprising. Arbenin responds—as most of us would in a situation of uncertainty—by falling back on familiar modes of behavior and outlook; that is, on the already familiar philosophy of the deck of cards.

Pushkin shows the defeat of his Byronic character, Aleko, through the latter's amoral and inconsistent actions. Lermontov goes even further by making his Byronic hero, Arbenin, experience and recognize the collapse of his philosophy. Arbenin undergoes an intellectual fall: having confronted the fact that his view of himself as the warrior against an evil universe has been inadequate and has led to the murder of an innocent person, he literally loses his mind. When he learns of his mistake he collapses mentally: "This proud mind has given in today" (*i etot gordyi um segodnia iznemog*) (3:114). His is the mistake of a proud mind, yet it is an epistemological and ontological mistake.

To view the world as a realm of benevolence is a naive and dangerous enterprise. Arbenin had witnessed how many naive ignoramuses were crushed by the cruelty of life. Yet, to take the opposite view, while tempting, is equally dangerous. In fact, the demonic allure of a gnostic outlook, which Lermontov described eloquently in the two early poems titled "My Demon" (1829 and 1831), seems to be the main temptation against which Lermontov himself, as well as his protagonists, must struggle:

> *Собранье зол его стихия. . . .*
> Он недоверчивость вселяет,
> Он *презрел чистую любовь,*
> Он все моленья отвергает,
> Он равнодушно видит кровь,
> *И звук высоких ощущений*
> Он *давит* голосом страстей,
> И муза кротких вдохновений
> Страшится неземных очей.
> (1:111; my emphasis)

> (*A multitude of evil is his element.* . . . He instills distrust; *he despises pure love;* he rejects all prayers; he views blood with indifference. He *crushes the sound of noble sensations* with the voice of passions, and the muse of gentle inspiration fears his unearthly eyes.)

This confrontation with the demon of gnosticism constitutes the conflict in several of Lermontov's major texts. *The Masquerade,* nevertheless, is Lermontov's first serious poetic response to the philosophy of evil's omnipotence. Arbenin, the first hero of his time, shares with Lermontov's later heroes their strength, pride, independence, self-reliance, and nobility. And, like them, Arbenin is made to struggle both with the existing evil that feeds his gnostic outlook as well as with the outlook itself. Through Arbenin's plight Lermontov reveals, however, that a gnostic outlook, tempting as it may be, proves its own undoing. By seeing evil everywhere, by suspecting it everywhere, Arbenin, regardless of all his pride, self-reliance, and refusal to submit to evil under pressure, succumbs to evil and is led to intellectual bankruptcy and to madness.

Chapter Four

The Enigma of Heroism in Lermontov's "The Song of Tsar Ivan Vassilyevich, His Young Oprichnik, and the Stout-hearted Merchant Kalashnikov"

> I cannot and will not retract anything, for it is neither safe nor right to go against conscience. I cannot do otherwise, here I stand, may God help me.
> —Martin Luther

> С человеком, который ставит свою честь выше жизни, с человеком, идущим добровольно на смерть, нечего делать: он *неисправимо человек.*
>
> (Nothing can be done with a man who values honor more than life, with a man who voluntarily accepts death: such a man is *incorrigibly human.*)
> (emphasis in original)
> —Alexander Herzen

IN RUSSIAN LITERATURE, the first decades of the nineteenth century were a time of Romantic involvement with folk culture and poetry, with national roots and national history. Russian writers began to share the conviction expressed by V. K. Kiukhel'beker: "The beliefs of our ancestors, the folk-mores, the chronicles, and folk tales are the best, the purest, and most authentic sources for our literature" (1979, 458).[1] Among numerous works resulting from such involvement, Lermontov's 1837 narrative poem "Pesnia pro tsaria Ivana Vasilievicha, molodogo oprichnika i udalogo kuptsa Kalashnikova" ("The Song" in the following pages) is just one more and, typically for Lermontov, a belated example of the genre.

Western scholarship has basically ignored the poem.[2] On the other hand, Russian scholars discuss the poem frequently, but tend to restrict their analysis to a discussion of folklore motifs in the poem.[3] A sensitive and provocative attempt to read the work on its own merits has been made recently by Lominadze (1985). His analysis contains many first-rate observations, but I disagrees with most of his conclusions.[4]

"The Song" should by no means be considered simply as a brilliant linguistic exercise in folklore imitation. The poem opens a carefully selected collection of twenty-eight of Lermontov's poems, prepared by the poet himself and published in 1840, the only collection published in his lifetime.[5] Apparently, this rather simple tale was quite important to the poet. Set in the time of Ivan the Terrible and written in the *bylina* form, "The Song" is the story of the merchant Kalashnikov, who kills his wife's attacker, the *oprichnik* (bodyguard of Ivan the Terrible) Kiribeevich, and then is executed by the tsar for his refusal to disclose his motives. What is there in this story that merits such attention from Lermontov?

This chapter takes a threefold approach in order to answer that question: first I analyze the structure of "The Song"; then I discuss it in the light of pertinent biographical data; finally I assess the poem as Lermontov's meditation on the nature of heroism, on its meaning and its relevance in a world openly hostile to individual heroism and nonconformism. Although Kalashnikov fights for truth and dignity and can be said to gain both physical and spiritual victory over his enemy, he is executed, leaving no tangible sign of victory behind. Lermontov's song is thus quite different from epic songs that celebrate universally acknowledged heroic acts. Throughout his mature work Lermontov presents to his readers a world in which an individual is the subject of hostility, manipulation, or malevolent forces; he thus raises the larger question, What constitutes heroic action in such a world?

The conflicts and tensions of "The Song" prefigure many conflicts that inform Lermontov's later work. By placing the poem first among twenty-eight Lermontov seems to suggest that it is here, in this poem, that the keys to understanding his mature work lie.

THE STRUCTURE OF "THE SONG"

The title of the work is ironic. Although the poem's obvious hero is the merchant Kalashnikov, the title introduces the characters according to an earthly gradation of power: the song is about the tsar, his servant, and the merchant. The epic singers introducing the story echo the order of the title:

Ох, ты гой еси, царь Иван Васильевич!
Про тебя нашу песню сложили мы,
Про твово любимого опричника,
Да про смелого купца про Калашникова.
(2:7)

(O you, tsar, Ivan Vasilievich! We composed our song about you, about your favorite oprichnik, and about the courageous merchant, Kalashnikov.)

Nothing is said about the relationships of the protagonists or about the tragic outcome of their interaction. The earthly gradation of power is ironically underscored in a similar manner throughout the poem. The singers seem unable to grasp the tragic side of the confrontation, and claim that the purpose of their performance is to entertain some unknown *boyar* and his "white-faced" wife: "Hey, fellows, sing! But tune the gusli's strings! . . . Let's entertain the dear boyar and his fair wife" (*Ai, rebiata poite, tol'ko gusli stroite! . . . Uzh potesh'te vy dobrogo boiarina i boiaryniu ego belolitsuiu*) (2:15). The singers' seemingly objective tone, nonchalant toward Kalashnikov and reverent to the tsar, foreshadows the world's indifference to the tragic events that are going to take place.

There are three parts to "The Song," each centered on a dialogue, or rather on an interrogation, a verbal confrontation.

The first part of "The Song" begins with a description of a feast at the court of Ivan the Terrible and presents the tsar as the source from whom all the actions and events emanate. Everyone participates in the tsar's festivity except the oprichnik Kiribeevich, who is so immersed in his thoughts that he fails to hear the tsar's reproach.[6] When finally, after the third attempt, Ivan's "angry word" (*groznoe slovo*) (2:8) reaches Kiribeevich, the latter is willing to accept a cruel punishment for his lack of attention: "If I have angered you—it is your tsar's will—give an order to execute me, to cut off my head" (*A prognevcd ia tebia—volia tsarskaia, prikazhi kaznit' rubit' golovu*) (2:9). This reference to execution resulting from the tsar's wrath describes the world in which the story of Kalashnikov is to unfold: events take place in a universe so fully controlled by the tsar that his wrath and an execution presuppose each other. Ivan enjoys and enforces absolute control. It is not enough for him to know that all of his courtiers are drinking and rejoicing: "and everyone drank glorifying the tsar" (*i vse pili tsaria slavili*) (2:8). He is more concerned with the fact that one of them was not drinking. He forces him to confess publicly the reason for his behavior. Such insistence on uniformity and conformity spreads from the tsar down the hierarchy, so that Kiribeevich ignores numerous women who cast glances at him, but has to elicit love from the "only one who does not look with admiration" at him (2:9). When viewed against such a background of assertion and dominance, Kalashnikov's nonconformism, his insistence on the privacy of his experience, his refusal to explain his behavior to the tsar, become even more heroic. Kalashnikov asserts the primacy of his individual responses: when he kills his enemy, Kalashnikov deliberately violates the spirit of festivity and challenges the pervasive atmosphere of uniformity.

Kiribeevich is characterized by the tsar as "a faithful servant." He belongs to the family of the tsar's servant (and leading henchman) Maliuta Skuratov and is not supposed to behave so disrespectfully; therefore he is asked to explain his behavior. Kiribeevich accepts the tsar's right to pry into his private life, bows to him, and then confesses his unrequited love for a beautiful woman, failing to disclose, however, the fact that the woman is married. Ivan forgives the oprichnik and then advises that he send some gifts to his love with a matchmaker and "not to get angry if she fails to love him" (*ne poliubish'sia, ne prognevaisia*) (2:10). The tsar's judgment seems rather fair under the circumstances, although it never occurs to him that the woman might have reasons to evade Kiribeevich. Thus, through deception, Kiribeevich reestablishes himself in the order of things, within the rank of participants in the tsar's grace. As a fair master, Ivan does not merely unleash his rage, but inquires into the reasons for his servant's misbehavior.

The second part introduces the merchant Kalashnikov depicted amidst his property, which he guards with the help of a German lock, a vicious dog, and an oak door. Kalashnikov is presented as a typical bourgeois placed within his possessions:

Запирает Степан Парамонович
Свою лавочку дверью дубовою
Да замком немецким со пружиною;
Злого пса-ворчуна зубастого
На железную цепь привязывает.

(2:11)

(Stepan Paramonovich closes his store with an oak door, locks it with a German spiral lock; and ties his vicious, growling, long-toothed dog to an iron chain.)

Lermontov describes Kalashnikov as someone who would keep his end of the bargain, yet would defend his own with the ferocity of his guard dog. Through the image of Kalashnikov Lermontov constructs an important fictional equivalent of English barons, whose insistence on their rights helped to draft the Magna Carta. And Lermontov was operating within the near vacuum of Russian cultural or literary models of such behavior.

Upon his return from the store, Kalashnikov does not find his wife Alyona home:

И дивится Степан Парамонович:
Не встречает его молода жена,
Не накрыт дубовый стол белой скатертью,
И свеча перед образом еле теплится.

(2:11)

(And Stepan Paramonovich is bewildered: his young wife does not greet him; the oak table is not covered with a white tablecloth, and the candle in front of the icon is almost out.)

Her absence endangers not only family custom but also religious observance. When the wife finally appears, confused and disheveled, Kalashnikov accuses her of infidelity, expresses his jealousy, and reminds her that they were married in front of the "holy icons." Like Kiribeevich, who before answering bows to his sole ruler, Alyona falls to Kalashnikov's feet, and says that she is not afraid of death or gossip but only of his rage. She is to her husband as Kiribeevich is to his tsar. She even addresses her husband as "my sovereign" (2:13). Like Kiribeevich before her and Kalashnikov after her, Alyona is willing to accept severe punishment for her misdemeanor but hopes to be given a chance to justify herself: "O my sovereign, my sun: either kill me right now, or listen to me" (*Gosudar' ty moi, krasno solnyshko, il' ubei menia ili vyslushai*) (2:13). Kalashnikov accepts his wife's explanation and decides to challenge Kiribeevich to a fistfight.

Kalashnikov's wife, Alyona, like Kiribeevich, temporarily angers her ruler and falls out of grace, but is reestablished again through her truthful confession. Although she is innocent, she accepts the role of the accused and tries to defend herself. Being wrongfully accused, she could have reacted with pride and challenged the rights of her accuser, but she does not; instead, she appeals to her husband to defend her. Both she and Kiribeevich view their rulers as sources of ultimate authority and power. But, as we shall see from the third part, Kalashnikov rebels precisely against such an attitude.

Throughout the poem Lermontov plays with the traditional folklore device exploiting the number three. The third event always differs from the first two. Only after the third summons does Kiribeevich answer the tsar and Kalashnikov come to the ring for the fight. Thus we can expect that the third interview will differ from the previous two.

The third interview occurs after Kalashnikov has killed Kiribeevich in the fistfight and is taken to the enraged tsar to explain his action. Two previous interrogations have resulted in the forgiveness and benevolence of a previously enraged ruler. It is reasonable to conclude that Kalashnikov could have saved his life by following the route taken by either of the previously accused: he could have lied, claiming that the murder was accidental, or disclosed the whole story to the tsar. Why didn't he?

Ivan the Terrible in "The Song" seems to be fair enough, and it is reasonable to infer that Kalashnikov could have been forgiven had he told the whole story to the tsar. Kalashnikov, however, denies the tsar even the possibility of administering justice. He chooses the worst possible defense by admitting that he had deliberately killed the oprichnik, yet refusing to say why: "I've killed him of my own free will, but as far as my reasons are concerned, I am not going to disclose them to you, only to God" (*Ia ubil ego vol'noi voleiu, a za chto, pro chto ne skazhu tebe, a skazhu tol'ko Bogu edinomu*) (2:18).

The similarities of the three interrogations are striking. In all three dialogues the participants are unevenly matched. There is an accused and an interrogator with greater authority and power. In the first place it is the tsar who questions his oprichnik, in the second place the merchant Kalashnikov questions his wife, and in the third the tsar questions the merchant. All three interrogators feel that they possess the God-given authority to question and accuse. In all three cases the accused have violated a certain law, thus angering their rulers. However, they have a chance to justify themselves, and in the first two cases they succeed: Kiribeevich through deception, Kalashnikov's wife through telling the truth. Both manage to mitigate the wrath of their accusers and to reestablish themselves in their good graces. In the third confrontation, however, Kalashnikov not only fails to pacify the rage of the tsar, but even increases the tsar's wrath by his refusal to provide an answer.

So the three-part structure of "The Song" puts Kalashnikov's rebellious answer into high relief. After observing Kiribeevich's and Alyona's behavior under pressure that is rather common, we contemplate Kalashnikov's unusual action. To appreciate fully the significance of his heroic act, the circumstances surrounding the genesis of "The Song" must be examined.

HISTORICAL AND BIOGRAPHICAL BACKGROUND OF "THE SONG"

There is no extant manuscript of "The Song," and the date of its composition is uncertain. It was first published in April 1838 in *Literaturnoe prilozhenie k Moskovskomu Invalidu* (Literary Supplement to the *Moscow Veteran*), a magazine edited by Anton Kraevsky, responsible for introducing most of Lermontov's poetry to the public. According to Kraevsky (most editors agree) the work was written in 1837 in the Caucasus during Lermontov's exile there.[7] Although the setting of "The Song" seems to be far removed from the events of Lermontov's life, this impression is deceptive. Lermontov's own experience enters "The Song" in many guises, some of which have not been recorded in scholarship.

A number of scholars have observed that events of "The Song" and the events surrounding Pushkin's death are linked: an enemy challenged to defend the honor of a wife, the ensuing duel, and the tsar as a participant and a partial cause of the outcome. The similarities are indeed striking. Even the solicitude that Nicholas I showed for the welfare of Pushkin's widow is similar to the care promised by Ivan the Terrible to the family of Kalashnikov.[8] One can hardly doubt that the dynamics of Pushkin's affair coincide with and partly inspire the outcome of Kalashnikov's story. But "The Song" is more than a paraphrase of the Pushkin affair, and one can hardly agree with John Mersereau, who sees in the work only a "veiled account of Pushkin's tragic duel and the circumstances surrounding it," rendered in the form of a talented imitation of folk song (Mersereau and Lapeza 1988, 298).[9] Lermontov had already written about Pushkin's death in "The Death of the Poet." I contend that it is not so much Pushkin's duel as Lermontov's own rebellious response to Pushkin's death and the consequences of this response that play the most important role in the genesis of "The Song."

Let us start, however, with one relevant actual event that, to my knowledge, critics have missed when analyzing various subtexts of the poem. This episode occurred in Saint Petersburg in April 1836 and preoccupied everyone at the time, according to the diaries of the Russian censor A. V. Nikitenko. (Lermontov was in Saint Petersburg at the time.) An official, Pavlov, murdered a certain Aprelev on the steps of a church just before Aprelev's wedding was to take place. This murder was Pavlov's revenge for his sister, who had borne two children with Aprelev. Despite Pavlov's pleas and threats, Aprelev had decided to marry another woman. That was not known at the time, as Pavlov refused to disclose his motives for the killing and dishonor his sister. Like Kalashnikov, Pavlov pledged to reveal his reasons only to God, as only God would understand and appreciate his actions. This is how Nikitenko describes Pavlov:

> Here is one more noble feature of his. During the trial they demanded *in the name of the tsar* disclosure of the true cause of his unusual action. He was promised some leniency for that. He replied: "Only God can understand and evaluate the cause of my action, and He will be the judge between me and Aprelev." (Nikitenko 1955, 183; emphasis in original)

Lermontov himself underwent a similar interrogation "in the name of the tsar." His own behavior on that occasion is even more telling for appreciation of the thrust of Kalashnikov's answer. Lermontov was arrested and interrogated after his poem "The Death of the Poet" became known to the authorities. According to Benkendorf's report to Nicholas I, Lermontov at first refused to name his accomplice.[10] Being threatened later with a cruel punishment and fearing its effect on his grandmother, however, Lermontov identified his friend S. A. Raevsky. He was tormented by this betrayal and blamed himself for the fate of Raevsky for a long time.[11] This is how he describes the situation in a letter to Raevsky:

> First I did not say anything about you, but then they *interrogated me on behalf of the tsar* (*doprashivali ot gosudaria*): they said that you are not going to be punished, but if I persisted, they would demote me to the rank of soldier. . . . I recalled my grandmother and I could not [resist]. I sacrificed you for her. . . . I cannot describe what I went through at that moment, but I am sure that you understand me and forgive and still consider me worthy of your friendship. (4:426; my emphasis)

Both Pavlov and Lermontov were subjected to interrogation "in the name of the tsar." Lermontov, however, gave in and, as a result, experienced the trauma of having denounced his friend. Undoubtedly, it haunted him and led to his putting into the mouth of Kalashnikov the bold answer he himself did not dare to make. Kalashnikov is interrogated not just "in the name of the tsar" but by the tsar himself. Thus the courage of his answer is even more pronounced.

The world of "The Song" is dominated by the presence of the tsar. Indeed, it is the tsar's world. In his attempt to seduce Alyona, Kiribeevich proudly refers to his service to the tsar as if it is his main weapon. Lermontov's presentation is confirmed by the studies of Karamzin. In his "Note on the Ancient and New Russia" (1811) Karamzin maintains that during Ivan the Terrible's reign the title "tsar's servant" was more respected than that of a prince:

> Within the country the autocracy strengthened. No one except the tsar could judge or reward: every authority was a continuation of the monarch's one. Life and estates depended on the will of tsars, and the most respected title was not that of a prince or boyar, but *the title of the tsar's servant* (*titlo slugi tsareva*). . . . The tsar became for all Russians an earthly god. (Karamzin 1991, 24; emphasis in original)

Lermontov re-creates the world of seventeenth-century Russia as it is described by Karamzin. The very word "tsar" occurs at least twenty-five times, by far the most frequently used word in the poem. The events of "The Song" emanate from the tsar. The expression "*Bogu edinomu*" (2:18) used by Kalashnikov in his refusal to answer the tsar is more than an idiom. These words put the tsar in his place by reminding him that there is only one God, that the tsar with all his power does not partake of divinity, and that there are certain aspects of human behavior over which the tsar does not have jurisdiction. Kalashnikov's answer challenges the sacralization of the monarch, and the attribution of a religious dimension to the state, traditions that were very much alive in Russia even at the time of Nicholas I.[12]

The pattern established by Kalashnikov's proud challenge to tsarist autocracy should not be taken simply as another Romantic attempt to reconstruct the atmosphere of the distant past. "The Song"'s presentation of the tsar-dominated world describes not just the time of Ivan the Terrible, but Lermontov's own. In articulating Kalashnikov's conduct, Lermontov confronts what was to become a pressing concern of his contemporaries, and of generations of Russians to come: how to deal with authoritarian power run amok. The originality of Lermontov's solution becomes more clear if considered against the background of Russian attitudes and expectations vis-à-vis their tsar. It is against this Russian identification of the tsar's will with that of God that Lermontov raises the fist of his Kalashnikov.

Several writers have observed that royal cruelty accompanied by blind admiration of the tsar flourished not only at the time of Ivan, but also during the more enlightened times of Nicholas I. The marquis de Custine (1989) quotes approvingly the view of the baron Sigismund Herberstein who traveled in Russia three centuries before de Custine:

> He [the tsar] speaks and it is done; the life and fortunes of laity and clergy, nobles and burghers, all depend on his supreme will. He is unacquainted with contradiction, and all he does is deemed as equitable as though it were done by the Deity; for the Russians are persuaded that their prince is the executor of the Divine decrees. Thus "God and the prince have willed," or "God and the prince know" are common modes of speech among them. Nothing can equal their zeal for his service. (Custine 1989, 95)

De Custine provides the following commentary:

> This letter, written more than three centuries ago, describes the Russians precisely as I now see them. . . . People and government are here in unison. That a man brought up in the idolatry of self, a man revered as omnipotent by sixty millions of men . . . should not undertake to put an end to such a state of things—this does not surprise me: the wonder is that among the voices that relate these things to the glory of this individual not one separates itself from the universal chorus, to protest in favor of humanity, against such autocratic miracles. It may be said of the Russians, great and small, that they are drunk with slavery. (95)

Describing a phenomenon more readily associated with the regimes of Ivan the Terrible or Stalin, de Custine (1989) lashes out at the reign of Nicholas I:

> This perpetual reign, and its perpetual worship, would be a real comedy, if upon such permanent dramatic representation there did not depend the existence of sixty millions of men, who live only because the man whom you see before you playing the role of the emperor, gives them permission to breathe, and dictates to them the mode of using this permission. It is the divine right, applied to the mechanism of social life. . . . There does not exist on the earth at the present time, not in Turkey, not even in China, a single man who enjoys and exercises such power as the emperor. (230)

Echoing de Custine's strategy of invoking relevant examples from the past, another Lermontov contemporary, the Russian émigré Ivan Golovin, opens *Russia Under the Autocrat, Nicholas the First*, with a description of one of his ancestors. At the beginning of the seventeenth century one Foma Golovin observed that he would "return to the country when these proverbs shall have ceased to be current in Russia: 'Everything that is mine belongs to the Tsar'; 'Near the Tsar, near death'; 'Do not fear the judgment, fear the judge'" (1970, 1). Golovin stresses the relevance of such proverbs to the contemporary period and then comments on Nicholas I's godlike power: "The tsar is the center of all the rays, the focus to which every eye is directed" (130). Golovin's proverbs provide a surprisingly accurate description of the universe of Lermontov's poem and function thus as the background against which the actions of Lermontov's characters should be assessed.[13]

While a foreigner, de Custine, recognized the totalitarian methods of Ivan the Terrible in the contemporary rule of Nicholas I, and if a rather average observer such as Ivan Golovin comments on them, the similarities could not have been missed by Lermontov. Lermontov places Kalashnikov within circumstances that had hardly changed in three centuries. The subjects of both Ivan the Terrible and Nicholas I need permission from their rulers to laugh or grieve, while their rulers feel free to control even inner life and to pry into the most private motives of their subjects. In his interrogation of the arrested Decembrists, Nicholas I would, in fact, unceremoniously ask and get answers to the most personal questions. Thus in all the interrogations of "The Song," questions are asked concerning private issues, and only Kalashnikov refuses to answer them. Lermontov describes resistance to the authorities' refusal to recognize the boundaries between public and private as a fundamentally heroic act.

Lermontov makes Kalashnikov transcend traditional ways of dealing with the tsar's authority. As in *The Masquerade*, Lermontov views Russian social life through the paradigm of the player/plaything (*igrok/igrushka*) relationship. In his lyric poetry he introduces a similar dichotomy by calling Russia "the country of slaves, the country of masters" (1:76) and describing his contemporaries as "contemptible slaves before power" (*pred vlastiu prezrennye raby*) (1:35). Yet these dichotomies cannot embrace the heroic behavior of Kalashnikov, who asserts his right to privacy in front of a ruthless tsar. Kalashnikov is neither a tyrant, nor a slave; neither a player, nor a plaything. Kalashnikov does not interfere in the private life of others, nor does he allow anyone to interfere in his own. As in the case of Arbenin, Lermontov presents a model of heroic behavior for readers who clearly lacked such models.

Lermontov frequently explores conduct that differs from either all-out rebellion or all-out surrender. One of his early poems is the translation of Schiller's "The Glove" (*Der Handschuh*, 1797), the ballad that deals with the conflict between human duty and human dignity, that traditional conflict of individualism that at the time of tsarist oppression acquired new urgency. A knight, having been ordered to perform a dangerous and useless task by his lady, leaves her after he carries it out. Schiller has obviously indicated to Lermontov one way of solving the conflict between the duty toward superior and the defense of one's own dignity. Likewise, Kalashnikov carries out his duties toward the tsar and God; he neither lies to them nor denies their authority. Yet, having done that, he defends his human dignity even if it means challenging the laws of both the tsar and God. When he wanted to present the behavior of common Russian people, the Polish poet Adam Mickiewicz, in the chapter "Military Parade" (*Przeglad wojska*) of the third part of his *Forefathers' Eve* (*Dziady*), created a series of terrifying portraits, if not caricatures, of the Russian virtues of patience and fatalism. One of such portraits is that of a dedicated servant who freezes to death while holding his master's coat. Mickiewicz is justifiably outraged by this incident, yet interprets it as emblematic of Russian heroism: "such death, such patience is the heroism of a dog, but not of a human being. . . . O poor Slavs, how I pity you, your heroism is the heroism of slavery." Lermontov, however, shows Mickiewicz and all the other critics or admirers of the "Russian virtues" that there is a way to be Russian and to manifest human, rather than a slave's, heroism.

Two of Lermontov's poems, "The Death of the Poet" (1837) and "Borodino" (1837), are also relevant to the genesis of "The Song." The connection between "Borodino" and "The Song" has been already noticed by Belinsky, who saw that both works contrast a heroic past with the mundane present. Another obvious and oft-observed connection is Lermontov's masterly imitation of the *bylina* style in "The Song," and of the speech of a simple soldier in "Borodino." The connection between the poems goes much deeper. Pushkin's shadow towers over these two poems even though they do not contain direct references to him. "Borodino" was first published in Pushkin's journal *Sovremennik* (Contemporary) in the second issue following his death (May of 1837), an issue closely connected with the memory of Pushkin, and it is now thought to have been written not only after Pushkin's death but also after Lermontov's composition of "The Death of the Poet."[14] Lermontov's "The Death of the Poet," "Borodino," and "The Song" form a cycle in which Lermontov attempts to come to grips with the fate of Pushkin.

The poems share a common theme: in all of them an attacker, perceived as a cultural and also as a religious invader, though he is harmed or killed, still succeeds in destroying a local hero or heroes. The puzzling name of Kiribeevich underscores this point; I believe that his name can be traced to Lermontov's tale "Ashik-Kerib," also written during Lermontov's 1837 exile in the Caucusus. "Kerib" in Turkish means "wanderer." Such a name clearly aligns Kiribeevich with another group of invaders, like the French soldiers in "Borodino" (who like Kiribeevich are also referred to in the text of the poem as "busurmans") or d'Anthes in "The Death of the Poet," who is called a "fugitive from far away" (1:21).

There is another common theme in these three Lermontov poems. The villains exhibit a rather lighthearted attitude toward serious questions of life. In "Borodino" the poet states that before the decisive battle the French soldiers were making merry while the Russian camp was quiet. "The Death of the Poet" involves a similar situation, the evil court irresponsibly pursuing what is described as "fun" (*potekha*), a word that figures prominently in "The Song." The court taunts the poet for the sake of *potekha:*

Не вы ль сперва так злобно гнали
Его свободный вольный дар
И для потехи раздували
Чуть затаившийся пожар.

(2:21)

(Was it not you who first maliciously persecuted his free and unrestrained gift, and for the sake of fun fanned the hidden fire?)

The singers of "The Song" claim to compose the song for the same purpose of "entertaining the good boyar" (*potesh'te vy dobrogo boiarina*) (2:11). The fistfight is also supposed to be entertaining: "Where are you, brave fellows? Why don't you entertain our father the tsar" (*Oi, gde vy, dobrye molodtsy? Vy potesh'te tsaria nashego batiushku*) (2:21). Kiribeevich also mentions the fight's potential for amusement: "I will just entertain our father the tsar" (*lish' poteshu tsaria nashego batiushku*). The courts of Ivan the Terrible and Nicholas I seem to be governed by "potekha"; that is, by moral irresponsibility, by an inappropriately playful attitude toward life.

Kalashnikov's attitude, on the other hand, is similar to that of the soldiers of "Borodino." He sees the point of festivity but rejects it: "Not for the sake of jokes or fun did I come here, you, son of an infidel. I came here to fight a terrible fight, the last fight" (*Ne shutku shutit', ne liudei smeshit' vyshel ia teper', busurmanskii syn. Vyshel ia na strashnyi boi, na poslednii boi*) (2:17). What is the moral seriousness that makes Kalashnikov violate the mood of festivity by murdering the tsar's favorite and then by refusing to explain his motives to the tsar himself?[15]

KALASHNIKOV'S TRUTH

Opposed to the notion of *potekha* and the attitudes it implies is that of "truth" (*pravda*). The word occurs in key moments of the poem. Given the complexity for any writer of grappling with the concept of truth, in the case of Lermontov one thing is clear: truth is always something deeply personal and internal. In his 1831 poem "My House" (*Moi dom*) Lermontov states what remained a conviction throughout his life: "there is a sense of truth in the heart of a man and this sense is a sacred seed of eternity" (*Est' chuvstvo pravdy v serdtse cheloveka, sviatoe vechnosti zerno*) (1:185). This sense of truth does not depend on external concepts of morality, law, or science, but on the voice of the heart.[16] Hence it can be ambiguous, contradictory, and shifting, but still preferable to external concepts because it partakes of eternity. This glorification of inner impulses is typical of many Romantic poets. As Blake observed: "Jesus was all virtue and acted from impulse, not from rules" (*Marriage of Heaven and Hell,* plates 23 and 24).

Kalashnikov follows the inner voice of his heart. Outraged by Kiribeevich's actions, he, like Arbenin, decides to punish his enemy personally and announces to his brothers that "such an insult is too much for his brave soul and heart to bear" (*A takoi obidy ne sterpet' dushe, da ne vynesti serdtsu molodetskomu*) (2:15). Then, in the same breath, he adds that in the event of his failure his brothers must go on fighting for the "sacred truth":

Буду на смерть биться, до последних сил;
А побьет он меня—выходите вы
За святую правду-матушку,

Не сробейте, братцы любезные!
Вы моложе меня, свежей силою,
На вас меньше грехов накопилося,
Так авось Господь вас помилует!

(2:15)

(I shall wage a mortal combat, and fight till my last breath, and if he beats me, you go to fight for the sacred mother-truth. Don't be timid, my dear brothers! You are younger than I; your strength is more vital. You've accumulated fewer sins, and so maybe the Lord will have mercy on you.)

Kalashnikov clearly equates the external notion of "sacred truth" with the voice of his heart and soul. But how "sacred" can such personal truth be? In the exchange with Kiribeevich, Kalashnikov calls him "infidel" (2:17) and accuses Kiribeevich of violating divine laws. The merchant's way of defending such laws is far from Christian, however: he is willing to kill his enemy.

Even though the voices of their hearts do seem sacred to many of Lermontov's rebellious characters, they do not correspond to the sacred in the traditional sense. Kalashnikov, for example, manifests very impious traits in his rage and pride. Not only does he challenge the tsar but also the tenets of Christianity. Here we are at the heart of Lermontov's paradox: his protagonists do challenge the earth and its rulers, but they do so on the grounds of their adherence to something other than external religious tenets. This paradox is symbolically rendered in the way both contenders address the tsar before their battle: while Kiribeevich bows only to the tsar, the merchant bows in succession to the tsar, the Kremlin, the churches, and the Russian people. Kiribeevich has only one law above himself, the law of the earthly power he serves and manipulates, while Kalashnikov does not differentiate among the external powers. A comparison with Pushkin is revealing. In *Boris Godunov*, the *iurodivyi* refuses to pray for Boris on the grounds of his religious convictions: "One cannot pray for the tsar, the Herod—the Virgin does not allow that" (*Nel'zia molitsia za tsaria Iroda—Bogoroditsa ne velit*). In Lermontov the situation is more painful; the merchant, like other Lermontov heroes, challenges the whole world order, both heaven and earth, on the grounds of some deeply felt personal vision of truth. Due to such a vision many of Lermontov's characters find themselves equally estranged from both heaven and earth.[17]

Only once in the course of "The Song" are we allowed a glimpse into the mental processes of any protagonist. Just before he strikes his fatal blow, Kalashnikov thinks of his adherence to the truth regardless of the consequences: "Whatever will be, will be; I will stand for the truth to the end!" (*Chemu byt' suzhdeno, to i sbudetsia; postoiu za pravdu do posledneva!*) (2:18). In the already quoted explanation to the tsar regarding the composition of "The Death of the Poet," Lermontov expresses a similar integrity: "I could not renounce it [the poem]: *truth* has always been sacred for me, and now, when I bring my guilty head for your judgment, I appeal to it with firmness, as the only defense of a noble man in front of *the tsar* and in front of *God*" (Manuilov 1964, 73; my emphasis).[18] Truth and one's nobility are presented as allies, opposed as they are to both earthly and heavenly realms.

The personal vision of truth might be "a sacred seed of eternity," but it does not correspond to external religious teachings. Kalashnikov commits murder and takes revenge, two rather ungodly actions. As his references to his "sinful soul" and "guilty head" testify, Kalashnikov understands that his unorthodox defense of truth violates the laws of both God and tsar.[19]

However, even if Kalashnikov is guilty as the tsar's or God's subject, as a free human being he feels justified in his controversial defense of truth, which he equates with the personal defense of his honor and dignity. He refuses to wait for justice from either God or the tsar. Kalashnikov proudly states to the tsar: "I have killed him of my own free will; but why I did it, I shall not disclose to you, only to God" (*Ia ubil ego vol'noi voleiu, a za chto, pro chto ne skazhu tebe, a skazhu tol'ko Bogu edinomu*) (2:18). Claiming that God is his sole authority, Kalashnikov expresses the hope of being understood and appreciated for his inner truthfulness, but there is no secure feeling of having God on his side. It is clearly not enough to see in his answer to the tsar only the echo of Christ's answer to the Pharisees: "Render therefore unto Caesar the things which are Caesar's; and unto God the things that are God's" (Matt. 22:21). By his rebellious answer and actions Kalashnikov adds to Christ's maxim: "But I shall also render unto myself the things which are mine." He knows that he cannot do otherwise, no matter what God or the tsar think of his actions. This is the core of his heroism and of his understanding of "sacred truth."[20] Kalashnikov, who dies defending his personal integrity and dignity, is the first real champion of individualism in Russian literature.

Lermontov, in fact, constantly underscores the primacy of the inner world, and stresses the need to protect the content of one's private life. His 1837 poem "I Don't Want the World to Know" (*Ia ne khochu, chtob svet uznal*) echoes the sentiment and even the diction of Kalashnikov:

> Я не хочу, чтоб свет узнал
> Мою таинственную повесть;
> Как я любил, как я страдал,
> Тому судья лишь Бог да совесть.
> Им сердце в чувствах даст отчет,
> У них попросит сожаленья . . .
> (1:29)

(I don't want the world to know my secret tale. How I've loved, how I've suffered, only God and my conscience can judge. My heart will give its account to them, and will ask their compassion . . .)

The speaker here asserts that only God and one's conscience can hold the content of the individual's inner world accountable. So when Ivan the Terrible inquires into the motives of Kalashnikov's action and asks him to reveal the reasons "according to truth and conscience" (*otvechai mne po pravde, po sovesti*) (2:18), he clearly oversteps the boundaries permitted to an earthly ruler. Ivan is entitled to demand a true answer, and Kalashnikov does not lie in response. Yet Kalashnikov's conscience hardly lies within Ivan's jurisdiction. Kalashnikov's refusal to answer is, therefore, his defense of what he rightfully considers his own: the content of his "conscience" (*sovest'*).

Norbert Elias (1991) has provided a fruitful way of discussing the issues of individualism: rather than getting lost in the abstract recounting and assertion of individual rights or responsibilities, he explores the historical changes and shifts within what he calls the "I-we balance" (153–239). According to Elias, in identifying themselves people tend to stress either individual differences (I-identity) or belonging to a group (we-identity). While both components are present within anyone's psychic makeup, the predominance of one or the other form of identity clearly depends on the particular historical and political situation. Commenting on contemporary Western societies, Elias (1991) writes: "It is characteristic of the structure of the more developed societies of our day that the differences between people, their I-identity, are valued more highly than what they have in common, their we-identity" (156). Kalashnikov asserts and defends his "I-identity," stressing the uniqueness and unconditional value of his inner world opposed to the "we-identity" of tsar-servants, the only identity encouraged within the poem. His individualistic effort is not appreciated by Ivan the Terrible. Kalashnikov is executed and buried in a "nameless grave"; that is, his "I-identity" is violently obliterated. Nevertheless, the poem resurrects and commemorates Kalashnikov's attempt to proclaim his "I-identity," and his refusal to be reduced only to a group identity. Herein lies Kalashnikov's moral revolution, the importance of which continues to be overlooked by a culture reluctant to acknowledge the value of its individual members.

VICTORY IN DEFEAT

Pushkin's Salieri states perfectly the painful conclusion that tormented not only Lermontov and his characters but many other rebels in Russian literature: "They say that there is no truth on earth. But there is no truth above either." Romantic poets resurrected a heroic dimension of rebellion and negation, shown, for example, in their fascination with Milton's Satan. They sympathized with heroic rebels like Satan, Cain, Manfred, Napoleon, and Prometheus. However, despite all this sympathy, in his drama "Cain: A Mystery" (1821), Byron underscores how Cain's rebellion leads to violent crime and alienation. Likewise, in his portrayal of Salieri, Pushkin responds to the Romantic glorification of rebellion and nihilism and warns of the dangers of such an attitude: Salieri turns into a selfish, envious murderer.

Lermontov, who by all accounts was strongly influenced by both Byron and Pushkin, could not help being skeptical of a one-sided glorification of rebellion, even a rebellion as justifiable as that of Kalashnikov. We saw in *The Masquerade* that Lermontov presents an extremely balanced and complex view of heroism. Lermontov's heroes are rebellious, but Lermontov sympathizes with them not because they are rebels, but because they are heroes and because they are defeated or destroyed. Prometheus, the suffering titan, is the figure most congenial to Lermontov, but Lermontov's Prometheus is never unbound; he remains chained to the rock.

In exploring the individualism of his protagonists, their perpetual struggle for autonomy and independence, their courage and self-reliance, Lermontov finds a convenient solution: he presents them not in triumph and victory but rather at their confrontation with defeat and loss. Lermontov's treatment of Napoleon is a case in point. In one of his poems devoted to Napoleon, the poet writes: "He perished as he had lived, without ancestors and without heirs, defeated, but still a hero" (*pogib kak zhil, bez predkov i potomstva, khot' pobezhdennyi, no geroi!*) ("Saint Helena," 1831) (1:215). In fact, all the poems that form Lermontov's Napoleonic cycle, whether "Aerial Ship" (*Voszdushnyi korabl'*, 1840) and "Last Housewarming" (*Poslednee novosel'e*, 1841) or the very early "Napoleon" (1829), "Napoleon (Meditation)" (*Napoleon* [*Duma*], 1830), and "Napoleon's Epitaph" (1830), concern Saint Helena. Napoleon's courageous acceptance of defeat allows Lermontov to mediate between glorifying and condemning the heroic individual. Like Napoleon, the majority of Lermontov's heroes are defeated, but they do not give up; they strive to remain true to themselves, manifesting a heroism of resistance rather than that of achievement.

Testifying to the authorities about "The Death of the Poet" Lermontov asserted an "inborn feeling of [his] young soul to defend any wrongly condemned person" (quoted in Manuilov 1964, 73). In his compassion toward suffering and misfortune Lermontov clearly prefigures Dostoevsky. As a 1831 poem put it: "Anything containing at least a drop of suffering cannot be a dream" (*I snom nikak ne mozhet byt' vse v chem khot' kaplia est' stradaniia*) (1:155). Suffering is the ultimate test of reality and thus of value for any event, for any action.

Lermontov, therefore, appears inconsistent in his sympathies for his characters: he often changes his attitude depending on whether they are winning or losing. Hence it is difficult to pinpoint his and, consequently, the reader's attitudes toward them. That his rebellious heroes—Pechorin, Arbenin, the Demon, and Kalashnikov—all fail clearly mitigates their destructiveness. The Demon, for example, is portrayed sympathetically throughout the poem.

When he declares himself the possessor of Tamara's soul, however, he loses his appeal: "But, heavens—who would have recognized him? How malicious was his gaze" (*No, Bozhe—Kto b ego uznal? Kakim smotrel on zlobnym vzgliadom*) (2:71).

Conversely, at the moment of his sudden death Kiribeevich gets a note of tenderness from Lermontov:

И опричник молодой застонал слегка,
Закачался, упал замертво;
Повалился он на холодный снег,
На холодный снег, будто сосенка,
Под смолистый под корень подрубленная.
(2:18)

(And the young oprichnik moaned lightly, trembled, and fell dead; he fell on the cold snow, on the cold snow like a pine tree, like a pine tree cut near its tarry root in a shady forest.)

The shift of the point of view is especially noticeable at the moment of Kalashnikov's execution. Beforehand an objective, almost upbeat tone prevails: "The executioner walks merrily back and forth, waiting for the valiant fighter, while this hapless fighter, the young merchant, bids farewell to his dear brothers" (*Palach veselo pokhazhivaet, Udalogo boitsa dozhidaetsia,— A likhoi boets, molodoi kupets, so rodnymi brat'iami proshchaetsia*) (2:19). But then the tone changes to one full of pity, tenderness, and compassion: "and his hapless head rolled in blood across the execution block" (*i golovushka bestalannaia vo krovi na plakhu pokatilasia*) (2:19).[21]

"The Song" ends with a reference to a group of folk singers who sing their songs when passing by the nameless grave of Kalashnikov. But if the grave is unmarked, what is the subject of their songs? Apparently, it is precisely that: a nameless grave, unknown sorrow, destroyed promise. Had Kalashnikov been victorious, Lermontov would not have had his singers sing of him.[22] When all is said and done, there remains only a song to commemorate Kalashnikov's heroism, the song sung by the singers and the poet himself.

Lermontov seems to follow a similar logic in his 1832 poem "The Field of Borodino" (*Pole Borodina*). In this poem Lermontov accepts the futility of the heroic sacrifice of Russian soldiers, but makes it, in a paradoxical turn, their greatest claim to glory:

Мои товарищи, вы пали!
Но этим не могли помочь.
Однако же в преданьях славы
Все громче Рымника, Полтавы
Гремит *Бородино*.
Скорей обманет глас пророчий,

Скорей небес погаснут очи,
Чем в памяти сынов полночи
Изгладится оно.
(1:184; emphasis in original)

(My friends, you have fallen, but it did not help. Still, in those glorious tales, Borodino thunders louder than Rymnik or Poltava. Sooner would the prophet's voice deceive, or the sky's eyes darken, than that word [Borodino] disappear from the memories of midnight's sons.)

Even if the deaths of Russian soldiers did not secure victory, their courageous sacrifice at Borodino speaks louder to a Russian soul than the victory at Poltava (1709) or the decisive victory over the Turks at the river Rymnik (1789). The memory of the soldiers' heroic stand, their refusal to surrender, is more permanent than the promises of heaven.

THE EVIL WORLD OF "THE SONG"

Lermontov's heroes are thus made to function in the universe, which punishes rather than rewards their heroic conduct. It appears to be created by an unjust or even evil creator, who deliberately destroys them. Such a perception of the world is crucial for the problematics of "The Song" and must be explored more thoroughly.

In one of its versions, the poem "The Death of the Poet" had an epigraph taken from the Russian translation of a French tragedy by Jean de Rotrou (1609–50), which contained an appeal to the tsar for the revenge and execution of a murderer. A week later, Lermontov, realizing that his hopes that the tsar would take swift revenge had not materialized, added the last sixteen lines of the poem. These lines contain a bitter attack on the tsar's court and express Lermontov's belief in a divine judgment that culprits in high places will not be able to escape. In "The Song," however, Lermontov's conviction of either earthly or divine justice is absent. Lermontov has moved to the opposite extreme, which can be summarized by Pushkin's lines from *Boris Godunov:* "As you won't be able to escape from heavenly judgment so you won't escape the earthly one." "The Song" shows the limitations or rather the inability of both tsar and God to administer justice. Thus it is not surprising that "The Song" begins the first and only collection of Lermontov's poetry published in his lifetime. It marks the beginning of a new period, a period of a rebellious stance vis-à-vis heaven and earth. The inspiration for such a stance comes from a personal understanding of truth, honor, and justice that neither domain can satisfy.

Lermontov often criticized his generation for its failure to defend its convictions, beliefs, and passions against force or persecution. In his celebrated 1838 poem "Meditation" (*Duma*) Lermontov describes his contemporaries as indifferent, weak, cowardly, and incapable of sacrifice:

К добру и злу постыдно равнодушны,
В начале поприща мы вянем без борьбы;
Перед опасностью позорно малодушны
И перед властию позорные рабы. . . .
И ненавидим ны, и любим мы случайно
Ничем не жертвуя ни злобе, ни любви.
(1:35)[23]

(We are shamefully indifferent to both good and evil; at the beginning of our calling we wither away without a struggle. Before danger we are shameful cowards, and before power we are shameful slaves. . . . We love and hate randomly, never sacrificing anything, neither for anger, nor for love.)

Kalashnikov's heroic conduct should thus be compared not only to the behavior of other characters within the poem, but to that of Lermontov's contemporaries as well. This message was not lost on Belinsky, who immediately interpreted the poem as a reproach to the present day (Belinsky 1978, 238–39). Already *The Masquerade* outlines Lermontov's attacks on his cowardly contemporaries and contrasts them with the protagonist Arbenin. At one point Arbenin declares: "I will prove that in our generation there is at least one heart for which an insult brings forth the fruit [of revenge]" (*Ia dokazhu, chto v nashem pokolenie Est' khot' odna dusha, v kotoroi oskorblenie, zapav, prinosit plod*) (3:66). The ability to sacrifice oneself and stand by one's own word, or fight for one's convictions, is exhibited not only by Kalashnikov or Arbenin, but also by the Russian soldiers of "Borodino": "and we promised to die and we stood by our oath in the battle of Borodino" (*i umeret' my obeshchali i kliatvu vernosti sderzhali my v Borodinskii boi*) (2:24). But what is the outcome of the heroic sacrifice of the Russian soldiers? What is the outcome of Kalashnikov's actions, and how is his heroism rewarded? And, ultimately, what kind of a universe do the protagonists of "The Song" inhabit?

The archetypal confrontation between a bragging champion and a righteous contender is the biblical battle of David and Goliath. Goliath represents a brutal, pagan, self-reliant force, while David firmly believes that God is with him and will help him. This confrontation is a clear antecedent to the fight of Kiribeevich and Kalashnikov. Both the bragging Kiribeevich and Goliath are killed by modest God-fearing contenders. The representatives of a proud brutal force die. But while David goes on to become king, Kalashnikov is executed. Nothing intercedes to save the merchant from the wrath of Ivan the Terrible.

In the text of "The Song" we encounter the following promise: "the winner of the fistfight will be rewarded by the tsar and the loser will be forgiven by God" (*kto pob'et kogo, togo tsar' nagradit, a kto budet pobit, togo Bog prostit*) (2:16). But the outcome is the opposite of what was promised: the loser, Kiribeevich, is killed, that is, at least in his earthly existence he is punished rather than forgiven by God. The winner, Kalashnikov, in his turn, is not rewarded by the tsar but is executed by him. It is important to note that in Russian folklore, as in the song "Mastriuk Temriukovich" from Kirsha Danilov's collection, Ivan rejoices in the victory of the Russian brothers over the bragging contender Mastriuk and admits to his wife that he would have rewarded the Russian fighters even if they had killed Mastriuk.[24]

Lermontov does not share the optimism of the folk song. In his universe, heroes are bound to repeat the fate of Pushkin, the eternal fate of rebels described in "The Death of the Poet" as: "And he rebelled against the opinions of the world—alone as before . . . and was killed!" (*Vosstal on protiv mnenii sveta—odin kak prezhde . . . i ubit!*) (2:21). The universe of Lermontov's poetry is a tragic one: its rulers are incapable of forgiveness. Here again the parallel with Pushkin is useful; in Pushkin's "Andzhelo" the culprit Andzhelo is ultimately forgiven by the ruler. Even more pertinent is Grinev's fate in *The Captain's Daughter* (1833–36). The champion of honor, Grinev, risks his life yet refuses to use Masha's name in his own defense. Masha, however, appeals to the empress and saves Grinev, while no one intercedes for Kalashnikov.

In fact, Lermontov's universe is more than tragic; it appears to be deliberately cruel, since its chosen beings, whether the poet-prophet of "The Prophet," or Napoleon, or the poet of "The Death of the Poet," are endowed with special gifts from above only to undergo additional suffering, degradation, and destruction. In the 1839 "Three Palms" (*Tri pal'my*), the trees complain to God about their uselessness. Their appeal is immediately answered: their loneliness is interrupted; the travelers whom they wish to help do arrive. But on the next day the same travelers mercilessly destroy the hapless trees. Nothing but ashes is left to commemorate their fate. The dynamics of Kalashnikov's challenge are similar: his desire is fulfilled—Kiribeevich is delivered to him, yet the merchant's heroism is rewarded with execution and "a nameless grave."[25]

The question that opens "Borodino" ("Tell me, uncle, was it not in vain that Moscow, burned down by fire, was surrendered to the French?" [*Skazhi-ka, diadia, ved' ne darom, Moskva, spalennaia pozharom, frantsuzu otdana?*] [2:23]) is never answered in the course of the poem. Critics from Belinsky on prefer to concentrate on the Russian spirit, realism, and other undeniably important features contained in the answer of the Borodino veteran, while the question of the first speaker remains open. Moscow was surrendered to the French after all. Was not the heroic sacrifice of the Russian soldiers just an exercise of self-destruction? People remember the battle at Borodino as they do many other heroic sacrifices of the Russian people, but what is the purpose of such heroism? Such questions underlie "The Song," as well as "The Death of the Poet" and "Borodino." At the end of each poem the defenders of higher truths against brutal forces are dead and defeated:

Pushkin, Russian soldiers, Kalashnikov. The predicament of many of Lermontov's heroes can be succinctly described in the line "And the world did not have mercy and God did not save!" (*I mir ne poshchadil—i Bog ne spas!*) from his 1832 poem, "He Was Born for Happiness and Hopes" (*On byl rozhden dlia schast'ia, dlia nadezhd*) (1:275). The concept of a cruel universe is so basic for Lermontov that he repeats this line almost verbatim in a much later poem, "To the Memory of Prince Odoevsky" (*Pamiati A. Odoevskogo*) (1839): "And society did not have mercy and God did not save!" (*I svet ne poshchadil—i Bog ne spas!*) (1:45).

GNOSTICISM AND HEROISM

The plight of Lermontov's heroes reveals not only their personal heroism but also discloses the hostile and cruel laws of the world they inhabit; it is clearly not Pushkin's "and-the-Duke-forgave-him" world. But how can one describe the universe of "The Song," a universe in which heroism, dignity, and courage are doomed to fail, while evil frequently triumphs? The metaphysical outlook conveyed by Lermontov's poem points to a feature of Romanticism that has only recently become the subject of scholarly attention: gnosticism. Lermontov's poem shares two key convictions of gnosticism: the earth is controlled by an indifferent or evil ruler, while a personal vision of truth is the source of action and salvation. Most critics, however, are unwilling to grant either that Lermontov depicts the world as created by an evil creator, that is, a gnostic world, or that anyone who manifests such blatant individualism and insistence on his personal vision, as Kalashnikov does, deserves praise or respect. Both admissions would be too unsettling and controversial for the Russian cultural tradition, or perhaps for most traditions. Those who are troubled by Kalashnikov's execution try hard to explain, justify, or reconcile his fate in terms of some higher purpose or providential plan.[26] Two typical examples are those of Lominadze, the most provocative yet symptomatic of recent criticism, and Dostoevsky's earlier response.

Lominadze (1985) correctly observes that the main tension of "The Song" lies in the fact that God's providence saves Kalashnikov in the battle with Kiribeevich but fails to save him from the execution ordered by a wrathful tsar (91). To resolve the contradiction, Lominadze posits the concept of "sacred Russia" (*Sviataia Rus'*), a term used by none other than Kiribeevich, and claims that the very existence of Russia as a saintly state demands the execution of such lawless merchants as Kalashnikov (156). Lominadze then backs off and tries to hide behind the notorious term "dialectics," which according to him should sustain two contradictory claims: the tragedy of Kalashnikov's death is not denied, but Russia nevertheless remains sacred. Obviously Lominadze is trying to have his cake and eat it too: "One cannot reconcile oneself with 'the cruel shameful death' of Kalashnikov, but, nevertheless, it does not stain the image of 'sacred Russia'" (166).

It is doubtful that Lermontov was either a thinker in the Stalinist mold, a pious Slavophile, or as masterly a Hegelian as Lominadze would have him be. Why should Lermontov even try to justify the sacred status of Russia? The word "sacred" (*sviataia*) occurs frequently in the text of "The Song"; the singers and Kalashnikov use it in connection with truth, churches, or icons, but not with the word "Russia." It is the deceitful Kiribeevich who refers to "sacred Russia."[27] In fact, the word "Russia" (*Rus'*) occurs only once in the text; that is, much less frequently than even the word "Moscow," let alone the word "tsar." Thus if there is an opposition along Lominadze's lines it is not between Kalashnikov and *Rus'* but between Kalashnikov and the tsar. Lominadze seems to confuse Russia with its ruler, echoing the pernicious mistake of Louis XIV (*L'état, c'est moi*) and probably of all Russian rulers. But it is precisely the fairness of such a substitution that Lermontov questions.

Dostoevsky is also impatient to resolve the tragedy of Kalashnikov's fate and bring the revolutionary thrust of his answer into the harmonious vision so detested by his own Ivan Karamazov. In 1877 Dostoevsky wrote:

> Lermontov has a tale about Kalashnikov. Belinsky, who by the end of his life had totally lost Russian sensitivity (the most talented of Westernizers), thought that in Ivan's words "I will order the ax sharpened" there is only the taunting, vicious joke of a tiger at the expense of its victim; while in the words of Ivan they signify mercy. You deserved execution—go then, but I also like you, and that is why I'll treat you as honorably as circumstances allow; but don't complain, I'll execute you nevertheless. Here, a lion spoke with a lion and knew it.
>
> N.B. You don't believe me? I can surprise you even further. You should know that Kalashnikov remained pleased with such mercy, and surely he viewed the death penalty as a just and fair punishment. All this is not in Lermontov, but it is so. (1972–90, 24:298)

Dostoevsky correctly notices a certain benevolence in Ivan the Terrible's treatment of Kalashnikov. The tsar allows the merchant to go to the execution block on his own, gives him time for a farewell, and promises to take care of his family. He also shows respect for his victim's integrity; he praises him for his honesty and tenderly calls him "young fellow" (*detinushka*) (2:19). Dostoevsky also correctly claims that Kalashnikov knows what to expect for his haughty answer. But even if Kalashnikov accepts the tsar's right to execute, is he really "pleased" with the sentence? Is Dostoevsky suggesting that Kalashnikov is not immune to the horrible disease diagnosed in Russia by the marquis de Custine: "The tyrant's dementia spread[s] so easily to the men who submit to tyranny; the victims become the zealous accomplices of the executioners" (Custine 1951, 313)?

However, even granting that Kalashnikov is resigned to march to his death, why cannot Lermontov question the cruel arrangement under which a hero is executed and even feels content with his own execution? Why does the tsar who is called "orthodox" in the text want to kill and not to forgive? What is "orthodox" or even lionlike about him then? Why should Lermontov or the reader be content with the outcome of execution even if Kalashnikov is? Dostoevsky's Ivan Karamazov poses exactly the same problem. Referring to the mother of a tortured child, Ivan states: "The suffering of the tortured child she has no right to forgive, she dares not forgive the torturer, even if the child were to forgive him."

One also wonders what Dostoevsky means by the phrase: "it is not in Lermontov"? That Lermontov, although he means it, simply fails to state in the text that Kalashnikov is satisfied with the tsar's justice? Or, perhaps, that Lermontov means something totally different and more painful, which he, Dostoevsky, must modify because he knows the truth better? For those who are disarmed by the friendly exchange between Kalashnikov and the tsar in which the tsar, praising the merchant and promising to reward his relatives, demonstrates his "autocracy with a human face," Lermontov adds a brutally realistic denouement: "And Stepan Kalashnikov was executed, subjected to a brutal and shameful death, and his hapless head rolled in blood across the execution block" (*I kaznili Stepana Kalashnikova smertiu liutoiu pozornoiu; i golovushka bestalannaia vo krovi na plakhu pokatilasia*) (2:19). In terms of the tsar and his world the sharp axe can mean grace, but why should it connote grace for Belinsky or the reader? According to Dostoevsky Belinsky is a Westernizer; he lacks Russian intuition and fails to see that a cruel execution can have another side. But this other side is also not the whole story. Why try to turn Kalashnikov into a propagandist of the Russian ideals of humility and obedience? Is it too disconcerting, too unsettling to grant Lermontov and his heroes the right to rely on an inborn sense of truth and honor in their confrontation with the universe?

Lermontov's heroes, whether Pechorin or Kalashnikov, care little about the judgments of the world as long as they do what they deem necessary. It is Kalashnikov's lot to defend the "mother-truth" (*pravdu-matushku*), and he does so. Whatever happens next, whatever verdict the tsar or the world pronounces, does not really concern him. As "I Do not Want the World to Know . . ." (*Ia ne khochu chtob svet uznal . . .*) states: "Reproach of fools, reproach of men, does not grieve a noble soul" (*Ukor nevezhd, ukor liudei / Dushi vysokoi ne pechalit*) (1:29). Therefore, to psychologize what Kalashnikov feels after the tsar's verdict is deliberately to misread the poem. Emphasis should be given to Kalashnikov's courageous answer, which leads to the cruel verdict, rather than what Kalashnikov feels about it. Dostoevsky, however, prefers to gloss over the rebellious answer that sets limits on the power of the Russian tsar and thus of the Russian state.

The comparison of Ivan and Kalashnikov to two lions blurs a great difference between them. The tsar merits praise for recognizing and respecting Kalashnikov's defense of his dignity, his freedom of conscience: "Good for you, young fellow . . . that you answered me according to your conscience" (*khorosho tebe, detinushka . . . chto otvet derzhal ty po sovesti*) (2:18). Ivan could have done worse, such as ordering that Kalashnikov be tortured until he discloses the reasons behind his actions. However, the Kalashnikov who—in "the country of slaves and masters"—answers the tsar as an equal and forfeits his life for it is by far a greater lion than Ivan the Terrible, who simply avoids petty vindictiveness and acknowledges Kalashnikov's right to privacy and integrity.

Lermontov's texts suggest his sympathy for gnosticism. Analysis of both "The Demon" and *The Masquerade* demonstrated awareness of both the attractions and shortcomings of such an outlook. If one views the world as unjust or evil and if one's only source of morality is inner impulse, the result (as with Arbenin or the Demon) can be murder and destruction. Paul Cantor in his provocative study of gnosticism in English Romanticism makes a similar point about Byron's "Cain," whose protagonist, filled with outrage at the moral inadequacies of the world and its creator, commits the first murder (1984, 139–40).

In "The Song," however, Lermontov is no longer concerned with exposing his protagonist's bankruptcy. Even though Kalashnikov, like other protagonists, takes the law in his own hands, he directs his anger against Kiribeevich rather than his wife, God, or the whole world. He stoically performs what he understands as his duty and is not really concerned with universal issues. Furthermore, while Arbenin could have rectified his situation had he listened to the Baroness or his wife, Kalashnikov appears to be doomed from the start; nothing could have saved him except a miracle. Arbenin perishes because he imagines the world to be more evil than it is. In "The Song" the world is evil. Because Kalashnikov's behavior is less objectionable than that of Arbenin, Kalashnikov's fate highlights the cruelty of his universe. His example, as well as that of the singers who celebrate his heroism in song, indicate a way of resolving the gnostic predicament that does not lead to destruction, murder, or madness. Kalashnikov manifests stoicism and resignation in the face of the real and imaginary evils of the world, and simply carries out his duty. Lermontov himself has learned from his character. Rather than railing at the injustices of the world, he recounts Kalashnikov's heroism, composes a song on the subject, and leaves it there. The poet's task is to put an inscription on the hero's nameless grave, to rescue a heroic act from oblivion.

Lermontov's great narrative poems, whether "The Song," "The Demon," or "Mtsyri," meet the moral challenge of gnosticism. These poems, like all of Lermontov's major works, play out various possible responses to existence in the gnostic world (the Demon who remembers lost bliss and is condemned by God to tormented life in this world is the perfect embodiment of the gnostic predicament). Lermontov's later texts actively articulate what was still implicit in "The Song": the only truly viable—that is, nonviolent—solution to life in such a world is the life of art and creativity, as opposed to the life of ceaseless rebellion and destruction. Such characters as Tamara, Mtsyri, or Doctor Werner (*A Hero of Our Time*) point to artistic outlook as the only tangible and honest outlook compatible with the existence in an evil world. At the age of sixteen Lermontov was already aware of the special role of art: "everything has betrayed me; poison is everywhere, only the sound of the lyre has been faithful to me" (*Vse izmenilo mne, krugom otravy, lish' liry zvuk, mne ne izmenen byl*) (1:101). The poet glorified art not because it provided a challenge to God and thus was attractive to artists who aspired to be gods themselves (a conventional view of Western Romanticism as articulated in the work of M. H. Abrams and Harold Bloom), but because only art enabled Lermontov to combine a gnostic outlook with nonviolence. Art indeed partakes of the inner impulse; it might acknowledge the hostility of the universe, yet does not result in external destructive behavior. For Lermontov, as for Pushkin, art creates and thus is incapable of resorting to violence and destruction: "genius and evil action are two incompatible things" ("Mozart and Salieri").

Lermontov's artistic output, among other things, was thus a rather successful way of confronting the gnostic outlook. Writing at the end of his career, Lermontov admits in his 1841 "Fairy Tale for Children": "the powerful image [of the Demon] haunted my mind for years . . . yet, having parted with other dreams, I also got rid of him through poetry" (2:95). It is poetry, the interraction with the "muse of gentle inspiration" (*muza krotkikh vdokhnovenii*) (1:111), that Lermontov sees as the last bulwark against the demonic temptation of gnosticism.[28]

Chapter Five

Futile, Fatal, or Heroic: Pechorin in "The Fatalist"

He is a real hero of our time. "What a hero and what a time," you will say. But that's the way things are.
—Ivan Turgenev, commenting on Bazarov

PECHORIN'S PROBLEM

The very title *A Hero of Our Time* presents a problem. Is Pechorin a hero? And if so, in what sense? What "time" does the author refer to in his title, and why does this "time" make Pechorin its hero? The novel's two introductions foreground the problem without resolving it. The narrator of the second introduction, the one who introduces Pechorin's diary, states: "Perhaps some readers will want to know my opinion of Pechorin's character. My answer is the title of this book. 'But this is malicious irony,' they will say.—I don't know" (64). Such a confusing and paradoxical statement from the narrator, who has just presented us with Pechorin's dubious escapades in "Bela" and "Maksim Maksimych," challenges us to discern and account for Pechorin's heroic qualities.

The "Author's Preface," which introduces the novel itself, does, however, offer an easy way out: "A Hero of Our Time is . . . a portrait composed of all the vices of our generation in the fullness of their development" (2). Unfortunately, many critics have taken these words at face value and consider the problem solved: there is nothing heroic about Pechorin, and all one has to do is to spell out his vices. It should not, however, be forgotten that the "Author's Preface" was added only to the second edition of the novel; like any later commentary this preface might at best suggest only a possible interpretation. Furthermore, the narrator's characterization of Pechorin, in the context of a thoroughly ironic preface that deals specifically with the reader's "faith . . . in the literal meaning of words" (1), is as ironic and ambiguous as anything in the two introductions. In other words, this preface cannot adequately meet the central challenge posed by the novel and its title: to determine those features that make Pechorin a hero of his time, and not just its typical representative. Although Pechorin may not be a universal hero, he is nevertheless a hero of a certain period. In this sense, Lermontov's aim is different from that of the authors of *La Confession d'un enfant du siècle* (Musset) or "The Knight of Our Time" (Karamzin). Lermontov explores what is heroic about Pechorin rather than what is simply typical. In what follows I take Lermontov's challenge seriously and attempt both to establish Pechorin's heroic features and to reconstruct Lermontov's view of his time.[1]

The scholarly literature on Lermontov's novel is vast. Numerous works by Russian and Western scholars have explored the historic, cultural, and literary background of the novel, Lermontov's psychological insights, as well as his narrative strategies. In the process, Pechorin has been condemned, exposed, glorified, and lectured from too many pulpits. Depending on the scholar's ideological agenda, Pechorin has been turned into a villain, a "superfluous man," a rebel. The examination of Pechorin's unique features is quickly overlaid if not substituted with the recitation of platitudes about the ills of society that he is supposed to represent. Pechorin's heroism is reduced to atheism, social protest, or sympathies for the Decembrist movement, an approach that marks many Soviet studies.

Western scholars, trying to avoid the excesses of Soviet scholarship, have gone to another extreme. They rarely acknowledge anything heroic about Pechorin, preferring instead to identify and condemn his sins, as if Pechorin had not done so himself. Especially unfortunate in this regard is Pechorin's admission of the joy he experiences when using others, an admission quoted by practically everyone who writes on the novel:

> There is a boundless delight in the possession of the young, barely unfolded soul. It is like a flower whose best fragrance emanates to meet the first ray of the sun. It should be plucked that very minute and after inhaling one's fill of it, one should throw it away on the road . . . my main pleasure . . . is to subjugate to my will all that surrounds me. (123)[2]

It is important not to take this passage out of its novelistic context. On the one hand, the exaggerated and highly rhetorical form of this confession makes Pechorin's purpose clear: he is parodying fatal Romantic characters, whose similar demonic confessions mesmerized readers of such popular texts of the period as Charles Maturin's *Melmoth the Wanderer* and Alfred de Musset's *Confession d'un enfant de siècle* (Manuilov 1966, 213). Yet Pechorin's, and ultimately Lermontov's, irony, which is directed at such clichés and at those titillated by them, is missed by readers who, like Princess Mary, take Pechorin's confessions literally. Furthermore, Pechorin frequently acknowledges emotions that prove too embarrassing for others to admit. When he confesses to being envious of Grushnitsky's success with Princess Mary, Pechorin asserts that this emotion is experienced by others, yet they are not frank enough to acknowledge it (90). Likewise, admitting his manipulative attitude toward others, Pechorin simply brings to the surface what those around him prefer to ignore.

Indeed, ruthless manipulation dominates the world of the novel: in one of the book's first episodes we see how the greedy Ossetians try to trick the inexperienced narrator, a newcomer to the Caucasus, into hiring six useless oxen. Later we witness the narrator himself trying to manipulate Maksim Maksimych into telling him an adventure tale; still later we observe Vulich as he connives to make the participants of a serious discussion on human responsibility witnesses to his irresponsible gamble with his own life. Similarly, the mysterious female smuggler tries to manipulate Pechorin and kill him, Grushnitsky manipulates the romantic expectations of Princess Mary, while Mary and the Captain of the Dragoons practice their manipulations on Grushnitsky. The implication of such events is clear: the whole world is engaged in one or another form of manipulation; Pechorin, however, becomes a scapegoat for bringing this fact to the surface and for being quite aware of it in himself. Or, as Belinsky (1978) puts it in attacking Pechorin's critics: "You condemn him not for his vices—you have more of them, and they are darker and more shameful than his—but for the courageous freedom, for the biting sincerity with which he discusses them" (3:118).

Ever since Pushkin's portrayal of Aleko in "The Gypsies" it had become a tradition in Russian literature to condemn individuals who seek license only for themselves while ignoring the autonomy of others. In the frequently quoted reproach to Aleko, the Old Gypsy remarks: "You want freedom only for yourself." Clearly, Pushkin's lessons were not lost on Lermontov, who in fact wrote a libretto based on Pushkin's text. Thus if we are to condemn Pechorin, we must base our critique of his actions on something more substantial than his self-proclaimed petty demonism. Lermontov's creation is too complicated for that; and yet Pechorin's musings seem to be so offensive to his readers' sensibility that his critics cannot wait to condemn and then dismiss Pechorin for his self-acknowledged egoism and manipulativeness.[3] The hypnotic power of the plucked-flower passage is such that it is cited even in books not directly related to Lermontov and Russian literature. Thus James D. Wilson, in his study *The Romantic Heroic Ideal* (1982), which is concerned with Western and American views of the issue, nevertheless manages to quote—and dutifully condemn—Pechorin for "becom[ing] a willing slave to an ego which pays little heed to the humanity of others" (53).

As if responding to such moralizing critics, Herzen (1954–66) writes:

> Moralists frequently and piously speak of the devastating vice of lust for power. . . . Lust for power, by itself, comes from a good source—from the awareness of one's human dignity. . . . Yet, moralists ignore a rather different feeling: love of subjugation, love of power and authority, a feeling based on

> self-contempt and obliteration of one's own dignity. This feeling is so common, so successful in epidemically infecting whole generations, whole nations, that one should discuss it, yet the moralists are silent. (2:92).

Herzen's words underscore one of the central issues of Lermontov's novel. Lermontov is no less aware than other moralists that lust for power is a devastating sin. He is more concerned, however, with the equally devastating, yet frequently ignored sins of surrender, subjugation, and obliteration of one's human dignity.

The most powerful attack on Pechorin is mounted, however, not by critics and scholars, but by the major Russian writers and thinkers of the nineteenth century. As if trying to avoid the challenge presented by Lermontov's problematic hero, authors ranging from Apollon Grigor'ev to Dostoevsky and Vladimir Solov'ev, and from Turgenev to Tolstoy and Chekhov, have preferred to present Pechorin-like characters either as vicious bullies or idle "superfluous men" consumed by a paralyzing "self-consciousness" (*refleksiia*). Such a persistent urge to parody or vilify Pechorin indicates that these writers were attracted to the enigmatic figure of Pechorin and felt the need to understand him. But in merely parodying him they refused to come to terms with the moral and intellectual challenges of Pechorin; Pechorin is in fact more complicated than either a demonic bully or a lazy *raisonneur.*

Dostoevsky, for example, thirty-five years after Lermontov's death, still felt the need to battle with Lermontov's creation, claiming that Pechorin belonged to a group of petty villains who began with Sylvio, the protagonist of Pushkin's short story "The Shot" (1830). According to Dostoevsky (1972–90) "Pechorin killed Grushnitsky only because he was not very attractive in uniform and failed to cut a dashing figure in the eyes of society women at the balls of Saint Petersburg high society" (22:39). In another misreading of Lermontov's text and its protagonist, Dostoevsky described his own Underground Man, rather than Pechorin of Lermontov's novel: "In Pechorin it [the Onegin type] has developed into insatiable bilious malice and an utterly strange, completely Russian confluence of two diverse elements: selfishness to the point of self-adoration, and malicious self-hatred. And still the same yearning for truth and action, and the same eternally fateful 'there is nothing to do'" (19:12).

Even when Pechorin is not condemned outright and when his uniqueness is acknowledged, it is in terms of quantity rather than quality. For example, William Todd (1986) concludes that Pechorin is a hero because he is "at one . . . with the values and patterns of the society that he represents and superior to the other characters in his ability to realize these values and patterns" (161). Yet if Pechorin is such a master of social games, and if he enjoys power and control, why does he not get anywhere with all his talents, connections, and skills? This question is rarely asked even by critics who grant Pechorin his talents and a certain superiority. Pechorin surely possesses impressive social skills, but what makes him a hero is the fact that he, even if capable of understanding and realizing the "values and patterns" of his society better than anyone else, refuses to play the game.

Although Pechorin's actions seem to resemble the actions of other characters in the novel, there is always a crucial difference, whether in the execution, motive, or impulse behind the action; and it is this difference that allows the narrator to dub Pechorin a hero. Lermontov's method of presenting his protagonists as similiar yet ultimately superior to those around them, finds its full expression in *A Hero of Our Time.* Each of the novel's five tales features a character who reacts to the challenges that face Pechorin in a manner that can be viewed as typical or conventional. Kazbich in "Bela," Pechorin's servant in "Maksim Maksimych," Yanko in "Taman'," Grushnitsky in "Princess Mary," and Vulich in "The Fatalist" act as foil to Pechorin and put his actions in sharp relief. Pechorin's deception in obtaining Bela should be considered against the background of Azamat, who exchanges his own sister for a horse; Pechorin's dismissal of the Taman' dwellers should be measured against Yanko who explicitly denies his responsibility toward the blind orphan and old woman (the mother of the girl whom he loves); Pechorin's formal politeness during the meeting with Maksim Maksimych should be compared to Pechorin's servant who treats Maksim Maksimych with haughtiness and condescension, stressing the wealth and social position of his master. Likewise, Pechorin's brave attempt to save the murderous Cossack from the lynching crowd should be contrasted to Vulich, who gambles with his life for no obvious reason. And finally, Pechorin's manipulation of Princess Mary should be approached in the context of Grushnitsky's attempt to manipulate Princess Mary by playing the role of a Romantic hero. Ultimately, Pechorin's cruelty must be condemned; surely he could have avoided killing Grushnitsky. Still we must first analyze what distinguishes him from the rest of the novel's characters.

Criticism that neglects the uniqueness of Pechorin has done a similar disservice to the concept of "our time." In his novel, Lermontov presents his own vision of this period. To establish what he means by "our time" we are better served by analyzing some of the materials provided by the text, such as the depiction of secondary characters, than we are with the writings of Belinsky, Herzen, or any other progressive or conservative cultural figure of post-Decembrist Russia.[4] Revealing as these writings are, they tell us less about the "our time" of the novel than, say, an obnoxious Captain of Dragoons, that nameless figure who plays such an unsavory but significant role in the novel's development. This captain, who is dismissed by Nabokov as "little more than a stock character of comedy" (1988, xviii), but recognized by Belinsky in his review of the novel as "incomparable" (1978, 3:148) speaks volumes about Lermontov's assessment of his time. Being no less aware of the "stock" features of his captain than Nabokov, Lermontov populates his book with such characters because he wants to make a serious and tragic statement about his "time," a time in which such characters thrive, succeed, and decide the fate of others. The ignoble and cruel world that Pechorin inhabits clearly informs his actions and thoughts. Yet to dismiss him as "a moral Quasimodo" (Dostoevsky) or "a ghost from the West" (Shevyrev) is to neglect the most interesting part of the novel: Pechorin's active interaction with his environment, which reveals not only his shortcomings, but also his merits.[5]

As if foreseeing his critics' desire to dismiss Pechorin as quickly as possible, Lermontov, with the foresight of a prophet, parodies such future refusals to come to terms with Pechorin. In the exchange between Maksim Maksimych and the narrator, simpleminded Maksim Maksimych happily resolves the mystery of Pechorin's anxiety and boredom: they are the result of the corrupting influence of foreigners and alcohol: "It was the French, was it, who introduced the fashion of being bored?—No, the English.—Ah, that's how it is . . . well, they have always been inveterate drunkards!" (41).

Such a simpleminded, if symptomatic, dismissal fails to confront fundamental questions posed by Lermontov's hero. What governs Pechorin's actions in this world of ruthless manipulation? What makes him tick? What prevents him, plagued as he is by all-encompassing doubts, skepticism, and uncertainty, from turning into one of his pedestrian doubles?

Pechorin's words, actions, and life embody all possible contradictions: moral, philosophical, social, and psychological. He is a huge question mark that, if it can not be answered, should at least be properly asked. We must therefore be wary of the cavalier ease with which all too many critics have dismissed Pechorin, branding him with one of those labels that blunts our analytical abilities; labels like "shadow from the West," "typical representative," "psychopath," "superfluous man," "petty demon"; or with such new and improved ones, like "male-chauvinist pig," and "an instrument of Russian colonial policies." We must delve deeper in order to account for the hero within.

"THE FATALIST": A STUDY IN HEROIC CONDUCT

> —Submit . . . you can't escape your fate!
> —I will not submit.
>
> —Lermontov, *A Hero of Our Time*

What is it that determines one's actions if one despises earthly joys, such as money and social power, but lacks faith in heavenly ones? Lermontov, in his 1829 poem "Prayer" (*Molitva*), describes just this predicament, one that was familiar to several of his protagonists: "Almighty, do not blame me . . . for the fact that Earth is too confining for me, and yet I am afraid to cling to you" (*Ne obviniai menia, Vsesilnyi . . . za to chto mir zemnoi mne tesen, k tebe zh priniknut' ia boius'*) (1:118).

Dostoevsky, critical as he was of Pechorin's pride and individualism, nevertheless unwittingly suggested one aspect of Pechorin's heroism. In his *Diary of a Writer* Dostoevsky (1972–90) states that the ultimate outcome of the loss of faith in immortality is disorientation, loss of moral barriers, crime, and suicide (24:46–50). Dostoevsky was also convinced that without convictions or foundations one would fail to act, as his portrayal of the Underground Man testifies. Pechorin, however, is a paradox: he is determined and active yet without firm convictions or foundations. Furthermore, regardless of his skepticism, Pechorin acts as if recognizing that not everything is allowed. Pechorin is thus a scandalous figure; by his very presence he undermines the future moral constructions of Dostoevsky. It is my contention that Pechorin's actions and morality are sustained by principles other than belief in immortality. The first of these, and one often neglected by critics, is Pechorin's adherence to the aristocratic code of behavior, to the rules of honor and obligation.

As if to answer Dostoevsky and to clarify this principle, the French aristocratic poet Alfred de Vigny writes in his "Diary of a Poet": La religion de l'honneur a son dieu toujours présent dans notre coeur. D'où vient qu'un homme qui n'est plus chrétien ne fait pas un vol qui serait inconnu? L'honneur invisible l'arrête." De Vigny then continues and charts a plan for a "contemporary novel": "Roman moderne.—Un homme d'honneur.—L'honneur est la seule base de sa conduite et remplace la religion en lui. . . . *L'honneur le défend de tous les crimes et de toutes les bassesses: c'est sa religion.* Le christianisme est mort dans son coeur" (Vigny 1935, 307–8; my emphasis).

In fact, Dostoevsky was well aware of the importance of honor and of the pernicious results that occur when respect for honorable behavior disappears. In *The Possessed,* Karmazinov directly associates the denial of honor with the forthcoming revolutionary cataclysms: "As far as I can judge, the essence of the Russian revolutionary idea consists solely in the negation of honor. . . . For a Russian man honor is but an extravagant burden. It has always been a burden, throughout history. One can attract him with the explicit 'right to dishonor' better than with anything else" (1972–90, 10:300). Yet, regardless of such awareness, Dostoevsky more frequently than not parodies or criticizes the code of honor. Such different characters as the Underground Man and Zosima are utilized by Dostoevsky to undermine this code, to present it as something Western, artificial, non-native, and clearly anti-Christian. Suffice it to recall the Underground Man's sarcasm directed at the literary origins of the *point d'honneur.*

Dostoevsky's hostile views are based on the sad treatment that the concepts of honor or chivalry had undergone on Russian soil. Romantic literature had made the concepts of honor and chivalry familiar and even fashionable. Walter Scott's novels turned knights, duels, and the rules of chivalry into everyday notions. The ideology of honor, even though largely exported from the West, was very much on the mind of Russian nobles, especially as they came in contact with a reality that was fundamentally incompatible with chivalry. Since Russia lacked the feudal tradition that sustained the institution of chivalry in the West, the concept of honor was bound to become muddled and confused. The crushing of the Decembrist uprising is an obvious example of this confusion. Nicholas I behaved like a vicious tyrant who saw any attempt to improve the Russian situation as a personal attack on him and thus perceived the Decembrists' aspirations mainly in terms of regicide or fratricide. He is known to have dismissed a Decembrist's appeal to his word of honor in the following manner: "What do I care about your disgusting 'word of honor'" (quoted in Gordin 1989, 449). The rebels, in their turn, got so confused in their sense of loyalty that they almost immediately started betraying those who trusted them.

Berdiaev seems to have put his finger on the problem when he laments the lack of "knightly principle" in Russia, assering that such a lack precludes "the development of a courageous personal spirit":

> The lack of courageous character and of that strength of personality that was forged in the West by the institution of knighthood is the most dangerous shortcoming of Russians, both common people and the intelligentsia. The very love of a Russian toward his motherland would take a form that would preclude the development of that courageous personal spirit. For the sake of that love, for the sake of clinging to the motherly breast, the knightly element was rejected in Russia. (1918, 28)

Berdiaev is painfully correct in connecting the "knightly spirit" to the spirit of individualism, or, in his terms, to the "courageous personal spirit" (*muzhestvennyi lichnyi dukh*). Not only do these two principles nourish each other, they have been subjected to a similarly hostile treatment in Russian literature, which clearly facilitated the rejection of both of them. While individualism is frequently depicted as selfishness or petty demonism, honor and chivalry are largely seen as abuses of power and strength. It is this misunderstanding and perversion of honor and chivalry that Russian writers of the nineteenth century almost universally convey in their presentations of duels.[6] Pushkin's "Covetous Knight," for example, depicts the surrender of knightly honor to the temptation of money; explaining his success at the tournament, Alber declares: "What was the cause of my heroism? Avarice." Instead of honor, Pushkin's knights exhibit greed, deception, and treachery.

Yet, even if the "knightly element" was doomed to be rejected in Russia, both Pushkin and Lermontov were considerably more sympathetic to the principle of honor than were later generations. For example, in *The Cap-*

tain's Daughter, Pushkin presents individual honor as a fundamental human attribute that must be preserved at all costs, depicting his protagonist, Grinev, as always acting honorably within the concrete historical circumstances of Russia. Likewise, Lermontov's entire oeuvre can be read as an attempt to formulate the rules of honorable behavior within situations painfully familiar to his Russian readers.

De Vigny, we recall, sees honor as fundamental to human psychic makeup: "La religion de l'honneur a son dieu toujours présent dans notre coeur." He asserts that inwardly felt dignity and integrity play a decisive role in governing human action. He then posits and plans to explore the independent existence of a moral act apart from traditional religion, and he believes that rules of noble behavior often pick up the slack where religion falls short.[7] In this, de Vigny clearly follows his countryman, Pierre Bayle, who already in the seventeenth century declared that a society of atheists would be no less moral than that of Christians: "L'Athéisme ne conduit pas nécessairement à la corruption des moeurs"; "je ne ferai pas difficulté de dire, si on veut savoir ma conjecture touchant une Société d'Athées, qu'il me semble qu'à l'égard des moeurs et des actions civiles elle seroit toute semblable à une Société de Payens" (1984, 5 and 77). Bayle bases his assertion on the belief that human actions are governed more by passions, temperament, or habit than by an overriding principle or principles (1984, 10). This position is often denied both in general, and in the particular case of Pechorin, whose amoralism has been equated with atheism ever since the novel first appeared.

Let us now look at how Lermontov's novel tries to resolve the dispute between Dostoevsky and de Vigny. It is my contention that although Pechorin may well be a skeptical, cruel, and heartless individualist, he is by no means an amoralist; what sustains his peculiar morality is the code of honor and chivalry. It is "The Fatalist" that most vividly illuminates Pechorin's paradoxical moral code, and as such offers a key to the novel's design and ideological thrust. Because several scholars have already argued that "The Fatalist" is the cornerstone of the novel,[8] I begin the analysis of the novel with this tale.

The problematics of "The Fatalist" are introduced at the very outset: Pechorin recalls how one evening a group of officers discussed predestination. As the novel's commentators have observed, such discussions were typical during this post-Decembrist period of "reconciliation with reality."[9] Lermontov, by referring to such discussions, signals that he wants to suggest his own solution to the problem of free will and predestination.[10]

It is clear that at the heart of such discussions lurks an immediate and very relevant question to its time: How should one act in a situation of oppression, tyranny, and hardship? Should one be resigned to one's fate, or try to resist it? After an exchange of anecdotes pro and contra predestination, one of the officers immediately asks the tale's key question: "and if predetermination actually exists, why then are we given free will and reason, and why must we account for our actions?" (182).

This important question, however, remains unexplored, because of Vulich's interruption: "At this moment an officer, who had been sitting in a corner of the room, got up and, slowly coming up to the table, surveyed all present with a calm and solemn gaze" (183). Indeed, Vulich has a marked tendency to do things that are out of place. The narrator recalls his payment for a lost hand at cards in the middle of a battle, a payment that even the winner describes as being "out of place" (184); or his untimely desire to strike up a conversation with a drunkard carrying a sword. Such actions manifest Vulich's intellectual blindness, his disregard for reason and responsibility.

Vulich's preoccupation with cards suggests that gambling for him is a substitute for responsible action. It is thus quite consistent with Vulich's character to turn the question of personal responsibility into a gamble. And it is telling that during their discussion, the officers throw their cards under the table, while Vulich, returning to the table, reintroduces the element of gambling into a serious discussion. Similarly, he later asks Pechorin to throw a card in the air as a signal for his rash experiment. Vulich dismisses the question of free will as "an empty argument" and, instead of discussing how one should live if everything is predetermined, concentrates on the predetermination of death by challenging the officers to test personally the existence of such predetermination. Such a test, in fact, can be resolved by a single action in the manner of Vulich, while the questions of life and responsibility cannot: they demand individual choices and solutions appropriate to each particular situation. Vulich thus brackets the problem and prefers to gamble instead. Indeed, Pechorin immediately notices that Vulich is not proving anything: he is merely gambling. Congratulating Vulich on his success, Pechorin states: "You are a lucky gambler" (187). But gambling is, in fact, a resignation of one's will, reason, and responsibility. Even the way Vulich picks up a gun from a wall is symbolic. The process is described as "taking at random" (*vzial na udachu*) (185); that is, Vulich already acts with a blind trust in luck, something that Pechorin clearly rejects and refuses to follow.

The concept of responsibility presupposes a free choice; Vulich, however, does not want to choose. His compulsive gambling, which on the surface might appear to be an interest in the uncertain, is, in fact, a desperate attempt to establish a definite relationship with fate, to divine one's luck. Vulich needs the certainty of predestination in order to avoid choice and thus responsibility. After Vulich has survived his test, he is visibly upset when Pechorin remarks that he was convinced that Vulich would die. He nervously tells Pechorin that his remark is out of place. However, it is rather Vulich's actions and his dramatic performance that are out of place here. Vulich takes Pechorin's remark seriously because he indeed believes in a predetermined hour of death and other false certainties. He is obviously as nearsighted and superstitious as Pushkin's Hermann, of whom Pushkin observed that, "in spite of his entertaining very little religious belief, he was extremely superstitious."[11]

Unlike the rest of the officers, who follow Vulich's escapades as if hypnotized, Pechorin scrutinizes Vulich's actions—and this is crucial—with maximum attentiveness. We learn, for instance, that Pechorin "had never taken [his] eyes off the pistol" (187), a manifestion of levelheadedness and readiness for the unexpected. He also observes Vulich's eyes: "I looked fixedly into his eyes" (185), as he reports it. Vulich meets Pechorin's eye with his own "calm and steady [immobile—*nepodvizhnyi*] gaze" (185). Such calmness in a person who holds a gun to his forehead is as out of place as everything else that Vulich does. Vulich's immobile gaze reveals someone who acts as if under a spell, rather than by his own will. As a gambler, Vulich surrenders himself to fate, that is, to blind and strange occurrences. This is the ultimate symbolism of Vulich's fatal meeting with the Cossack. The blind and cruel chance that sends the Cossack toward Vulich is, in fact, what Vulich resigns himself to, and thus he is given it. The exchange between Vulich and the Cossack: "Who are you looking for, man [brother—*bratets*]? You!" (191) can be reversed as well, as it is not only the Cossack who has been looking for a victim, but also Vulich who has been looking for a Cossack, that is, for a blind murderous fate. Even the term "brother" is significant; it underlines that the two are mirror images of each other: half-crazed, self-destructive maniacs.

The exchange with the Cossack is more than an ironic commentary on the accidental and cruel nature of death; it also reveals how character contributes to fate. The Cossack was on a rampage, but it is Vulich who addressed him, otherwise the Cossack would have passed him by. The Cossack, death incarnate, is on his murderous course, and those who treat death lightly, without caution, as Vulich does, fall prey to it. By having Vulich repeat the fate of the slaughtered pig, whom the Cossack had killed earlier, Lermontov emphasizes that Vulich's fatalism is as effective in the face of danger as the behavior of a pig. Vulich did not just call to the Cossack at the moment of their encounter: all his previous gambler's life has been an invitation to the Cossack.

The encounter with the Cossack demonstrates the complex interplay between chance and necessity, between human character and external causality, and it shows that such a complex interplay can not be easily resolved, which is what Vulich wishes for. The exchange between the Cossack and Vulich is all the more important because it is not a realistic one; as Eikhenbaum has noted, there can be no one to report it. Eikhenbaum attributes this to a failure present throughout the novel: the absence of realistic motivation (1987, 272). However, as has been seen throughout this chapter, Lermontov's aim in *A Hero of Our Time* was not primitive verisimiltude. Because the dialogue sheds symbolic light on Vulich, it has to be there.

The importance of the Cossack as fate personified is stressed once more when Pechorin himself confronts the Cossack. Moreover, the contrast between Pechorin's and Vulich's encounter is striking. Through his encounter with the Cossack, Pechorin reintroduces the question of free will and responsibility and offers his own solution to it. By capturing the Cossack, Pechorin commits a free and heroic action that only superficially resembles that of his double, Vulich. Even if Pechorin competes with Vulich in his game, he clearly rewrites the rules.

Strangely, scholarly study on this subject seems to be in general agreement that Pechorin's capture of the Cossack has neither moral nor social foundation but is, in fact, just a mindless emulation of Vulich. In a rather typical statement, Gary Rosenshield describes Pechorin's action as follows: "It is the act of a daredevil. If a motive is required, Pechorin's need not to be outdone by anyone is more than sufficient. He wants to know if he has the courage to do something as dangerous as Vulich" (1988, 94).[12]

Nothing could be further from the truth.

In contrast to Vulich, Pechorin's actions are not self-centered; they involve other individuals and their tragic plight. In his confrontation with the Cossack, Pechorin deals with a real and not self-imposed danger. Moreover, Pechorin does not gamble but responds to the human drama unfolding in front of him: the Cossack is going to be shot before his mother's eyes. Furthermore, as opposed to Vulich, Pechorin uses all his will, reason, skills, and responsibility in his confrontation with the Cossack, and stays alive. The difference in the outcome of these confrontations underlines the difference between Pechorin's and Vulich's attitudes toward the question raised by the officer: will, reason, and responsibility are obviously not required in order to die: they are required in order to live. Pechorin's actions are similar to Vulich's only on the surface: on a deeper level they are as different as life and death.

The first thing that strikes Pechorin upon his arrival at the scene where the Cossack has barricaded himself in the hut is the tragic face of the Cossack's mother: "I noticed at once the striking face of an old woman which expressed frantic despair. She sat on a thick log, her elbows propped on her knees and her hands supporting her head: it was the murderer's mother. Now and then her lips moved. . . . Was it a prayer they whispered or a curse?" (191).

The despair on the mother's face is the force that spurs Pechorin to immediate action. In a similar vein he jumps to the defense of Princess Mary, when a drunk officer accosts her at the ball. Having witnessed Mary's "imploring glance" (*umoliaushchii vzgliad*) (114), Pechorin, risking a duel, saves her from scandal. Such actions of Pechorin reveal the kind of morality glorified by G. K. Chesterton in his introduction to *Oliver Twist*. Commenting on Dickens, Chesterton writes: "He did not dislike this or that argument for oppression: he disliked oppression. He disliked a certain look on the face of a man when he looks down on another man. And the look on that face is the only thing in the world that we really have to fight between here and the fires of hell" (1989, 267).

The Cossack *essaul* (Cossack captain) comes up with two ways of getting the Cossack: first he asks the mother to plead with her son to surrender, informing her that his refusal angers God and has kept the officers waiting for two hours already; when the mother refuses, the *essaul* offers to shoot the criminal through a crack in the window. The word used to describe shooting is *pristrelit'*, which does not mean simply "to shoot at" but has an implication of "shooting down like a dog," as it is usually used in the idiom *pristrelit' kak sobaku* (Dahl's dictionary defines *pristrelit'* as "to finish up with a shot a wounded, sick, or useless animal or beast"). And all that takes place in front of the eyes of the Cossack's mother. It is obvious that the presence of the mother is more than an homage to realism on Lermontov's part. Any mother is a marked symbol for Lermontov, himself a real-life orphan who populated his oeuvre with numerous orphans striving to relive the moment of a motherly embrace. In Lermontov's celebrated poem "The Cossack Lullaby" (1838), a Cossack's mother promises to pray for her son, even though she foresees and accepts his inevitable departure: "I'll be suffering from anxiety and yearning, I'll be waiting hopelessly, I'll be praying all day long, and I'll be divining at nights" (*stanu ia toskoi tomit'sia, beznadezhno zhdat' stanu tselyi den' molit'sia po nocham gadat'*) (1:38). It is clear that the presence in "The Fatalist" of the Cossack's mother who prays for her reckless son is an important signal, alerting us to a human tragedy which is unfolding before Pechorin's eyes.

Among contemporary scholars, only Emma Gershtein has noted the presence of the Cossack's mother in the tale, but even she fails to connect her presence to Pechorin's action. She restricts herself to the rather sentimental and bombastic, but nevertheless astute, observation that "a woman has returned to the novel not in the role of a lover, but rather in a new function, as a mourner and intercessor" (1976, 51). I would only substitute the oversentimental "a mourner and intercessor" (*plakal'shchitsa i zastupnitsa*) with the more simple "mother."

Earlier, inspired by Vulich's escapade, Pechorin had mused on his contemporaries' loss of convictions and pride; he had failed to note, however, that while he himself lacked conviction, he did have pride, and it is this pride and sense of honor that precludes him from accepting the solution offered by the *essaul:* to shoot the son like a mad dog in front of his mother's eyes. Pechorin immediately decides to risk his own life to remedy the situation. Pechorin might present the case as a duel with Vulich, or fate, while in fact it is an act of utter nobility. According to the *essaul*'s logic, it is better to kill a person in the presence of his mother than let the officers wait a few hours. Pechorin does not need such favors from the *essaul.* Such a shooting is unfair and dishonorable. Like many other unfair and dishonorable actions—

one can recall similar episodes from "Princess Mary," such as harassing the princess by sending a drunkard to invite her to a dance, or spreading malicious rumors of Princess Mary's fall in the absence of men who can defend her honor—it provokes an immediate reaction from Pechorin: he is willing to risk his own life in order to correct the dishonorable acts of others. Pechorin, as we all know, is perfectly capable of killing a human being, but not in the manner suggested by the *essaul*.

By avoiding the dishonorable slaughter of the Cossack, Pechorin obviously uses his principles, strength, and talent for a good cause. What he discovers is as solid a conviction as one can find, but he deliberately glosses over it. He downplays his own heroism and goes on discussing his skeptical outlook. Why? Is it because Pechorin constantly tries to convince himself that he is something he is not, as Vera puts it, or is it, as he acknowledges, because his life is "a chain of sad and frustrating contradictions to heart or reason" (89)?

I believe that Pechorin's refusal to turn his honorable act into a conviction has deeper reasons than a mere penchant for contradictions. Pechorin elaborates a paradigm of behavior that is based on uncertainty and skepticism rather than on abstract principles or convictions. At the end of "The Fatalist" Pechorin states explicitly that it is uncertainty that gives him strength and decisiveness: "I like to have doubts about everything: this inclination of mind does not impinge upon resoluteness of character. On the contrary, as far as I am concerned, I always advance with greater courage when I do not know what awaits me" (192). Pechorin here clearly supersedes Arbenin and his destructive pursuit of certainty. In an emblematic verbal gesture Pechorin opposes predetermination (*predopredelinie* in Russian) to indeterminacy (*neopredelennost'*) and celebrates the latter, by referring to the "indefinite (*neopredelennoe*) albeit, real rapture that the soul encounters in any struggle" (188).

In response to the temptation of "fatalism" or of any other illusory conviction, Pechorin asserts the transcendental value of freedom, thus sharing a view articulated by Lermontov as early as 1832 : "I will not give up my freedom for the sake of a delusion" (*ia svobody dlia zabluzhden'ia ne otdam*) ("I Won't Abase Myself Before You" [*Ia ne unizhus' pred toboiu*]) (1:252). Even though Pechorin does not know what to live by, he will not accept a deliberate, even if comfortable, illusion; such scruples immediately set him apart from the rest of the novel's characters, and in fact, from the majority of Russian literature's heroes, obsessed as they are by the search for some guiding ideology.[13]

If one's convictions and actions are encouraged by the sign of heaven, then what is the use of human will, reason, and responsibility? The Bible condemns such a search for signs of certainty, and Pechorin in his assertion of skepticism and doubt coupled with inner resolve asserts a fundamental value of Christianity, freedom of the will. Such freedom can and should exist only in uncertainty.

Through Pechorin Lermontov promotes a new ethics of behavior, based on indeterminacy.[14] "The Fatalist" reveals the hidden mechanism behind Pechorin's activity: his philosophy of action. Pechorin refuses to follow any predetermined program or ideology, but if chance throws him into a situation of tension and confrontation he reacts to the challenges offered with the utmost care and reacts according to his own personal principles. In that sense, Pechorin is quite similar to Henry Martin, the protagonist of Walter Scott's *Old Mortality,* to which Pechorin refers. Ulph (1972) is quite convincing in pointing out this similarity.

Pechorin's behavior finds its parallel in the actions of Lermontov's earlier hero, Kalashnikov. The merchant, we recall, challenges both the earthly and heavenly empires and skillfully kills his enemy Kiribeevich not because of some abstract revolutionary principle, but because his personal sense of honor and dignity has been encroached upon by the tsar's world and could not be remedied by the heavenly one.

Pechorin's heroic combination of thorough skepticism and decisive action might not be a revelation in the post-Nietzschean existential West. But in terms of Russian reality, Pechorin raises problems that Russian culture has yet to come to terms with, prone as Russians are to search desperately for a master ideology to relieve them of the responsibility of living in a world of uncertainty and choice. Hence, fatalism, the reliance on some preordained course—whether charted by God, science, or materialist philosophy—is, in Russian terms, the most dangerous of beliefs. Lermontov displays true insight by bringing this problem to the foreground.[15]

Long before "The Fatalist," the novel reveals both how tempting and dangerous fatalism can be. In "Bela" we encounter a parody of Vulich; this in the person of a mindless Russian coach driver who without any precaution travels across a dangerous mountain ridge. The narrator makes a point of observing the differences in behavior of the two coachmen, one a Yaroslavl peasant and the other an Ossetian: "the Ossetian led his shaft horse with all possible precautions, having unhitched the outside horses beforehand, while our easygoing Russ did not even bother to get off his box seat." The narrator, even though worrying about the well-being of his trunk, nevertheless seems to agree with the driver's statement: "Why, sir! With God's help, we'll make it no worse than they" (31) and comments, "We might well not have made it; but then again we did, and if all people reasoned more, they would be convinced that life is not worth worrying about so much" (31). His comment is in fact a sign of how prone Russians are to fatalism, resignation, and passivity.

Pechorin clearly objects to such a state of affairs: he acts with all possible precautions; he is not ready to surrender his will to anyone, including God. Ominously, however, it is the murderous Cossack who states the proud conviction of Pechorin. To the *essaul's* request that he give in to the inevitable power of circumstance—"submit to your fate"—the Cossack answers: "I won't submit" (192). The Cossack's actions show Lermontov's awareness of the possibly fatal consequences of unrestrained rebellion; nevertheless, it is clear that Pechorin is trying to mediate between the Cossack's absolute rebellion and Vulich's absolute resignation to fate.

Contemplating the temptations of fatalism, Pechorin admits that he has accomplished little and is now exhausted from previous aspirations and metaphysical quests. That is why, provoked by Vulich's theatrics into pondering the metaphysical subtleties of predestination, Pechorin quickly abandons it: "But I stopped myself in time on this dangerous path; and as I have, for a rule, never to reject anything decisively, nor trust *blindly* in anything, I brushed metaphysics aside and began *to look* under my feet" (189; my emphasis). This act, this insistence on looking as opposed to blindness, proves immensely useful, as it helps Pechorin to notice a dead pig under his feet. In light of the intoxication of his contemporaries with Hegel and Schelling, with spiritualism, ghosts, and other otherworldly emanations, Pechorin's remark that brushing metaphysics aside has prevented him from stepping on a dead pig is both ironic and prophetic. It is a funny and bitter comment on the fate of those who continue to be engaged in metaphysical investigations, who do not notice slaughtered pigs under their feet and ultimately share the pig's fate. In other words, Pechorin's faith in Providence lasts only till he sees a victim (a pig), and as he does not want to become another victim, he lets this faith go and proceeds home with "more caution" (190). Ultimately, it is the usefulness of any metaphysical construct, of any ideology, that Lermontov questions. In the long run, metaphysical truths become delusions; they introduce slippery certainties that take away one's readiness for and awareness of the unexpected, which is born out by Vulich's failure to be ready for the Cossack.

Contempt for metaphysical certainties is manifested even in the very last words of the tale. When Pechorin narrates the story of Vulich to Maksim Maksimych, the latter's comment is a brilliant statement of ambiguity: "Why the devil did he talk to a drunk at night! . . . However, this must have been what was assigned to him at his birth" (194). Maksim Maksimych in his explanation appeals both to predestination and to human error, but which was the cause, we will never know. One must learn to make choices in the face of uncertainty; otherwise a choice will not be free. The novel ends with a wonderfully ironic statement: "Nothing more could I get out of him: he does not care, generally, for metaphysical discussions" (194). Surely, Maksim Maksimych is a simpleminded soldier, not versed in the abstractions of metaphysics; his statement, however, contains all the metaphysics required for a free act. It implies both the need for reason and responsibility (one should avoid talking to sword-carrying drunkards), but also acknowledges the possibility of some higher intervention. As for further metaphysical discussions, it is not only Maksim Maksimych but also Pechorin and Lermontov who do not particularly care for them.

Similar to Pechorin, Lermontov likes to doubt everything, including Pechorin's heroism. Once "The Fatalist" is over we are forced to contemplate the fate of Pechorin and his death under obscure circumstances somewhere in Persia. We return to the ambiguity of the novel's second preface: Is it a bitter irony to call Pechorin a hero? The choice is ours.

ILLUSIONS, CERTAINTY, AND FREEDOM

The spasmodic search for ultimate and definitive truths is typical not just for Vulich or for the Yaroslavl peasant, who passively and fatalistically rely on God's help, but for the ideological quests of the period: from the Slavophiles to the Westernizers; from Belinsky with his Hegelianism to the Lovers of Wisdom (*Liubomudry*) with their Schellingianism; from Count Uvarov's slogan of "Autocracy, Orthodoxy, and National Spirit" to Bakunin's anarchism. All these ideologies attempt to establish and promote universal truths—truths that in turn crush freedom of choice, of doubt, and paradoxically, of action.

Pechorin's profound observation on the symbiosis between indeterminacy of philosophical foundations and decisive and resolute action flies in the face of the main refrain of Lermontov's contemporaries, whose favorite activity was to bemoan the loss of convictions. Although such complaints could easily be gathered into a lengthy volume, suffice it here to provide several fairly typical examples. In the epilogue to his *Russian Nights* (1844) Vladimir Odoevsky (1981) observes: "The distinguishing feature of the contemporary moment is not skepticism as such, but the desire to find a way out from it, to believe in something, to hope for something . . . a desire, all the more painful because nothing can satisfy it" (199). In his frequently quoted poem "Our Century" (*Nash vek*) (1851) Feodor Tiutchev dutifully complains that the corruption of modern man consists in the fact that he is perishing without faith, yet fails to search for it:

Не плоть а дух растлился в наши дни,
И человек отчаянно тоскует . . .
И сознает свою погибель он
И жаждет веры . . . но о ней не просит.

(Today it is spirit and not flesh that is corrupted, and man feels a desperate anxiety . . . and realizes his own perdition, and thirsts for faith . . . yet does not ask for it.)

Even such a famous rebel as Alexander Herzen maintains in his *Dilettantism in Science* (1841): "a multitude of people are left without their past convictions and without a present . . . with an inner striving but without that cornerstone of moral existence without which man cannot live" (1954–66, 3:7).

It is clear that we are dealing with a common topos, a formulaic complaint that betrays a desire to mimic rather than to think and communicate. Against such an attitude of his contemporaries and posterity, of whom Dostoevsky is the most notable example, Lermontov creates a hero who refuses to be engaged in a vain search for convictions and even more vain process of complaining, but in fact suggests that such a lack of ideological convictions is a source of strength rather than weakness.

The originality of Lermontov's thought and design continues to be missed by the novel's commentators. Complaints about loss of faith go well into the twentieth century as the novel's numerous critics fail to learn anything from the courageous lessons of Pechorin. In a rather typical statement, Russian Symbolist critic Iuli Aikhenval'd considers Pechorin's remark on his generation's loss of convictions the most profound statement of the novel and provides the following moralistic gloss upon it: "Yes, while man has faith he has strength, will, and an interest in life. But now . . . poets dub a hero of our time a person who is bored, uneasy, does not live himself, and kills others" (1929, 144). Such an influential Russian thinker as Lev Shestov echoes this sentiment. Even if he correctly observes that Pechorin kills hope and faith, Shestov adds that Lermontov surrenders to his own hero by failing to create values capable of withstanding Pechorin's skepticism, as if that had been Lermontov's original purpose. For Shestov, the creation of illusory schemes and systems is not a sign of weakness, as it is for Lermontov, but rather a sign of intellectual courage and strength: "Lermontov frequently tried to tackle the same issues as did Pushkin, but each time he did so Lermontov failed to conquer the problem: rather the problem conquered him. . . . Lermontov gave in, effaced himself before his own creation, Pechorin. . . . Pechorin kills all faith, all hope" (1990, 198–99).

The blindness of such interpreters as Aikhenval'd or Shestov is all the more surprising given that their readings contradict the actual text of the novel. As early as the "Author's Introduction" the "medicine of caustic truths" is contrasted with sweets that give one indigestion, indicating that nontruths, those pleasant but deceitful illusions, are a sickness, rather than a cure. Throughout the book Pechorin and ultimately Lermontov constantly subject illusions, hopes, and expectations to the attack of bitter truths, expressing an almost compulsive need to treat "sweet delusions" with caustic medicine. Pondering the reasons for his preoccupation with Mary and Grushnitsky, Pechorin remarks:

> Is it an outcome of that nasty but unconquerable feeling which urges us *to destroy the sweet delusions* of a fellow man, in order to have the petty satisfaction of saying to him, when he asks in despair, *what is it he should believe:* "My friend, the same thing happened to me and still, you see, I dine, I sup, I sleep

in perfect peace and *hope* to be able *to die without cries* and tears." (122–23; my emphasis)

Like the Demon, "whose gaze destroys hope" (*ia tot chei vzor nadezhdu gubit*) (2:61), Pechorin destroys the hopes of others: the only hope he offers is the hope of dying courageously. Pechorin is well aware of the petty demonism of his behavior as he admits to playing with others the games that were played with him ("my friend, the same thing happened to me"). But there is another level on which his lessons lose their demonic overtone: the courageous gazes of Pechorin and the Demon do not so much—or not only—destroy the hopes of others; first and foremost they are directed inward. Pechorin and the Demon scrutinize their own false hopes. Pechorin's petty concerns with the naive aspirations of Mary and Grushnitsky do not undermine either his, or especially Lermontov's, program of shattering the naive and illusory approach to life. Lermontov's sympathy for such a project is revealed in his 1833 letter to M. A. Lopukhina:

> Alas, the period of my dreams has passed, as did the time when I had faith; all I need now is material pleasures, tangible happiness. . . . When I saw how my beautiful dreams had flown away, I told myself that there was no use in creating new ones. It is much better—I thought—to learn to live without them. I tried, I looked like a drunkard who slowly tries to accommodate himself to life without wine! My efforts were not wasted, and soon I saw in the past nothing but a series of insignificant and all-too-common adventures. (4:407–8)

Lermontov views naive expectations as a dangerous affliction; their action is similar to wine, a substance that hardly prepares one to confront life's challenges. Furthermore, instead of making life more interesting, they turn it into a series of banalities shared by many. Nineteen-year old Lermontov suggests, paradoxically and originally, that it is illusions and dreams that we share in common, and not actual experiences.

In "The Fatalist" Pechorin admits that illusions, when turned into convictions and faith, used to help people to be resolute in their actions (188). Yet the certainty that served as the foundation of such convictions was false, dreamlike, and the reliance on such phantoms has led to weariness and passivity:

> In my early youth, I was a dreamer; I liked to fondle images, gloomy and iridescent by turn, that my restless and avid imagination pictured to me. But what was left me of it? Nothing but weariness, as from a night battle with a phantom, and a vague memory full of regrets. In this vain struggle, I exhausted the ardency of soul and the endurance of will, indispensable for real life. (188)

As if attempting to cure his readers of blind reliance on expectations, from relaxing one's gaze even for a second, Lermontov fills his novel with expectations that never come to fruition; such is the rhythm of the world as Lermontov came to see it. One should be warned before it is too late that hopes are bound to be frustrated. To harbor expectations is intellectually futile and psychologically damaging: their frustration leads to disillusionment and apathy. Whatever hopes are offered by life or texts, one should not hope, for hopes result in illusory schemes; they promise false certainties that life with its uncertainty is bound to frustrate.[16]

Lermontov's novel thus embodies a massive critique of expectations and illusions of any kind. In the course of the novel, metaphysical, social, literary, and personal expectations are ruthlessly frustrated. Maksim Maksimych, narrating the touching death of Bela, refers to the doctor's pronouncement that Bela was not going to make it through the day—but then he adds that the doctor was wrong. The narrator, taken with Bela, is suddenly filled with hope: "'She recovered?' I asked the junior captain, grasping him by the arm and involuntarily feeling glad. 'No,' he answered, 'the doctor's mistake was that she lingered two days'" (44). Such is the fate of all expectations in Lermontov's world: Maksim Maksimych waits for Pechorin in vain, while Pechorin expects to find Undine in vain; Mary waits to see a hero in Grushnitsky, while Vulich waits for a sign from heaven. It is not just that these expectations are not fulfilled; rather, they are fulfilled in a sardonic and cruel way. Maksim does finally meet Pechorin; Pechorin does encounter Undine; Vulich does find his death; even Grushnitsky gets to participate in a duel, thereby fulfilling the expectations that his heroic overcoat raised in Mary. But what a cruel twist is given to all these events! Those familiar with Lermontov's oeuvre should not be surprised, however. Were the three palms of the eponymous poem (1839) not awarded with the same sardonic fate, in response to the expression of their hopes and aspirations?

Illusions and expectations are similar to Grushnitsky's crutches; they might help Grushnitsky to recover from his wound and even elicit sympathy from Princess Mary, but in the long run they should be discarded, especially if one wants to learn to stand on one's feet firmly and not be thrown off the cliff, as was Grushnitsky, or cut down as were the three palms.

Through Pechorin, Lermontov articulates a program rather unusual in its day: he suggests that one should give up hopes and expectations and begin to act instead. Pechorin's profound words at the end of "The Fatalist" put the matter succinctly: "I like to have doubts about everything: this inclination of the mind does not impinge upon resoluteness of character. On the contrary, as far as I am concerned, I always advance with greater courage when I do not know what awaits me" (193–94). Pechorin is quite successful in situations of uncertainty. As his actions in "The Fatalist" testify, he keeps his eyes open, takes precautions, while remaining ready for any turn of events.

The rest of the novel's characters—whether Vulich, Grushnitsky, Maksim Maksimych, or Princess Mary—clearly fail to actualize Pechorin's program. Indeed, there is an important exchange on this subject between Pechorin and Grushnitsky. Grushnitsky reproaches Mary for encouraging his expectations: "Why then give hopes?" To which Pechorin answers: "Why did you hope? I can understand people who desire something and strive for it, but who wants hopes (*a kto zhe nadeetsia*)?" (135). Pechorin's rebuttal is valid whether it is applied to Grushnitsky himself, or to Mary's expectations of theatrical love and passion, or the readers' expectations of traditional heroes and adventures.

Moreover, the events of the novel suggest that blind trust and naive expectations are not just false or debilitating: they are morally dangerous. Mary's initial response to Grushnitsky, a response fueled by her illusions, triggered a chain of events that resulted in Grushnitsky's death. When Grushnitsky complains that Mary gave him hope, he is right; she did encourage him and thus she is to be partly blamed for his death, as even her mother recognizes: "my daughter, though innocently, was the cause of that" (178). Similarly, Pechorin's own expectations of Bela—the wish that she be an angel sent by fate—leads to another tragedy. It is thus important to underscore that in "The Fatalist," Pechorin gives up on destructive illusions associated with erotic love. It is significant and symbolic that Pechorin makes Nastia, his love interest in the story, wait for him rather than he waiting for some kind of miracle to occur as the result of their affair. Pechorin has learned from his mistakes.

Pechorin's attack on illusions has thus both a pragmatic and moral dimension, and is obviously directed not only against the characters within the novel, but also outside it; that is, against Lermontov's contemporaries. The sorry example of the Decembrists vividly reveals the relevance of Lermontov's program of shattering illusions and expectations. The Decembrists did a great deal of damage, both to themselves and others, first expecting an easy victory to their ill-prepared coup, and then blindly hoping for forgiveness from the avenging monarch.[17]

Commenting on the naive expectations of the Decembrists, the source of which was the confusion of actions with expectations, life with theater, Iuri Lotman writes: "Viewing real life as a performance not only offered a person the possibility of choosing his type of individual behavior, but also filled it with the expectation that things were going to happen. Eventfulness, that is, the possibility that unexpected phenomena and turns of events would happen, became a norm" (Lotman and Usenskii 1984, 160). In other words, the Decembrists' propensity for theater and role-playing preconditioned them to wait for a miracle; that is, for something that happens in a play or novel, but not in real life. Lotman's observation explains the mechanism that enabled the Decembrists to confuse the need for striving and acting with theatricality and Romantic expectations. One does not put on the mask, say, of a Karl Moore simply to continue to live like a clerk or an officer. One begins to expect things to happen as they happened to the brave robber. But one should not play a noble criminal in real life unless ready to face not only the glory of victory but also the treachery, shame, and gallows of defeat.

Lermontov does not want his readers "to abandon hope," nor does he demand cynicism or resignation. Instead, he challenges his contemporaries' refusal to come to terms with the harshness and unfairness of their society, a refusal accompanied by mindless trust in the utopian promises of various literary, intellectual, and social schemes. Lermontov was well aware that Romantic ideals are not a panacea, and, indeed, in certain situations and circumstances should be avoided. Explaining French hostility toward Romanticism he writes: "Why can the French not tolerate Romanticism? Because an untimely guest is worse than a Tartar" (4:371). This remark explains Lermontov's own intolerance toward the rhetoric of hopes and ideals that dominated Russian Romanticism in the 1830s. Interest in what Pushkin called "the elevating deception" (*vozvyshaiushchii obman*) had gone too far; it was time to disembark from "The Frigate 'Hope' "—a rather symptomatic title of Alexander Marlinsky's extremely popular tale of the period—and substitute actions for hopes. Instead of creating new dreams "it is better . . . to learn to live without them" as Lermontov put it in the already quoted 1833 letter to Lopukhina.

The "Author's Introduction" warns us against blind trust in the literal meaning of words, or more broadly, of appearances. To stress his point, Lermontov compares the reading public to a provincial person taken in by the seemingly friendly exchange between the diplomats of two hostile nations. Lermontov, however, is aware that his bitter lessons will not by themselves cure his audience or give it the right vision. "However, do not think . . . that the author of this book ever had the proud dream of becoming a reformer of mankind's vices. . . . Suffice it that the disease has been pointed out; goodness [God] knows how to cure it" (2). Lermontov's evasive "God knows" (*Bog znaet*) stresses that he does not and cannot know how to cure the illness. But Lermontov's ironic narrative invites us to take his words both literally and figuratively. And if taken literally, his words reveal another truth: only God knows the cure, for only God possesses the complete knowledge of facts, the full vision of the persons behind the masks, while humans are bound to look "through a glass darkly." But to the extent that the human being is aware that his or her assessment of a situation is not godlike and necessarily contains elements of uncertainty, and if correctives are constantly incorporated into judgment, many moral mistakes can be avoided. In that sense Lermontov is correct to claim that to pinpoint the illness may be tantamount to curing it.

"The Fatalist" explores the psychologically debilitating effect of blind reliance on metaphysical certainties and denounces the illusions and false aspirations that plagued Lermontov's generation. Yet, as exemplified in such diverse texts as Pushkin's *Evgenii Onegin* and *Belkin's Tales*, in Belinsky's criticism, or Dostoevsky's "Notes from the Underground," literature itself became one of the main sources of debilitating certainties, false expectations, and idle hopes. With their possibilities severely limited by the suppressive regime, it was in the domain of literature, and in the ideology of Romanticism in general, that Lermontov's contemporaries tried to satisfy their thirst for action and resistance.

Many leading Russian writers and critics warned of the dangers of basing life on a literary model or paradigm. They criticized the frivolity of popular Romantic literature, its promotion of unrealistic expectations, its negative impact on behavior. But these warnings did not make this literature less popular or less influential. The fact that even later writers felt the need to explore the harmful impact of Romantic literature in years to come is very telling. For instance, Turgenev discusses the impact of Romantic literary expectations in his "Knock . . . Knock . . . Knock . . ." while Dostoevsky returns to its debilitating role in his "Notes from the Underground." Both of these works explore the connection between literary expectations and the dysfunctional behavior of their protagonists. Although they were written much later, both texts return specifically to the 1840s as the time of the highest intoxication with popular Romantic literature.

It is clear that Lermontov, as a skeptical thinker and critic of harmful expectations, could not neglect such an important source of lies and false hopes as contemporary literature, especially as it was embodied in the work and ideology of Alexander Bestuzhev. Known by his pen name, Marlinsky, the former Decembrist, Bestuzhev became in the 1830s the most popular and influential peddler of Romantic fantasies, expectations, and illusions. In the next chapter I shall explore how Lermontov's novel and particularly its longest tale, "Princess Mary," undermined Marlinsky's dominance on the cultural scene and exposed the Russian public's dangerous embrace of the treacherous certainties encouraged by Romantic literature.

Chapter Six

Lermontov versus Marlinsky; or, Why Grushnitsky Had to Be Thrown off the Cliff

"PRINCESS MARY" AND *A HERO OF OUR TIME*

"Princess Mary," by far the longest tale in *A Hero of Our Time*, dominates both the novel and its scholarly discussion. Critics ranging from Shevyrev to Eikhenbaum have insisted that *A Hero of Our Time* is "Princess Mary," and view the rest of the tales as secondary to this main one. Belinsky, on the basis of Pechorin's self-revelations—"Princess Mary" is written in the form of Pechorin's diary—asserts that "Princess Mary" solves the mystery of Pechorin, while the other tales of the novel construct it (1978, 3:393). Dostoevsky, in his comments on Lermontov's novel, tends to focus on the Pechorin of "Princess Mary"; Dostoevsky's portrayal of the Underground Man is, in fact, modeled on the content of Pechorin's diary.[1]

Although it has recently become a commonplace to maintain that all the tales constitute integral parts of the novel, and although "The Fatalist" and "Taman" have been fruitfully explored and their significance established,[2] "Princess Mary" still shapes and informs not only attitudes toward Pechorin, but the readings of the four other tales. What in these tales might have been interpreted as Pechorin's heroism suddenly becomes, from the perspective of "Princess Mary," deception, manipulation, pettiness, or viciousness. Critics of Pechorin feel justified in their accusations, due to the seeming sincerity of Pechorin's confessions. Since the events of "Princess Mary" are presented without the protective distancing of a narrator's voice, readers who have faith "in the literal meaning of words" (1) presume that Pechorin's diary must necessarily explain his enigma. Yet, as was already well known to Heine—and Lermontov refers to his comment on the insincerity of Rousseau's *Confessions*—a confession does not necessarily contain "the truth," and a diary entry is probably as "constructed" as any other narrative.

"Princess Mary" seems less artful and more sincere than the other tales due to its thinly veiled emotions of hostility and anger. In an unpublished draft of the "Author's Introduction" Lermontov angrily responds to the attacks against his hero and addresses his readers with almost naive indignation: "and

I'll tell you that you all are almost like him [Pechorin], some are better, but many are much worse" (4:470). Such a personal and bitter attack is clearly out of place in Lermontov's ironic novel, and thus it is not surprising that he removed it from the preface. Nevertheless, this passage indicates to what degree Lermontov's bitterness toward society and its mores—a bitterness that Lermontov so clearly manifested in *The Masquerade*—informs, if not directs, Pechorin's own bitterness and aggressiveness. The author, who made "our time" part of the title of his book, has clearly much to say about his time. In this sense, Lermontov's novel continues the argument of *The Masquerade,* a play that presents Arbenin's mask-wearing environment in a most unflattering light. Perhaps because Lermontov failed to get his play published, he felt obliged to return to and develop this theme. In "Princess Mary" we are invited to explore another masquerade, another emblem of Russia's social ills.

MARLINISM AS A PHENOMENON OF RUSSIAN CULTURE

It will be recalled that the name of Prince Zvezdich, a character who together with the Baroness epitomizes the failings of Russian society and thus provides the foil to Arbenin, comes from Alexander Marlinsky's tale "The Trial" (1830). This is hardly a coincidence. I contend that the main thrust of "Princess Mary" is Lermontov's attack on his society's dangerous embrace of the cultural fashion I call—borrowing the term from the history of Russian literature—*marlinism.* Marlinism found its source in the work and personality of Alexander Bestuzhev-Marlinsky (1797–1837), an epigone of Byron and Scott and the most popular Russian writer of the 1830s. It is Lermontov's work in general and his novel, *A Hero of Our Time,* in particular, that finally undermined Marlinsky's reign over the Russian cultural scene and exposed the unhealthy symbiosis between Marlinsky's fashionable writings and the conduct of the Russian public.

The phenomenon of marlinism and its role in the cultural history of Russia deserves a much more penetrating scrutiny that it has received so far. Rather than viewing marlinism as a particular narrative style, as is usually done, I shall treat it as a mode of behavior with cultural, social, and moral implications exemplified first and foremost by the actions and writings of Alexander Marlinsky. In what follows I shall discuss the reasons for the popularity of marlinism and explore the phenomenon of marlinism as reflected through the critical prism of Lermontov's novel. I shall show that marlinism was, as it were, a "forced masquerade"; that is, a highly theatrical, melodramatic, and pseudoheroic mode of behavior that arose in response to the pressures of post-Decembrist Russia. This masquerade offered a surrogate solution to Russia's tragic problems: its lack of basic freedoms and the trauma of the

Decembrist fiasco. Lermontov, who attempted to debunk such surrogate solutions in his drama *The Masquerade,* resumes his attack in "Princess Mary," with far greater skill and success.

As early as 1839, having read only the novel's first tale, "Bela," Belinsky immediately compared it to the writings of Alexander Marlinsky. Belinsky in fact characterizes "Bela" as an "antidote (*protivoiadie*) . . . to the reading of Marlinsky's tales" (1978, 3:188). Belinsky thus interprets Lermontov's text as the cure for Marlinsky's poison even before Lermontov himself formulates, in the preface to the novel, the concept of bitter truths needed to cure his readers' oversweetened stomachs. Both Belinsky and Lermontov thus view the popular Romantic tales of predictably melodramatic adventures as unhealthy and destructive.

Such popular Romantic texts create illusions and unrealizable expectations that, if relied upon, can easily result in disaster. In "Taman'," Pechorin causes irreparable damage when he allows himself to mistake a ruthless beggar for a literary figure, Undine. Similarly, spurred by exotic narratives, he imagines Bela to be "an angel sent . . . by compassionate fate" (40). Even if understandable, such mistakes are rather costly. In his sketch "Caucasus' Veteran" (*Kavkazets,* 1841) Lermontov is explicit about the harmful role of literary expectations on human behavior. He refers to the Russian noblemen who went to the Caucasus in search of romantic adventures similar to those they had first heard of in Pushkin's "Prisoner of the Caucasus" or in Marlinsky's writings. Lermontov describes the sad plight of an officer whose dreams are now lost: "He is not advancing in the ranks. He has become moody and silent, just sits and smokes his small pipe; he also reads Marlinsky when off duty and says that it's very good. . . . For a time he had dreamed of a captured Circassian woman, but by now he has forgotten that almost unrealizable dream" (4:144). In the context of the officer's lackluster career and sullen mood one might wonder what is so good about reading Marlinsky. Lermontov's words present Marlinsky as a peddler of cheap escapism, of unrealizable fantasies that one entertains during free time in order to forget the misery of everyday existence.

In order to appreciate fully the urgency and skill of Lermontov's attack on popular literature as exemplified by Marlinsky, we must now take a closer look at the phenomenon of marlinism. Here is how Turgenev summarizes Marlinsky's popularity in his short story "Knock . . . Knock . . . Knock . . ." (1871):

> Marlinsky is considered old-fashioned now and nobody reads him, people make fun of his name. But in the thirties he was regarded as a great literary genius, and no one, not even Pushkin, could compare with him, according to the views of young people of that time. He not only enjoyed the reputation of being the foremost Russian writer, but, what is much harder to achieve and

> which happens much less frequently, he left his mark on his own generation. Heroes *à la* Marlinsky were to be found everywhere, but especially in the provinces and especially among infantry and artillery officers. (1968, 220)

Preoccupied with the state of Russian art, Turgenev felt an urgent need to attack Marlinsky. In order to describe the phenomenon of marlinism in painting he even coined the phrase "*briullovskii marlinizm*" by merging the names of the painter Karl Briullov and Marlinsky. Turgenev encouraged new artists to overcome this dreadful phenomenon (1987, 160).

In his 1834 essay "Literary Reveries" written at the height of Marlinsky's popularity, Belinsky, while remaining critical, nevertheless acknowledges that "he [Marlinsky] enjoys nowadays a tremendous authority; today everyone genuflects before him, and if they do not universally acclaim him as the *Russian Balzac,* it is only because they are afraid that he will take it as an insult. Instead they are waiting for the French to call their Balzac a *French Marlinsky*" (1978, 1:107; emphasis in original). A year earlier, a prominent literary figure, Nikolai Polevoi, had commented on Marlinsky: "one can say decisively, that among novelists living today, no one compares to him in artistic power" (quoted in Stepanov 1966, 200).

The reason behind Marlinsky's popularity is not immediately obvious. To Belinsky his weaknesses as a writer were immediately clear, and in the same "Literary Reveries" mentioned above he was the first to attack Marlinsky for his emptiness and falsehoods. Nevertheless, Marlinsky's popularity was still on the rise even in 1840 when Belinsky wrote a long essay solely to debunk him. Even that was not enough: as late as 1852 Leo Tolstoy felt the need to debunk a Marlinsky-type hero in one of his earliest stories, "The Raid."

For his part, Lermontov satirizes the melodramatic mode of behavior and interaction popularized and epitomized by Marlinsky when he describes one of the key figures of "Princess Mary," Grushnitsky:

> His speech is rapid and ornate; he is one of those people who, for every occasion in life, have ready-made pompous phrases, whom unadorned beauty does not move, and who solemnly drape themselves in extraordinary emotions, exalted passions, and exceptional feelings. To produce an effect is rapture to them; romantic provincial ladies go crazy over them. (84)

Belinsky immediately detects the presence of Marlinsky in this description: "I should add to this sketch that they [people like Grushnitsky] admire the works of Marlinsky, and whenever conversation moves beyond everyday concerns, they try to speak with the phrases taken from his tales" (1978, 3:110). According to several observers and commentators, the character of Grushnitsky was, in fact, based on one N. P. Koliubakin, an acquaintance of Marlinsky who conducted himself "somewhat in the spirit of his [Marlinsky's] heroes" (quoted in Manuilov 1966, 170).

In the terminology of Russian literary history, marlinism has been defined and discussed as a particular narrative style in which bombastic, highly metaphorical, or even outlandish phrases combine with melodramatic events and adventures. As one of the first critics of Marlinsky's style, Belinsky characterizes it thus: "Not a single character in his tales ever said anything straight, but always theatrically, always with an epigram, pun, or comparison; in short, in Marlinsky every kopeck becomes a ruble, every word is adorned with curls" (1978, 1:108). To limit one's study of marlinism to the analysis of narrative style is hardly adequate, however, as according to both Lermontov and Turgenev, marlinism, in addition to being a literary style, was a mode of highly dramatic behavior. The main objective of such behavior was to "produce an effect." Marlinsky's imitators needed, therefore, an audience, such as provincial ladies, who would appreciate and encourage their histrionics. Like any fashion, marlinism involved and implicated both those who acted it out and those who participated in it as audience.

Being a cultural phenomenon, marlinism involved the concrete behavior of its numerous adepts, including that of its creator, Alexander Marlinsky himself. As we know from the works of Iuri Lotman, the peculiar characteristic of the Russian 1830s was the blurring of the boundaries between life and fiction, so that for many authors of the period, life and fiction constituted a continuous text. The salient features of Marlinsky's life therefore embody and vividly reveal various aspects of marlinism.

Marlinsky's prominence both on the literary and historical stage has tended to push into the background the fact that he was a controversial, if not an unsavory character, a person whose actual behavior has been and still is overshadowed by the cultural myths that surrounded him. For generations of Russians Marlinsky has remained an emblem of the writer-Decembrist, a martyr for progressive ideals. Thus while his writings and especially his "flowery style" were criticized or even ridiculed, his life has never been carefully scrutinized. Marlinsky might be called the "Teflon Decembrist," since those who write about him either ignore or make excuses for many unpleasant facts of his biography.[3]

It was he who, with his naive poetry and slogans, drew many young people, including his three brothers, the poet Alexander Odoevsky, and such well-known personalities as A. I. Yakubovich and P. G. Kakhovskoi (one of the five executed Decembrists), into the Northern Secret Society. On the day of the uprising he moved from barrack to barrack begging soldiers to choose death over surrender.[4] The very next morning, however, he voluntarily appeared before the investigation committee and denounced himself and many others who had trusted him—from Ryleev to his own brothers. The investigating commission singled him out as "the first to reveal that certain members of the Northern Society . . . were disposed to the criminal intentions of . . . the extermination of the Imperial family" (quoted in Leighton

1975a, 141).[5] In exchange for his confession he received a more lenient sentence than most other Decembrists. In fact, his sentence continued to shrink, being reduced from execution to twenty years of exile, to soldier's service in the Caucasus, so that within three years he indeed found himself in the Caucasus, where he resumed his literary career under his pen name, Marlinsky. His brothers' lot, by contrast, was not so fortunate: Pyotr, only sixteen when the uprising took place, was arrested and exiled; taunted, and persecuted by a commanding officer, he permanently lost his mind by 1831. One manifestation of his madness was a virulent hostility toward his brother, Alexander, as reported by S. Golubov (1938, 368). But was it a sign of madness?

Marlinsky himself failed to draw any conclusions from his ordeal. After the tragic events in which his best friend, Ryleev, was hanged and his own family destroyed, Marlinsky's writings hardly show any change. Once in the Caucasus, he continued to intoxicate the minds of others with his Byronic tales of exotic adventures, and with his rhetorical exaltation of the "sublime and beautiful." Commenting on the apolitical nature of Marlinsky's tales, Nikolai Chernyshevsky remarks: "the most thorough investigation would not find a trace of principles which were unquestionably dear to their author as a human being" (1939–53, 3:201). While remaining the most privileged of the exiled Decembrists, Marlinsky was very successful in using his romantic aura of persecution, as well as his fiery eyes and curly black hair, in carrying out numerous amorous conquests. Since the wives of other Decembrists were often his prey, it is clear that, among other things, Marlinsky was quite indifferent to the cult of friendship so beloved by the Decembrists, and so eloquently described by his own pen. His love conquests included one Olga Nestertseva, a teenage girl, whose age was somewhat between sixteen and nineteen, depending on how politically correct Marlinsky's biographer wants to be. On 23 February 1833 this girl was found mortally wounded in Marlinsky's bed. According to his and her own deathbed testimony, she was accidentally shot by the gun Marlinsky kept under his pillow. This occasion afforded Marlinsky ample material for complaints about fate's continuous injustice toward him, so that even such a seemingly skeptical, but in fact, gullible person as Prince Mirsky argues that this incident left Marlinsky traumatized and unable to write for several years (Mirsky 1958, 120). In reality, his literary output did not diminish at all. Only a week after his melodramatic complaints about this tragic event, Marlinsky wrote a letter to his publisher, Nikolai Grech, in which he rather cheerfully discussed his new novel and other publishing ventures.

Marlinsky was the only Decembrist writer permitted to resume his career. Beginning in the early 1830s his tales began to appear in *Son of the Fatherland.* This journal was edited by Nikolai Grech, who enjoyed strong government connections. Another figure associated with official views, F. V. Bulgarin, was one of his best friends and defenders. Although officially never fully forgiven, Marlinsky was nevertheless not ostracized. The opportunists Grech and Bulgarin could safely remain his correspondents and publishers. In fact, government circles had hardly any reason to object to the renewal of Marlinsky's career.[6]

In his memoirs, written in 1876, Turgenev recalls how Marlinsky rode the wave of pseudopatriotic, pseudo-Romantic works that dominated the literary scene in the 1830s. Quoting his own unpublished notes from the 1850s, Turgenev explains that Marlinsky's popularity was the result of "certain European influences":

> Under the influence of special events and circumstances in European life of that period (from 1830 to the 1840s) an opinion slowly took shape here that we were a great, unshakably firm state fully in control of its destiny and that art was to be a worthy forerunner and prophet of that greatness and that power. At the same time a group of people appeared, clearly gifted but whose talent bore the mark of rhetoric and superficiality. . . . These people appeared in poetry, art, journalism, and even on the stage. . . . (Their names . . . come to the mind of any reader—such names as Marlinsky, Kukol'nik, Zagoskin, Benediktov, Briullov, Karatygin). (1983, 34–35)

It is clear, however, that the superficial and pompous art of Marlinsky and like-minded authors (Kukol'nik, Zagoskin, and Benediktov), painters (Briullov), or actors (Karatygin) had less to do with European influences of the 1830s than with the brutality with which the tsarist regime crushed the Decembrist uprising in the 1820s. Turgenev's silence on the subject of Decembrism is indicative of the national trauma and of the fact that the whole affair was banished from public discourse.

As I suggested in the first chapter of this book, the resurgence in the 1830s of a certain type of 1820s behavior was not coincidental. It was a reaction, in part at least, to the events of the Decembrist uprising. The Byronic tales or poems that were already passé in the twenties, as the works of Pushkin testify (see his treatment of Lensky, for example), came back to life in the thirties. Lermontov himself was diligently reworking such poems in the early period of his development, while the rest of the country began to read them with renewed interest.

It was at this time that Marlinsky's tales burst onto the scene, capturing the imagination of its numerous readers. Turgenev, who would later turn into a tireless critic of marlinism, admitted to kissing Marlinsky's name when it appeared on the pages of magazines (1987, 167). It would seem that there is only one way to account for this explosion in popularity: Marlinsky's tales provided readers with a way to relive the hopes and aspirations of the twenties—and much more safely, one might add. Thus it is not surprising that Pushkin, who continued to develop, was overlooked by his contemporaries, while Marlinsky, who produced the same Romantic tales that were popular before the uprising, became even more popular in the thirties. Testifying to Marlinsky's tremendous popularity, Gogol has his Khlestakov brag to the provincial ladies: "Everything that appeared under the name of Baron Brambeus, "Frigate 'Hope'" and *Moscow Telegraph*—I wrote it all." In typically grotesque fashion Khlestakov claims that such diverse yet popular Romantic entities of the early thirties, as the journal (*Moscow Telegraph*), the author (Senkovsky), and the tale (Marlinsky's "Frigate 'Hope'"), were all written by him.

Marlinsky wrote about Gothic locales and exotic adventures, great passions and the struggle for freedom, and the public enjoyed these things vicariously. Characters in Marlinsky's fiction feel persecuted not by a cruel political regime, but rather by stereotypes of Romantic and Gothic evil, be they villains, fate, or social conventions. The stories end not with the humiliation and pain of Siberian exile, but either happily or with melodramatic destruction. These tales, despite their pompous rhetoric, were innocent entertainment: consumers of these extraordinary adventures remained perfectly ordinary and obedient citizens. "With age they become peaceful landowners, or drunkards; sometimes both" (84) observes Pechorin about people like Grushnitsky, this typical product of marlinism. From fictional works such as "The Frigate 'Hope'" to his critical articles, Marlinsky continues to recite Romantic platitudes, while attacking skepticism and emotional restraint. He fails to admit that his own unabashed riding on the frigate of "hope" led to treachery, disillusionment, and death.

It is clear that Marlinsky's fictions, or rather "sweets that ruin the stomach," could hardly be approved by Lermontov, a writer matched only by Tolstoy in his zeal to expose falsehood. How much Lermontov knew of Marlinsky's duplicitous behavior is unknown. Yet he obviously knew enough to parody Marlinsky's 1830 society tale, "A Trial," in his *Masquerade*. By connecting the name of Marlinsky's protagonist, Zvezdich, to Prince Zvezdich, a person who used masquerade as a license for irresponsible behavior, Lermontov pointed to another weak person, who totally reversed his intentions and convictions the very next day after the failure of the Decembrist uprising. Marlinsky, it seems, also had his masquerade of intoxicating liberal slogans and then returned to the previous hierarchical structure he had dreamed of undermining.[7] Incidentally, as Marlinsky himself admits in one of his letters to the authorities, the very first condition of entering the Decembrist secret society was to give "a word of honor not to reveal what he would learn" (quoted in Kotliarevsky 1907, 126). Yet neither Marlinsky nor Zvezdich manifest any difficulties in either giving or breaking their words of honor. The name Zvezdich is connected to Marlinsky in another way too; it refers to *Poliarnaia zvezda* (Polar Star), the popular journal in which Marlinsky's tales were published during the pre-Decembrist period.

Indeed, Lermontov's association of masquerades with Marlinsky is far from coincidental. Marlinsky—similar to Baroness Strahl—was adept at utilizing the masquerade rules of his society: at one moment playing the part of a bloodthirsty rebel; at another, that of servant to the tsar and a Russian patriot; at still another, a persecuted artist. Mickiewicz, recalls his visit to Ryleev, during which he saw many prominent Decembrists, solemnly participating in what appears to be a rather childish performance: "Bestuzhev [Marlinsky] . . . cross-legged, Turkish fashion, on a Persian carpet . . . the civilians wore voluminous cravats *à la* Byron; some were dressed like Directoire dandies" (quoted in Sutherland 1984, 91–92). And this group, Mickiewicz continues, would cease conversation in order to recite, with the utmost seriousness, verses that called for regicide, after which they would solemnly drink to the success of their aspirations. Incidentally, the poem that the Decembrists recited, "And the Blacksmith Walks Out of His Smithy" (*Kak idet kuznets da iz kuznitsy*), was coauthored by Marlinsky and Ryleev. The poem calls for the unconditional execution of every figure of authority, be it the tsar or members of the clergy.

An excerpt from Marlinsky's diary provides a revealing glimpse into his world: between describing his adventures at balls and brothels, he notes: "stayed home all afternoon. Memorized Shakespeare's speech of Brutus. Drank a lot of champagne and paid for it with a headache in the evening" (quoted in Mikhail Zetlin 1958, 117–18). Marlinsky's preoccupations are revealing of his attitudes: balls, champagne drinking, womanizing are the things of the same order as the republican speech of Brutus; it is all part of a game, a performance. One is thus not surprised that the more sober members of the Russian literary community, such as the then well-known author A. E. Izmailov, would characterize young Marlinsky as "Zavirashka"; that is, "a person who gets carried away by his lies" (Levkovich 1978, 171 and 182). Had Marlinsky read *Julius Caesar* to the end, he would have discovered Brutus's blindness to the concrete realities of Rome, and to the consequences of his naive idealism; he would have discovered how out of place Brutus's revolutionary rhetoric was. It is significant that as the events following Brutus's conspiracy unravel, the unruly mob kills the poet Cinna, only because he bears the same name as one of the conspirators. The true makers of words always suffer when the irresponsible abusers of language take over the stage.

Since his unpublished play could hardly undermine the authority of Marlinsky, Lermontov resumed his attack on marlinism in *A Hero of Our Time*. Referring to the marlinian background of Lermontov's novel, Vadim Vatsuro observes: "For a reader of the 1840s, who witnessed the blossoming of marlinism, the inner polemical thrust of 'Princess Mary' must have appeared significantly greater than it appears to us now" (1964, 355).[8]

As an example of this inner polemical thrust, one can note the similarities between Marlinsky's opening of his essay "On Romanticism" (published in 1839 in an almanac edited by Nestor Kukol'nik, another Marlinsky-type writer disliked by Lermontov) and the musings of Pechorin in "Princess Mary" (3 June), in which he parodies and challenges the banalities of Marlinsky.

> *Marlinsky:*
> What is a feeling but an incarnated thought? What is intelligence, but an experienced thought (*opytnost' mysli*)? What is will, but thought turned into action? Hence the person who is endowed with thoughts strives to feel, to know, and to act (Bestuzhev-Marlinsky 1981, 2:465).

> *Pechorin:*
> And what is happiness? Sated pride. . . . Ideas are organic creations. Someone has said that their very birth endows them with a form, and this form is action; he in whose head more ideas have been born is more active than others. . . . Passions are nothing else but ideas in their first phase of development; they are an attribute of the youth of the heart; and he is a fool who thinks he will be agitated by them all his life. (123–24)

Marlinsky considers emotions and feelings the final result, the incarnation of thought. Pechorin, while mimicking Marlinsky's style, reverses the equation and calls passions "an idea in the early stage of its development." Passions for Pechorin are "underdeveloped" thoughts, to which he refuses to attribute signs of maturity. And he then directly attacks Marlinsky's brand of Romanticism by calling a person preoccupied with passions and feelings a fool (*glupets*).

It is also interesting to compare Pechorin's characterization of Grushnitsky: "He is fairly witty, his epigrams are frequently amusing, but they are neither to the point, nor venomous" (84) with Belinsky's comment on Marlinsky: "nature has abundantly rewarded him with wit, amusing and good-natured, which prickles but does not hurt, tickles but does not bite" (1978, 1:109). The similarity is rather telling, and it seems that by allowing Pechorin to echo Belinsky's words of 1834, Lermontov makes it clear that the real object of Pechorin's attacks is Marlinsky rather than Grushnitsky.

NONINDIVIDUALS: GRUSHNITSKY, MARY, AND MARLINSKY

Although critics, beginning as early as Belinsky, have noted the anti-Marlinsky subtext embedded in Lermontov's novel, none has gone beyond general comments or sketchy comparisons. While *A Hero of Our Time* scrutinizes and criticizes marlinism on many levels, I believe that the most comprehensive attack occurs in the plotline describing Grushnitsky's interactions with Princess Mary. No one has yet investigated the social and cultural implications of their relationship. I propose to interpret it as Lermontov's comment on, and criticism of, the phenomenon of marlinism. Seen from this perspective, Mary's fascination with Grushnitsky reenacts and exposes the speciousness of the reading public's infatuation with Marlinsky.

In other words, it is insufficient to analyze "Princess Mary" solely in terms of Pechorin's personal hostility toward his double, Grushnitsky. Unfortunately, this is the case with the majority of critical works,[9] whose narrow concentration on psychology obscures important dimensions of the novel. It also disregards the fact that there are aspects of Grushnitsky's behavior that Pechorin and, by implication, Lermontov, simply cannot accept.

Significantly, the initial target of Pechorin's anger is neither Mary nor Grushnitsky alone but the two taken together; it is in their symbiosis that the issue of marlinism is first raised. They enter the story at almost the same moment and spur Pechorin's emotions by the sympathy they arouse in each other. Their interaction represents a microcosm of society as Lermontov perceives it: one person is acting and pretending, while another is taken in.

Grushnitsky and Mary are similar to each other in their lack of experience and naïveté. Pechorin notices how much they enjoy sentimental conversations with each other.[10] Pechorin calls their budding sympathy "the beginning of the [comedy] plot" (*zaviazka est'*) (95), and he is right: the couple is engaged in performance. At their first meeting in Piatigorsk, Pechorin has hardly exchanged a few words with Grushnitsky when Mary and her mother pass by:

> at this point the ladies moved away from the well and came level with us. Grushnitsky had time to assume a dramatic attitude with the help of his crutch, and loudly answered me in French: *Mon cher, je haïs les hommes pour ne pas les mépriser, car autrement la vie serait une farce trop dégoûtante.* (87)

In fact, Grushnitsky is already engaged in *une farce trop dégoûtante;* his pretentious declaration of hatred and contempt for mankind is nothing but a stock, well-worn phrase of Romanticism. One recalls a line from Marlinsky's "Mulla-Nur": "there was a time when I hated people, there was a time when I despised them" (Bestuzhev-Marlinsky 1981, 1:127); or from Kiukhel'beker's *Izhorski:* "I used to despise people; from now on I will hate them" (Kiukhel'beker 1967, 311). Pushkin (1937–59) utilizes a similar formula in his poem, "Angel" (1827), in which a demon witnessing the beauty of an angel declares: "Not everything did I hate in this world, not everything did I despise in it" (*ne vse ia v mire nenavidel, ne vse ia v mire preziral*) (3:59). Lermontov, in fact, reverses Pushkin's phrase, in the description of his own Demon: "and everything that he saw before him he either despised or hated" (*i vse chto pred soboi on videl, on preziral il' nenavidel*) (2:47). Grushnitsky is, indeed, what Belinsky—in his characterization of Grushnitsky—calls: "the most contemporary type, the representative of those idealistic phrasemongers that one encounters nowadays on every corner" (1978, 3:411).

In any case, Grushnitsky finds in Mary a very responsive audience, for she repays his declamation with "a long curious glance" (87). Half an hour later, witnessing another interaction between them, Pechorin describes it as a "scene" (*stsena*), and its two participants as "actors" and even "dramatis personae" (*deistvuiushchie litsa*). In this encounter, dropping his glass on purpose, Grushnitksy assumes a pained expression and feigns a limp as he attempts to pick it up. His ploy to attract Mary's attention succeeds brilliantly, and Pechorin observes: "Princess Mary saw it all better than I. Lighter than a little bird, she skipped to him, bent down, picked up the glass, and handed it to him with a movement full of inexpressible charm" (88). Mary then makes sure that her mother who, according to Romantic conventions, must be hostile toward the romantic feelings of her daughter, does not notice Mary's action. She thus initiates another performance: "a minute later she left the gallery with her mother . . . , but as she passed by Grushnitsky, she assumed a most formal and dignified air, she did not even turn her head, did not even take notice of the passionate glance with which he followed her" (89).

Critics often note that Pechorin describes human situations in theatrical terms; he is thus accused of being manipulative and cynical. But, after all, the interaction between Mary and Grushnitsky *is* a performance, exactly of the kind Shakespeare described in one of his sonnets as "I lie with her and she with me." If mutual deception and role-playing are the essence of his society's social relations, if its members participate in and understand only plays, Pechorin might as well be entertained by the show: "Fate is obviously taking care of my not being bored" (95). Ominously, though, Pechorin remarks: "The dénouement of this comedy will be our concern" (95). And later he indeed ceases to be an observer, interfering in Mary and Grushnitsky's play, with tragic results for both of them. It should be stressed, however, that Pechorin interferes as an actor and not as a director, since he runs the dual risk of being killed by Grushnitsky and of falling in love with Mary. Thus his interference is of a very different kind than that of the Captain of Dragoons who, remaining behind the scenes, sends a drunkard to insult Mary and directs Grushnitsky to his death.

Many other scenes involving Mary and Grushnitsky are performances as well. Mary and Grushnitsky are constantly engaged in mutual deception and role playing. In the final analysis, they are two sides of the same coin. Had there not been a Mary to encourage mask-wearing, there could have been no Grushnitsky to flaunt the mask and play the role. Although Mary's defenders like to present her as a helpless victim, does not Lermontov suggest that it is her responsibility to put aside her romantic dreams and expectations in order to look at what is behind the various masks of her suitors?

Grushnitsky and Mary leave the book almost simultaneously: both are crushed by Pechorin and both pronounce similar phrases expressing their hatred for him. Before his death, Grushnitsky returns to the naive Romantic phrase about hatred and contempt with which he appeared on the scene: "*je haïs les hommes pour ne pas les mépriser*" (87). This time, however, he uses it more appropriately: "I despise myself and hate you" (171).

The truth of Pechorin's treatment, although hateful, is driven home. Grushnitsky is made to recognize his own baseness. Likewise, Pechorin's interference forces Mary to acknowledge her mistakes and shortcomings. When at their final meeting Pechorin asks her: "Even if you loved me, from this moment on you despise me?" she answers: "I hate you" (180). She does not use the word "despise" suggested to her by Pechorin, because, on a deep psychological level, she, like Grushnitsky, feels contempt for herself. Both of them, as well as numerous readers after them, hate the messenger for revealing their own weaknesses and inadequacies. By the time Lermontov was writing his first foreword, he was well aware of the public's dislike of Pechorin and its reasons: "Is it not, perchance, because there is more truth in this character than you would desire there to be?" (2).

Lermontov's satire was not missed on astute readers like Belinsky. Nevertheless, as Lermontov's preface to the second edition of *A Hero of Our Time* acknowledges, the majority of readers missed the ironic thrust of his novel: "Our public is still so young and naive that it fails to understand a fable unless it finds a lesson at its end. It misses a humorous point, and does not feel irony" (1).

This inability was not limited to the general public alone. No less a figure than Wilhelm Kiukhel'beker, the well-known writer and Decembrist, was himself fooled both by Grushnitsky as a character and Marlinsky as a writer. Commenting on "Princess Mary" Kiukhel'beker observes: "Grushnitsky is invaluable, there is so much truth in his character. . . . It is a pity that Lermontov has wasted his talent depicting such an obnoxious (*gadkii*) creature as his obnoxious Pechorin" (Kiukhel'beker 1979, 415). Leaving this evaluation of Pechorin aside, why is Kiukhel'beker so enamored of Grushnitsky?

Like so many other of Lermontov's readers, Kiukhel'beker takes seriously what Lermontov parodies in the novel. Similar to Princess Mary, Kiukhel'beker mistakes Grushnitsky's mask of heroism for the real thing and is taken in by Grushnitsky's performance, by his impersonation of the typical, frequently repackaged, and easily recognizable Romantic hero. Kiukhel'beker's enthusiasm for Grushnitsky betrays a naive and unsophisticated reader, a former Decembrist with the Decembrist predilection for naive slogans, naive actions, and no less naive literature. Not surprisingly, Kiukhel'beker was unwavering in his admiration of Marlinsky, followed the publication of his tales religiously, and admitted in his diary that he is "ready to acknowledge Marlinsky as the deepest of our thinkers and the most inspirational of our writers" (1979, 340).

In fact, Kiukhel'beker, like any other Russian reader, might have been forewarned by Grushnitsky's very name, which even if a mask, is still transparent. This bombastic name reminds one of Marlinsky (or Lensky), and thus of many other Romantic heroes. However, in this case, the "poetic" name has a very prosaic root: *grusha* (a pear). Incidentally, according to Vladimir Dahl *grusha* refers not only to a fruit but also to an obscene gesture, *kukish*, *dulia*—in English, to give someone the finger—a meaning that Lermontov clearly utilizes. Grushnitsky's name, therefore, properly defines his formula: a fashionable poetic facade disguising a very prosaic or empty interior. Grushnitsky thus represents the key aspects of marlinism as Lermontov understood it: emptiness, ostentatious declaration of heroism, and a disparity between rhetoric and actions. He is a variant of the already familiar Prince Zvezdich.

Grushnitsky's formula is vividly reenacted in his use of his soldier's overcoat. While an emblem of heroism, this coat in fact serves as a mask, hiding his mundane strivings for epaulettes and a wealthy wife. Grushnitsky's overcoat (*soldatskaia shinel'*) is mentioned at least twenty times in the novel and is one of the first things that we learn about him. After their initial greeting Pechorin observes: "Grushnitsky is a cadet. He has been in the service only one year; he wears, following a peculiar kind of foppishness, a soldier's thick coat" (*tolstuiu soldatskuiu shinel'*) (84). Pechorin explains what he means by "a peculiar kind of foppishness" when he informs us that Grushnitsky wants to become the hero of a novel. The heroes of such novels, including those of Marlinsky, are supposed to be persecuted, misunderstood, and ostracized. Conveniently enough for Grushnitsky, the discourse that associates the soldier's uniform with Romantic heroism and persecution was firmly rooted both in Russian reality and fiction.

The Romantic dimension of the soldier's greatcoat is depicted by Nikolai Pavlov in his popular tale "Iatagan" (1835). Its plot hinges upon the protagonist's rise and fall from the rank of cadet to an officer and back to a soldier. Pavlov stresses the Romantic power conferred on this character by his soldier's uniform—a power the heroine of the tale is incapable of resisting:

> But in a strangely illogical way she adorned the stern rank of Bronin with all the roses of imagination, so it seemed that an officer's uniform would only diminish his charm, and not add to it. She did not see in him a crude soldier under a gray overcoat; he was for her a soldier of romances, a soldier of the stage. . . . He was for her a person, demoted not because of the usual proceedings, but the victim of envy, persecution; a person against whom the universe had conspired. And the princess kept on defending him. (Pavlov 1985, 64)

The princess of Pavlov's story is a clear antecedent of Princess Mary and her romantic attitudes. Pechorin parodies such attitudes brilliantly when he describes Princess Mary to Grushnitsky: "[She] will start persuading herself that she is miserable, that she loved only one man, meaning you, but that Heaven had not wished to unite her with him, because he wore a soldier's greatcoat, although under that thick gray garment there beat a passionate and noble heart" (102).

For many noblemen a soldier's uniform was a sign of real persecution: from exiled Decembrists to Lermontov's friend Raevsky, who was demoted to the rank of private for his role in distributing Lermontov's "Death of the Poet." Grushnitsky, however, is not demoted or persecuted. He simply appropriates the soldier's overcoat and its heroic associations with exile and rebelliousness.

Even though "there is no art to read the mind's construction in the face," let alone in the mask, the particular choice of mask can be revealing. The fact that Grushnitsky dons the mask of a Romantic hero because it is fashionable reveals that he is a person who follows the crowd rather than an individual capable of making difficult moral choices. Grushnitsky is a weak, immature person—Pechorin describes him as "a boy" (*mal'chik*)—who cannot stand on his own. It is no accident that he appears on crutches. He needs a support, be it the support of crutches, or of literary rhetoric, or of the Captain of Dragoons who, we remember, leads Grushnitsky to his death. Grushnitsky approaches life the way he rushes into battle—with his eyes closed. "I have seen him in action: he brandishes his sword, he yells, he rushes forward with closed eyes. Somehow, this is not Russian courage," remarks Pechorin (85).

Blindly following either his own childish instincts for revenge or directions from the Captain of Dragoons, Grushnitsky persists in avoiding moral choices to the very end. Forsaking his ostentatious nobility he gets involved in spying, setting traps, and spreading malicious rumors about Mary. There is an indisputable cruelty to Pechorin's killing of Grushnitsky after the latter finally chooses to rebel against the captain and allows Pechorin to recharge the gun. However, this fact does not alter Lermontov's condemnation of Grushnitsky for his refusal to act with independence, honor, and dignity. Enticed by the Captain of Dragoons, Grushnitsky does take a shot at an unarmed man, after all. Lermontov demonstrates convincingly that a person who refuses to exercise moral choices, who acts as a hero because it is fashionable and costs him nothing, under different circumstances easily becomes an instrument of evil. Lermontov has probably observed a similar paradigm of behavior in Pushkin's *Eugene Onegin*. Onegin, we recall, sounds very noble and honorable when rejecting Tatyana, yet forgets all his nobility and dignity and becomes Zaretsky's puppet at the time of his duel with Lensky.

Lermontov, as it turned out, was prophetic in his estimation of the role played by the Grushnitskys in Russian society; he himself fell victim to another Grushnitsky. Lermontov frequently teased his fellow officer N. S. Martynov; on one occasion he mocked Martynov's excessively martial outfit and attempt to look fashionable, that is, heroic. Unfortunately, marlinism has the ability to strike back at its critics: Martynov killed Lermontov in a duel.

Innokentii Annensky, who as a critic was prone to vague pronouncements, nonetheless hits the nail on the head in his assessment of Grushnitsky: "There is no need to see Grushnitsky as a satire, even less so as a parody of a hero. It is simply a thought, and a sad one at that, about a man, who is afraid to be himself, and who while thinking, does not want to think things through" (1979, 139). Incidentally, Nikolai Bestuzhev uses a similar concept in his characterization of his younger brother, Alexander: "You've acquired the habit of thinking but not of thinking through—two totally different things" (quoted in Golubov 1938, 40).

Grushnitsky, we conclude, is a nonentity who wears the mask of a heroic person. The fact that this mask happens to mimic Pechorin is secondary. Pechorin dislikes Grushnitsky not so much because Grushnitsky copies him, but simply because Grushnitsky is *a copy*. Grushnitsky goes through life hiding behind fashionable masks, without ever questioning the masquerade in which he participates, the roles he plays, or the rules he obeys. On a realistic level, Grushnitsky's actions are hardly commensurate with his destruction. Nevertheless, by killing Grushnitsky, Lermontov stresses the need to eradicate the profound ills affecting his society, such as blind obedience to fashion, persistent fear and refusal to be oneself, immaturity, weakness under pressure. Given all the later Russian preoccupation with social, ethnic, and other communal guilt, Lermontov's lesson remains as fresh as ever. It puts the blame squarely where it belongs: at the doorstep of the individual.

MARY AND THE READER

Lermontov's oeuvre constantly investigates such diverse yet connected cultural phenomena as post-Decembrist reaction, marlinism, and masquerades. Troubled by and concerned with the current Russian situation, as his play *The Masquerade*, the poem "Meditation" (*Duma*) (1838), or the novel *A Hero of Our Time* reveals, Lermontov felt the need to strike marlinism down, to disclose the potential dangers of this disease that had afflicted Russian society since the Decembrist uprising and that had manifested itself in gradual masqueradization of all social and cultural institutions of his time.

In *A Hero of Our Time* Lermontov found a perfect vehicle with which to strike a blow against marlinism: Through Pechorin he was able to promote his own cultural concerns and to achieve his literary goals. *A Hero of Our Time* exposes and destroys the Marlinsky-type hero, and thoroughly undermines Marlinsky-type narratives. It is clear that what we observe in the initial interaction between Grushnitsky and Mary is more than a mating game between two potential lovers. The melodramatic actions of these two characters are in full accord with the prescriptions of marlinism. Mary's infatuation with Grushnitsky reenacts and satirizes the cultural events of Lermontov's time, when the majority of the Russian reading public was carried away by the bombastic declamations of Marlinsky's tales.[11] There are thus certain parallels between Pechorin's and Lermontov's enemies, strategies, and tasks. While Pechorin attacks Grushnitsky and Mary for their symbiosis and participation in the social masquerade, Lermontov attacks the symbiosis between Marlinsky's writings and the popular literary tastes of his day.

It is Mary who, in her naïveté and reliance on cultural clichés, supports and encourages Grushnitsky's masquerade, and it is the Russian reading public that supported Marlinsky's pseudoheroic narratives. Just as the false hero Grushnitsky is dethroned by Pechorin before Mary's eyes, Lermontov's novel dethrones Marlinsky in front of his devoted readers raised on ultra-Romantic tales.

Princess Mary is an easy prey to Grushnitsky's histrionics because she, similar to the Russian reading public, has been raised on popular Romantic tales; tales that are far removed from the concerns of everyday life. Mary, "innocent as a dove" (96) and whose preparation for life consists of reading Byron in English and a knowledge of algebra, will be constantly frustrated in her attempts to understand people. She always jumps ahead with incorrect interpretations of people's actions, her interpretations inspired by fashionable literature. Mary never tries to look beneath her suitors' Romantic facade but prefers to treat them in terms of a fashionable literary discourse. Having been disillusioned by Grushnitsky, Mary fails to question her own role in Grushnitsky's masquerade; she thus falls prey to the rather blunt and obvious masquerade of Pechorin. She sheds tears over his dramatic confession and views his aura of mysteriousness as his most attractive characteristic, until finally, following literary paradigms, she declares her love for him in the following melodramatic manner: "Perhaps you are afraid of obstacles on the part of my family. . . . It does not matter . . . my entreaties will convince them. . . . Or is it your own situation? . . . But I want you to know that I can sacrifice anything for the one I love" (148).

Pechorin utilizes Mary's inexperience to make his point. His strategy with her is rather simple: by doing two opposite things (such as kissing her and then remaining silent and indifferent) he will leave her hanging between the two interpretations that popular Romantic literature provides for such contradictory behavior. As a result, Mary will face many sleepless nights in her attempt to decipher Pechorin's confusing messages. There is a telling moment when Pechorin, on his way from Vera's bedroom, looks into Mary's room and sees her awake, late at night, holding a book but staring above it, into space. Apparently she is trying to use the book as a means of resolving her confusion; however, she looks above it, as if trying to negotiate the events of her life with the content of the book—and she is obviously failing. Mary, in fact, finally admits her helplessness to Pechorin, symptomatically couching her admission in Marlinsky-type language: "Either you despise me or love me very much" (144). Princess Mary clearly fails to come to terms with such a problematic hero as Pechorin.

Initially Mary had expected Grushnitsky to be a hero, and had it not been for Pechorin, Grushnitsky would have succeeded; he looked and talked like the heroes of her imagination. Pechorin, however, interrupted this process of mutual fascination, first by becoming in Mary's imagination "the hero of a novel in the latest fashion" (95) and then by frustrating the expectations she associated with such a hero. He thus arouses hostility from Mary, as well as from numerous readers: he is not what they expected, and that causes disappointment and anger.

Pechorin's ability to control Mary is based on her utter predictability, which is a result of her relying on popular literature as a guide to real life. Pechorin realizes that he has "found [her] out" (*otgadal*) (120), because she acts in accordance with the rules established by such literature. Blending Romantic slogans, sentimentality, and melodramatic plots, the fiction of Marlinsky, Pavlov, or Bulgarin would often describe the behavior of a heroine who has just heard the hero's confession of being persecuted and alienated. Thus, having heard Pechorin's confession, Mary acts accordingly: "at that moment I met her eyes: tears danced in them, her arm leaning on mine, trembled, her cheeks glowed, she was sorry for me!" (128).

Although his treatment of Grushnitsky kills rather than cures him, Pechorin's shattering of Mary's naïveté and sentimentality can hardly be seen as an irredeemable tragedy. By the end of the tale, Mary is not ruined, but puzzled. Pechorin leaves Mary, as he leaves the reader, with a certain task to perform: to face the caustic truths of events, to ponder their meaning, and draw unpleasant conclusions both about them and oneself. To greet such truths with the words "I hate you" (180), as Mary, Grushnitsky, and numerous readers do with Pechorin, is not enough.

Mary's frustration with Pechorin, her inability to fit him into familiar literary patterns finds its parallel in the exasperation of the novel's readers, who with each consecutive tale become more confused about the nature of the text and its protagonist. Both Mary and readers approach Pechorin with ready-made formulas, and thus try to fit him into already familiar emotional states, such as love, contempt, or hatred. This almost universal frustration with its protagonist finds expression in such diverse readers as Kiukhel'beker, Nicholas I, the Slavophiles, and Apollon Grigor'ev, all of whom tried somehow to bracket Pechorin, to discern and posit other heroes in the book, whether Grushnitsky, Maksim Maksimych, honest Circassians, or even "honest smugglers." Such a reaction was, in fact, assumed in the novel itself, when in his search for literary exoticism the narrator of "Bela" continually questions Maksim Maksimych about Kazbich, as if Kazbich "should be" its main hero.

Lermontov puzzles his readers with an enigma: a hero whose heroism is both highlighted and undermined. As early as the "Author's Introduction," Lermontov stresses that Pechorin is drastically different from Romantic characters and their imaginary adventures. In the course of the novel Pechorin discards false heroes, such as Grushnitsky or Vulich, for what can be seen as Pechorin's greater heroism. At the same time, some of Pechorin's actions clearly undercut his heroism and thus present us with a puzzling and confusing pattern of behavior. Pechorin seems both to puzzle and to test us, as he tests characters within the novel.

Here I part from Walter Reed's formulation that, in Lermontov, "demythologizing is followed by a remythologizing in a new key" (1974, 125). Lermontov, indeed, demythologizes the old Romantic hero but the ingenuity of his approach lies in the fact that he refuses to remythologize.

In "The Fatalist" Pechorin stresses his ultimate embrace of uncertainty, and that is what Lermontov wants his readers to do: to doubt all expectations, all masks, and not to create new certainties and new illusions. Mary, whose illusions about Grushnitsky were quickly shattered, did not wait long to develop a new set of illusions about Pechorin, illusions that prove even more harmful to her. As we remember, "The Fatalist," and thus the entire book, ends on a note of high ambivalence, including ambivalence toward the possible heroism of Pechorin. Thus there is no remythologizing in the novel; any mythologizing is the creation of a new mask, a new certainty, a new genre. What we are left with is a hero who not only undermines the heroism of others, but whose own heroism is presented in highly ambivalent terms. Pechorin continues to demand from us a free and individual response and herein lies his uniqueness.

Scholars ranging from Eikhenbaum and Ginzburg to Mersereau, Bagby, and Eagle have fruitfully explored how Lermontov subverts the genre expectations of his readers and parodies popular genres of the Romantic period. Indeed, Lermontov constantly mocks such texts as well as the expectations of their readers.[12] One can recall how the narrator of "Bela" was visibly disappointed upon learning that Pechorin was happy with Bela. This is because the narrator's expectations were based on Romantic adventures already familiar to him from Byron, Pushkin, and Marlinsky. Instead of an epic battle between Kazbich and Pechorin, featuring daggers, blood, and a self-sacrificing heroine to boot, the narrator learns of happy love and its consequent boredom and dissapointment. In the end, Lermontov provides the reader with all the Romantic trappings: the dying heroine, her love and devotion, Pechorin's pursuit of Kazbich—but it does not happen as we expect. Lermontov frustrates his readers' expectations, or rather fulfills them in his sardonic manner by totally rewriting familiar events, by filling them with twists and ambiguities.

Like Pechorin, who parodies, challenges, and destroys his rivals, Lermontov subverts the fashionable Romantic narratives of the type popularized by Marlinsky. Discarding their trite and false heroes, he puzzles his readers with an enigma: a hero whose heroism is both asserted and undermined, and a narrative form that is tantalizingly close yet indisputably different from typical society tales ("Princess Mary"), from narratives of travel that exploit a combination of exotic and erotic motifs ("Bela"), or from tales of supernatural adventures ("Taman'"). Pechorin dons so many masks that he lays bare the device of masquerading. He reveals Romantic posturing for what it is: a mask. The complex, contradictory, and unpredictable structure of Pechorin is paralleled by similar qualities in the novel itself. Even if a particular tale can be seen as parodying and thus referring to a concrete literary genre of Romantic literature, Lermontov's conglomerate, after we take into consideration all the forms it parodies, is simply too complicated to be defined.

It is thus hardly surprising that critics still argue about the genre of *A Hero of Our Time*, some claiming that it is a novel, some defining it only as a collection of tales unified by the same protagonist and so on. Without any desire to enter into this thorny discussion, I only observe that Lermontov's book testifies to the truth of Tolstoy's profound remark, that all significant Russian literary works do not fit the preexistent scheme of literary genres. In fact, Tolstoy's friend Gol'denveizer records that Tolstoy included *A Hero of Our Time* in his list of "nonconformist" Russian classics.

Viewed from the perspective of the social and cultural masquerade embraced by Russian society in the aftermath of Nicholas I's oppression, Lermontov's agenda becomes clear. Lermontov fills his novel with all kinds of frustrated expectations (and not just literary ones) not in order to produce an ironic, meta-literary narrative, or to participate in "literary struggle" with previous forms and genres, but in order to awaken the Russian public from its romantic slumbers. Shattered expectations, illusions, and lives are there to demonstrate how hopes, expectations, and other certainties debilitate one's ability to be oneself, to resist, to act freely and responsibly. The reader is made to undergo the same treatment as the characters within the novel.[13]

Furthermore, the shattering of Mary's and the reader's expectations and illusions has not only cultural but also psychological, moral, and political dimensions that have rarely been acknowledged by those who study the way in which Lermontov undercuts the generic expectations of his readers. Lermontov was acutely aware of the implicit compact between the author who fulfills expectations and the reading public that demands such fulfillment. Literary expectations force authors to reconstruct, reinterpret, or suppress certain facts. Any responsible writer has to have inner strength to resist the temptation and to offer bitter truths instead of sweet, expected falsehoods.[14] Moreover, the temptation to please one's listeners, to put on the mask they want to see, is present not only in book writing but in any form of speech. Unfortunately, by giving into it, one inevitably becomes somebody else's plaything (*igrushka*), a concept familiar to us from *The Masquerade*. Lermontov began to see integrity and courage—as manifested by resisting and disappointing the expectations of others—as fundamental to any hero. Pechorin must use all his strength to remain calm when he abandons the crushed Princess Mary; nevertheless, he perseveres, as he knows that to do otherwise would be dishonest both to himself and to Mary: "she . . . covered her eyes with her hand, and it seemed to me that tears glistened in them. . . . This was becoming unbearable: another minute, and I would have fallen at her feet" (179). This scene is an obvious rewriting of Onegin's rejection of Tatyana, in which Onegin makes pleasant and elevated pronouncements, enchanting Tatyana even further only because he feels the need to remain a "nice guy" (*dobryi malyi*); that is to say, a person who plays along. Pechorin, on the other hand, resists the temptation of fulfilling the expectations of others, and so does Lermontov in all his mature work.

Lermontov's oeuvre points to a fundamental malaise of Russian culture, a malaise vividly exemplified by Grushnitsky in Lermontov's novel and by Marlinsky in real life. In a society where the free expression of individuality is strongly discouraged if not suppressed, one tends to do what is expected and acceptable; that is, to wear fashionable and familiar masks. Like any deception, however, this masquerading is unhealthy and in the long run destructive. Lermontov indeed viewed his novel as a medical diagnosis of this affliction: "the disease has been pointed out" (2). Even if he refuses to spell out the cure, the events of the novel suggest that as a first step toward curing Russia, marlinism—the refusal to act freely and responsibly, the habit of hiding behind fashionable masks, slogans, or illusions—has to be jettisoned: Grushnitsky is thrown off the cliff.

The urgent need to discard marlinism was not felt by Lermontov alone. Attacking the phenomenon of marlinism in art, Turgenev observed rather severely that in order for art to exist, marlinism had to be destroyed: "Art will emerge here only when Briullov is killed, as Marlinsky was killed: *delenda est Carthago, delendus Brulovius*. . . . Briullov—that phrase-monger, . . . that drum, that cold yet noisy rhetorician" (1987, 160). Turgenev also acknowledges Lermontov's contribution to that process. Commenting on the fate of heroes *à la* Marlinsky Turgenev observes: "this type, as we all know, lasted a long time, up to the time of Pechorin" (1968, 220). Similar to Princess Mary, who became bored with the dramatic sentimentalities of Grushnitsky, Lermontov's readers, it seems, also had difficulty returning to Marlinsky.

Chapter Seven

Mtsyri's Refusals: The Making of Lermontov's Paradoxical Hero

А может, лучшая победа
Над временем и тяготеньем—
Пройти, чтоб не оставить следа.
Пройти, чтоб не оставить тени

На стенах . . .
Может быуь—отказом
Взять? Вычеркнуться из зеркал?
Так: Лермонтовым по Кавказу
Прокрасться, не встревожив скал.

(Perhaps the best victory / over time and gravity— /
is to pass by without leaving a trace, / to pass by
without leaving a shadow / on the walls . . . /

Perhaps by refusal / To win? To cross oneself out
of the mirrors? / Like Lermontov in the Caucasus /
To pass by without disturbing the cliffs.)
—Marina Tsvetaeva, "To Steal Away . . ."

THE NARRATIVE POEM "Mtsyri" is often hailed both as Lermontov's masterpiece and the culmination of the tradition of the Russian Romantic narrative poem (*poema*).[1] Although this observation may be chronologically valid, I do not think it does full justice to Lermontov's design and execution. Just as Pechorin may embody the death knell of marlinism without being its literal culmination, so Mtsyri renders the tradition of the Russian Romantic narrative poem obsolete by far surpassing the heroic personalities that this tradition has heretofore produced.

The poem, indeed, culminates Lermontov's own ventures into the genre of the Romantic poem. Similar to all of Lermontov's mature works, "Mtsyri" reworks the themes first articulated in his earlier poetic ventures: "Confession" (*Ispoved'*, 1830–31) and "Boyarin Orsha" (1835–36), in particular. Lermontov clearly felt satisfied with the result: "Mtsyri" is the only one of Lermontov's narrative, or "Byronic," poems that he included in his 1840 collection of verse. Furthermore, it is highly significant that Lermontov concludes this collection with "Mtsyri." There is a clear sense of accomplishment and possibly closure associated with the poem: on several occasions the poet read it in Petersburg salons; one such occasion was the celebration of Gogol's name-day on 9 May 1840. By contrast, it will be recalled that "The Demon" was never published during Lermontov's lifetime, and there is no evidence that he wanted to see any other of his earlier Romantic narrative poems in print.

While Western scholars have basically ignored the poem,[2] Soviet scholars, such as Mann and Maksimov, have approached "Mtsyri" in terms of its generic features. Such an approach is obviously an important, if ultimately inadequate, enterprise; besides its other limitations, it fails to note that all the previous Russian Romantic poems of note were written at least ten years before Lermontov's. The best that criticism has offered heretofore is an acknowledgment of various contradictions in the poem, without any attempt at explaining them.[3] In fact, not only are some aspects of the poem puzzling or contradictory, the very reason for writing such an unabashedly Romantic poem so late in Lermontov's career is unclear. Is not "Mtsyri" an anachronism then? Why did Lermontov return to the genre of the Romantic poem after a decade of experiments in verse and prose?

Thus, regardless of all the praise, the poem's meaning, as well as the nature of its protagonist, continues to elude critics. Belinsky, who admired the character of Mtsyri as well as many passages of the poem, nevertheless remained skeptical of it; he characterized its main idea as "youthfully immature" (1978, 4:542). Belinsky's attitude is echoed in later scholarship: Mtsyri's strivings and actions are often dismissed as childish or irredeemably romantic.

While exploring Lermontov's poem on its own merits and placing it within its Russian and European contexts, I also interpret it in terms of Lermontov's own development. As his last completed narrative poem, "Mtsyri" is certainly his final, and perhaps most sophisticated and paradoxical presentation of the Romantic hero.

MTSYRI'S NAME: THE INITIATION OF A HERO

The reader, encountering the poem for the first time, is bound to be puzzled by its mysterious title. The strange non-Russian word *mtsyri,* though, is accompanied by the author's own footnote, which explains it in the following manner: "*Mtsyri* means in Georgian a 'non-ordained monk,' something like 'a novice'" (2:74). Lermontov's explanation warns us that the Russian equivalent of the word "mtsyri" is only an approximation: "something like 'a novice.'" Indeed, as background studies indicate, "mtsyri" in Georgian also means "a stranger, an outsider" (Manuilov et al. 1981, 324–27), a meaning that Lermontov clearly intends.[4]

However, Mtsyri's alienation is not indicated alone by the Georgian meaning of the word "mtsyri." Indeed, since "Mtsyri" is a Russian-language poem, the protagonist is immediately estranged from his Russian readers, for whom the word "mtsyri" is meaningless. This tension and confusion is compounded by the ending of his name, which evokes the Russian nominative plural. A title such as "The Novice" (*poslushnik*) would have been more "native," as it is rooted in the Russian language and culture and presupposes a certain social and cultural position. Thus, the very title of the poem becomes an emblem of Mtsyri's plight: his name is as alien to the Russian language as Mtsyri is to his environment.

Similar to the way Russian spelling reshapes the look and the sound of the Georgian word "mtsyri," Mtsyri himself is reshaped by the foreign language and customs imposed upon him: "but later he got used to captivity, began to understand the alien language, and was baptized by a holy father" (*no posle k plenu on privyk, stal ponimat' chuzhoi iazyk, byl okreshchen sviatym ottsom*) (2:76). This statement suggests that the captivity of Mtsyri is more than physical; his "powerful spirit" (*moguchii dukh*) (2:75) is also captured by somebody else's language and religion. Mtsyri, who was previously mute—"he wondered silently and alone; he turned food down with a gesture" (2:75)—is now introduced to a foreign language and to the foreign cultural concepts that such an introduction entails. Mtsyri's domestication is not completed, however: he never forgets that he is a captive.

Mtsyri's name is not the only characteristic that estranges him from the reader. There is also the fact that he fails to be a dangerous Romantic hero, such as Lermontov's own Arbenin, Pechorin, or the Demon. Indeed Mtsyri is not evil, and thus, as he ironically remarks, will be of no use to his readers: "but I did not do evil to others and thus it would not be of much use for you to learn about my deeds; besides, is it possible to tell the story of one's soul?" (*no liudiam ia ne delal zla i potomu moi dela ne mnogo pol'zy vam uznat', a dushu mozhno l' rasskazat'?*) (2:76). The line "is it possible to tell the story of one's soul" crops up in the two variants of "Mtsyri," "The Confession"and "Boyarin Orsha." The preceding line is different in "Mtsyri," however. Instead of the phrase "you must know about my deeds even without my help" (*moi dela i bez menia ty dolzhen znat'*) (2:160 and 330), which occurs in the previous variants, Lermontov offers an ironic and sad commentary on Mtsyri's lack of evil.

Furthermore, when Mtsyri fails to approach a beautiful Georgian woman whom he sees, he misses the opportunity to embark on an erotic adventure, an unforgivable sin for a hero of any Romantic poem. By contrast, Byron's "Giaour," another outsider with a strange name, experiences a dramatic and tragic love affair, something that immediately makes him familiar to the literary expectations of his readers.

In other words, Mtsyri is consistently presented as a stranger, a riddle to be deciphered. One of the keys to this riddle lies in the fact that Mtsyri is an orphan. His story is in fact the culminatation of a group of texts that explores the theme of cosmic abandonment, concentrating on the plight of an orphan: a person torn between memories of lost bliss and present anxieties. The concept of metaphysical orphanhood, so central to the Romantic imagination, is one of Lermontov's key images. As he wrote elsewhere: "I was born here, but my soul belongs elsewhere" (*Ia zdes' byl rozhden no nezdeshnii dushoi*) (1:214). Practically all of Lermontov's writings feature orphans, who especially dominate his early work. Fernando, the orphan-hero of Lermontov's earliest play, "The Spaniards" (*Ispantsy*) (1830), complains of his cosmic abandonment:

> Так, так, совсем забытый сирота!
> В великом Божьем мире ни одной
> Ты не найдешь души себе родной!
> Питался я не материнской грудью
> И не спал на ее коленях. Чуждый голос
> Учил меня родному языку.
> И пел над колыбелию моей.
>
> (3:120)

(Yes, yes, a completely forgotten orphan! / In God's great world you will not find a single soul dear to you. / Not a mother's breast fed me. / I did not sleep on her knees. / A strange tongue taught me to speak / And sang over my cradle.)

To be sure, orphans are present in the later works (such as the blind boy in "Taman" or the wife of Kalashnikov), but their role is less pronounced. In "Mtsyri," however, Lermontov not only returns to this crucial concept but does so with a vengeance. Mtsyri appears to lose everything: parents, friends, motherland, language, religion.

This kind of loss, cosmic in proportions, has often been viewed in the Christian tradition as an expression of the soul's estrangement from the body. As his archetypal poem "The Angel" testifies, Lermontov fully partakes of this tradition. In "Mtsyri" he again makes use of it, having Mtsyri acknowledge that his spirit is a prisoner in his own body: "from early childhood this fire / has secretly lived in my breast, / but now it has run out of food / and burned through its prison" (*etot plamen' s iunykh dnei taiasia zhil v grudi moei, no nyne pishchi net emu i on prozheg svoiu tiur'mu*) (2:92).

In "Mtsyri," though, Lermontov confounds the issue: Mtsyri's spirit burns through its material prison (his chest) in order to recapture the blissful moment of a material past, rather than of a spiritual future. Mtsyri views bliss in heaven as nothing but *priiut*, a temporary shelter, or an orphanage; he is willing to exchange such an orphanage of heaven for a few childhood minutes in his native land:

> Пускай в раю,
> В святом заоблачном краю

Мой дух найдет себе приют . . .
Увы, за несколько минут
Между крутых и темных скал,
Где я в ребячестве играл,
Я б рай и вечность променял.
(2:92)

(Let my spirit find its shelter in the sacred region beyond the clouds, in paradise. . . . Alas, I would exchange both paradise and eternity for several minutes among the dark and steep cliffs where I used to play as a child.)

Mtsyri's passionate striving for his lost homeland is reminiscent of the biblical Jews; like them, he "sighs and gazes at the East, / yearning for his homeland" (2:75). To convey Mtsyri's plight, Lermontov thus utilizes not one but two archetypal images of loss: the loss of the soul's heavenly home in the body, and the loss of a material homeland, Jerusalem, in the desert. Both images deal with captivity and the loss of homeland; thus Christians could spiritualize Jewish loss by turning a real physical place into a spiritual one, heavenly Jerusalem. Lermontov seems to reverse the process: he directs Mtsyri's spiritual longings toward the bliss of childhood, toward an earthly paradise, among the cliffs of his homeland. In other words, Lermontov depicts Mtsyri as equally estranged from both heavenly and earthly domains. He is thus in in a typically gnostic predicament, simultaneously sustained and tormented by the memory of a lost bliss.

Mtsyri's position in the universe seems to be defined by loss. Indeed, he is located—or, rather, suspended—between the spiritual and physical, between nature and civilization, between a heavenly Jerusalem and an earthly homeland. Mtsyri's borderline state is underscored by his being a novice; that is, neither yet a monk nor fully of this world. This indeterminate, liminal existence presupposes the possibility of a transition to another state (a novice turning into monk, for example); that is, an act of initiation. One cannot remain a novice indefinitely; one must either join the monastery or return to the world. Mtsyri, as his failed escape testifies, does neither: he neither returns to the world nor joins the monastery. He remains "a novice." From an external perspective Mtsyri fails the initiation: he fails to escape, to cross the border, to merge with a group of potential compatriots. Likewise, Mtsyri fails to take an oath and join another group, that of the monks. Mtsyri himself evaluates his own actions as a personal failure:[5]

Да, заслужил я жребий мой!
Могучий конь в степи чужой,
Плохого сбросив седока,
На родину издалека
Найдет прямой и краткий путь. . . .
Что я пред ним? Напрасно грудь
Полна желаньем и тоской;

То жар бессильный и пустой,
Игра мечты, болезнь ума.

(2:89)

(Yes, I deserved my fate! A powerful steed will throw off a poor rider, and in an alien and unfamiliar steppe find a straight and speedy way back to his fatherland. What am I in comparison? In vain my chest is filled with desire and yearning; it is an empty and powerless fever, a play of fancy, an affliction of the mind.)

Mtsyri's courageous actions suggest, however, that he cannot be dismissed so easily. Mtsyri's name signals not only the failure of someone who remains a novice, but the success of someone who has achieved a new identity. Rather than remaining a "novice," or "nonordained monk," Mtsyri in fact acquires a new identity; that of an outsider, a stranger (the second meaning of the word). Mtsyri thus completes his journey on earth, successfully completing his initiation by living up to his name. The tension between these two ways of looking at Mtsyri's fate constitutes the thematic core of Lermontov's poem.

This tension is introduced early on. Already in the second section Mtsyri's life story is summarily recounted: we learn of his childhood, when he is captured and left for dead in the monastery, of his languor and homesickness, and of his failed attempt to flee from the monastery on the eve of taking the monastic oath. The bulk of the poem, however, describes his struggles and desires, as if to suggest that there is another way of looking at his failed escape, another view of Mtsyri's life and sufferings.

This other view is stated explicitly when Mtsyri explains his flight in terms of a philosophical quest. Mtsyri wants to escape in order to "find out whether the earth is beautiful and whether one is born into this world for freedom or imprisonment" (*Uznat' prekrasna li zemlia, / Uznat' dlia voli il' tiur'my / Na etot svet rodimsia my*) (2:80). The word "*prekrasna*" clearly means not only "beautiful" but also "good"; that is, "anything worthy of praise," as Dahl defines it in his dictionary. Mtsyri thus tries to solve the key questions of existence: Is the earth beautiful? Should life be praised or cursed? Is one born for freedom or prison? Significantly, Mtsyri connects these questions; the question of life's ontological value is connected to the question of man's destiny and freedom.

On his first morning of freedom Mtsyri finds himself, symbolically, lying at the edge of a precipice, looking into an abyss, while surrounded by a wonderful garden:

Я осмотрелся; не таю:
Мне стало страшно; на краю
Грозящей бездны я лежал,
Где выл, крутясь, сердитый вал;
Туда вели ступени скал;
Но лишь злой дух по ним шагал,

Когда, низверженный с небес,
В подземной пропасти исчез.
Кругом меня цвел Божий сад;
Растений радужный наряд,
Хранил следы небесных слез. . . .
В то утро был небесный свод
Так чист, что ангела полет
Прилежный взор следить бы мог.
(2:81)

(I looked around, and—I won't hide it—I was terrified. I was lying at the edge of an ominous abyss, where an angry wave howled and rolled. Steps, formed of cliffs, led down to it: only an evil spirit had stepped on them as he disappeared into the chasm of the underworld after being cast down from heaven. Around me a heavenly garden was blooming; the rainbow-like raiment of plants preserved traces of heavenly tears. . . . The morning air was so transparent that it would have been possible to trace the flight of an angel with a diligent gaze.)

In this vision Mtsyri discovers the essence of freedom: its ambivalence. From inside a monstery, abysses such as these could of course not be seen; but neither could divine gardens and the pure sky in which "it would have been possible to trace the flight of an angel" (2:81). Freedom is presented as openness to both "an evil spirit" and "an angel": it is life on the edge or borderline; here one must make sure not to fall into the abyss, while simultaneously tracing the flight of a heavenly angel.[6]

If success is measured by accomplishments, then the outcome of Mtsyri's adventure must be deemed a failure; in that case one is born for prison. Mtsyri himself admits that he has failed in his task and sadly remarks that he "will die as he lived, a slave and an orphan" (2:77). But here Mtsyri manifests a seeming inconsistency: if a gnostic outlook is the correct one—that is, if we are born for prison, if life is cruel and evil—then what is to preclude us from cursing such a world? And yet, Mtsyri dies without cursing it; "ne proklianu" (I shall not curse) (2:93) are the last words of the poem.

Mtsyri's refusal to curse suggests that he has discovered a different criterion for evaluating the success of his search, a different proof of the beauty and goodness of Earth. The questions of theodicy and freedom are solved not by theoretical evaluation of results, but by one's actions, by the actual experience of life:

Ты хочешь знать, что делал я
На воле? Жил! и жизнь моя
Без этих трех блаженных дней
Была б печальней и мрачней
Бессильной старости твоей.
(2:80)

(You want to know what I did when I was free? I lived, and my life without these three blissful days would have been more sad and gloomy than your feeble old age.)

In his three days of flight, of "life," Mtsyri discovers what remains hidden from the majority of Lermontov's heroes. The world as he has never experienced it before opens up before Mtsyri; he acquires a sense of the beauty of the earth, of its goodness, which gives him the courage and strength to die without a curse on his lips. Mtsyri completes his initiation, his philosophical quest only upon this final courageous act of his life.

Mtsyri's narrative reveals the inadequacy of the terms "slave" and "orphan" for self-characterization. Mtsyri cannot be understood in traditional Romantic terms, as an active and violent character who troubles his surroundings and leaves his imprint upon them. Even if Mtsyri does not escape his prison, he does not surrender to it either. Mtsyri's struggle offers a different answer: although one may be born and die *in prison,* this by no means implies that one is born *for prison.* Lermontov suggests that the measure of heroism is the thoroughness of human resistance to prisons, rather than the ability to conquer and to create prisons for others.[7]

Mtsyri's name, the allegorical nature of his confrontations, as well as the poem's cosmic imagery and symbolism, suggest that Lermontov is creating his own cosmic myth, revising his view of success and heroic achievement and offering a solution to the gnostic predicament. Mtsyri escapes the monastery to be free, that is, to be exposed to both good and evil; his initiation consists of balancing on the edge, in applying all his strength and skill in order not to fall down into the abyss of evil:

Тогда к потоку с высоты,
Держась за гибкие кусты,
С плиты на плиту я, как мог,
Спускаться начал. Из-под ног
Сорвавшись камень иногда
Катился вниз. . . .
И я висел над глубиной.
(2:82)

(Then, holding onto the supple bushes, I descended from the heights toward the stream, jumping from one plane to another. Beneath my feet a random stone would roll down. . . . And I was suspended over the depths.)

Instead of a sanctioned initiation, which involves crossing a certain border, accomplishing a task, and joining a group, Mtsyri's is based on his proud and continuous resistance to evil. From his childhood refusal to eat the food of captivity, to his deathbed refusal to curse the world that held him captive, Mtsyri refuses to give in, to submit to evil, to conclude that the universe is ugly rather than beautiful. While perceiving the abyss, he enjoys the heavenly garden, a feat quite rare among Lermontov's protagonists. The Demon, we recall, manages to either despise or hate God's marvelous creation, while Arbenin zeroes in only on evil and ultimately surrenders to it. Mtsyri is confused over what he wants, as every human being probably is, but is certain of what he has to reject. It is obviously very easy to fall into the depth of evil; one has only to stop using all of one's efforts to stay in balance.

Through this image of Mtsyri on the brink of an abyss, Lermontov offers another view of initiation and heroism: one is always on the edge, forever choosing, forever confronting questions of human freedom and earthly goodness. One can, indeed, go through a traditional initiation if one's purpose is to join a group; but to solve the key questions of being, one must remain an outsider (*mtsyri*), suspended between good and evil, continually striving for the former, continually rejecting the latter.[8] Mtsyri's entire life is an initiation, as opposed to the traditional ritual, which ends after certain tasks are accomplished. In depicting Mtsyri's plight Lermontov anticipates a way of thinking that in many respects resembles existentialism. As if commenting on the plight of Mtsyri, Ortega y Gasset (1968) writes: "Man always travels along the precipices, and whether he will or not, his truest obligation is to keep balance" (199).

Lermontov, however, looks not only forward in time but back as well. In his portrayal of Mtsyri, the poet can be said to be re-creating the paradigm set by Milton in "Paradise Regained." In this "brief epic," as Milton called it, Christ's resistance to Satan is depicted in terms of a refusal to accept Satan's most tempting offers. And it is such a refusal that guarantees, for Milton, the possibility of paradise regained. Similar to Milton's ideal, Mtsyri first and foremost rejects evil: "I did no evil to people" (*no liudiam ia ne delal zla*). Lermontov clearly lacks Milton's deep religious faith; there is not even a hint that Mtsyri's heroism is rewarded with paradise regained. Nevertheless, Lermontov offers an interesting alternative to his own Byronic heroes, such as Arbenin, Pechorin, or the Demon: this escapee from a monastery, this conqueror of a wild leopard, nevertheless continually and skillfully avoids evil.

Let us now consider the elements of Mtsyri's initiation, his proud refusals to enjoy the comfort provided by the monastery walls, to enter the hut of a beautiful woman, and to curse the world after it has played its evil tricks on him. These actions, or rather the choices that Mtsyri makes, should offer us important clues to Lermontov's new vision of heroism.

MTSYRI AND WALLS

The events of Jewish history, to which the poem's epigraph alerts us, provide an important background to the poem. The source of the epigraph is identified in a rather general way: *Pervaia Kniga Tsarstv* (literally, "the First Book of Kingdoms"; that is, 1 Samuel). Such a general reference invites us to explore the context of the book as a whole. 1 Samuel describes an important transition in the political system of the Jewish state: the movement from the rule of Judges to that of Kings. This book portrays the ambivalence of the Jews toward the new institution of kings and shows their attempt to work out new relationships between God, his appointed judge, and the king. Thus in 1 Samuel 8, the Jews demand to be given a king regardless of the judge Samuel's warnings of possible abuses of royal power. In fact, they prefer to give up their freedom and direct relationship with God in favor of a king who will both defend them and decide for them, which displeases Samuel: "But the thing displeased Samuel, when they said, Give us a king to judge us. And Samuel prayed unto the Lord. And the Lord said unto Samuel . . . they have not rejected thee, but they have rejected me, that I should not reign over them" (1 Samuel 8:6–7). The remaining books of Samuel and Kings, called in Russian the "Books of Kingdoms" (following the Greek translation of the Bible), describe what might be called the rise and fall of the Jewish kingdoms. Here we witness the struggle, siege, and ultimate capture of the Jews by the Babylonian King Nebuchadnezzar. The Second Book of Kings ends with the tragic fall of Samaria and Jerusalem, the destruction of Jerusalem's walls and its temple, and the captivity of the king.[9]

Similarly, kings (tsars), conquests, captivity, and destruction of the church figure prominently at the beginning of Lermontov's poem. Already in the first chapter we learn that the Georgian tsar, being "overburdened by his crown" (*udruchen svoim ventsom*), gave up his kingdom to Russia. The narrator then states that "God's grace descended upon Georgia!—Since then it has bloomed in the shade of its gardens" (2:75). But the previous description of the neglected and ruined monastery, which had been intact only a few years before, clearly undercuts this assertion of grace and prosperity:

Теперь один старик седой . . .
Сметает пыль с могильных плит,
Которых надпись говорит
О славе прошлой и о том,
Как, удручен своим венцом
Такой-то царь в такой-то год
Вручал России свой народ.
. . . .
И божья благодать сошла
На Грузию. Она цвела
С тех пор в тени своих садов,
Не опасаяся врагов,
За гранью дружеских штыков.
(2:75)

(Nowadays only a gray old man . . . sweeps the dust off the tombstones, whose inscriptions speak of ancient glory and of a time when such-and-such tsar, overburdened by his crown, delivered his people to Russia. And God's bliss descended upon Georgia. It flourished in the shades of its gardens, not fearing its enemies behind the blades of friendly bayonets.)

These first images already point to the tension between opposing views of initiation and success: the Georgian king regains prosperity but at the cost of his crown and freedom; God's grace is accompanied by the destruction of the monastery, by its unattended ruins and graves.[10] The king is commemorated, yet his name is not given; together with his crown the king gives up his identity, while Georgia's prosperity is achieved with bayonets. The king, "overburdened with his crown," prefers walls of Russian bayonets to the responsibility of office. His grave, on which a description of his surrender is inscribed, refers, however, to "former glory," suggesting that glory is no longer present here.[11]

A growing ambivalence toward the saving power of Russian bayonets is expressed in the following description: "once a Russian general was approaching Tiflis on his way from the mountains. He was carrying a captured boy. The boy had become ill" (2:75). This description, if not by causal relation, then at least by a relation of contiguity, clearly connects Russian military power to captivity and illness: instead of grace, Russian bayonets have brought captivity and illness.

The dying boy, however, is cured. Just like the walls protecting Georgia, the friendly walls of the monastery help—or seem to help—Mtsyri to recover: "he remained among the protective walls, saved by the friendly treatment" (2:75). Even though the walls are initially depicted as "protective" (*khranitelnye*), the rest of the poem problematizes this notion. In the long run, the walls turn out to be destructive or even self-destructive, as the ruins of the monastery testify. Protective walls may bring temporary prosperity and comfort but they inevitably lead to destruction. The fate of the monastery also hints at an answer to Mtsyri's inquiry into the connection between freedom and the earth's beauty: the confining walls of bayonets slowly corrupt the beauty they are supposed to defend; a prosperous garden gives way to gravestones; imprisonment divests earth of its beauty.

Indeed, the imagery of walls, cells, and other restricted spaces dominates Mtsyri's passionate monologue, which starts with the following complaint: "I did not live long and I lived in captivity" (*Ia malo zhil i zhil v plenu*) (2:76). Monastic life itself, as Mtsyri describes it, is a form of captivity, almost an imprisonment behind walls. In his monologue Mtsyri claims that there is nothing within the monastery's walls that can satisfy his passions: "what among these walls could have you offered as a substitute for the brief but intense friendship between my burning heart and the storm" (*chto sred' etikh sten mogli by dat' vy mne v zamen toi druzhby kratkoi, no zhivoi, mezh burnym serdtsem i grozoi*) (2:80). The monastery itself is always connected with walls in Mtsyri's mind: "our monastery shone with its jagged wall" (*nash monastyr' sverkal zubchatoiu stenoi*) (2:90). During his wanderings Mtsyri loses his way and finds himself surrounded by the "eternal forest." Trying to find a way out, he reaches a meadow, which is surrounded by "an impenetrable wall" (*nepronitsaemoi stenoi*) (2:86). Finally emerging from the forest walls Mtsyri is returned to the monastery's walls. Moreover, for Mtsyri, walls are not merely external in nature; he calls his own body a "prison" that keeps the raging fire within. Even in his death Mtsyri is preoccupied with walls and is terrified that they will silence the story of his life: "and the tale of my bitter torments will not attract the sad attention of anyone among these silent walls" (*i povest' gor'kikh muk moikh ne prizovet mezh sten glukhikh vnimanie skorbnoe nichie*) (2:92).

Mtsyri's struggle with walls is best summarized by his own observation on the eternal struggle between the mountain river and the stones surrounding it: "Even though it was without words, I comprehended that conversation, relentless murmur, eternal argument with the stubborn heap of stones" (2:81). Mtsyri thus recognizes his own predicament in this eternal struggle of stones and rushing water. He, indeed, struggles with walls to the end: he dies inside the monastery, but to the very last he dreams of escape. He desires to die with his eyes on the mountains, listening to the sound of the wind, hearing in these sounds the song of his motherland. Mtsyri never gives up his longings; like the waves, he continues to beat against the stones.

The structure of the poem underscores the dynamics of Mtsyri's unending argument with walls. Mtsyri's narrative of his escape interrupts the gloom of the first two chapters but in the last three chapters we return to his captivity: Mtsyri is now dying inside the monastery. Mtsyri's narrative is thus framed by the descriptions of his confinement. Mtsyri's tale of his three days of freedom is thus one more way to resist walls. Mtsyri refuses to give in; he verbally re-creates his escape in order, as he puts it, "to live again, at least in imagination" (*chtob zhit' khot' myslenno opiat'*) (2:82). Mtsyri's narrative symbolically re-creates Lermontov's conception of the poetic process: the failure to escape captivity is counterbalanced by a poetic narrative of escape, enabling the poet to reexperience freedom.

By submitting to the monastery, by giving in to its walls, Mtsyri not only renounces his own desires but is screened from that exposure to good and evil that is the essence of freedom and life. He thus views his three days of wandering as true life and refuses to accept any substitute for his desire to live in the "miraculous world of troubles and battles" (*chudnyi mir trevog i bitv*) (2:77). Mtsyri proudly states: "Through dark nights I nurtured this passion with my yearning and tears. Now I loudly admit it before heaven and earth and do not beg for forgiveness" (2:77).

There is a revealing contrast between Mtsyri's attitude to freedom and the one expressed by Baratynsky in his 1833 poem "Why Does the Slave Need Dreams of Freedom?" (*K chemu nevol'niku mechtaniia svobody*).

Like Lermontov, Baratynsky employs images of waves and the shoreline to describe the nature of the human predicament: "life, which beats into our hearts like a powerful wave, but which is fitted into narrow borders by fate, is burdensome for us" (*tiagostna dlia nas, zhizn' v serdtse b'iushchaia mogucheiu volnoiu i v grani uzkie vtesnennaia sud'boiu*) (1989, 164). Clearly, both Lermontov and Baratynsky express the Romantic yet tragic desire to escape the bonds of narrow confinement: the narrow borders (*grani uzkie*) of Baratynsky remind one of Mtsyri's "blades of friendly bayonets" (*grani druzheskikh shtykov*) (2:75). But while Lermontov's Mtsyri refuses to renounce his desires, Baratynsky, even if with ironic resignation, nevertheless calls for surrender:

> Уделу своему и мы покорны будем,
> Мятежные мечты смирим иль позабудемь
> Рабы разумные, *послушно* согласим
> Свои желания со жребием своим—
> И будет счастлива, спокойна наша доля.
> (1989, 164; my emphasis)

> (We will be submissive to our lot, we will subdue or forget our rebellious dreams; reasonable slaves, we will *obediently* make our desires conform to our fate, and our lot will be happy and tranquil.)

Baratynsky's phrasing suggests the reason for Lermontov's dislike of the word *poslushnik*, which has the same root as *poslushnyi* (obedient, submissive). Mtsyri is anything but obedient. (Compare Lermontov's disdain for obedience in his famous 1841 poem, "Farewell, Unwashed Russia": "Farewell . . . to you too, sky-blue uniforms [that of secret police] and also to you, you people who submit to them" [*proshchai . . . i vy mundiry golubye, i ty, poslushnyi im narod*]) (1:76). Baratynsky sees confining walls as an invitation to surrender (in fact, having translated his poem into French, Baratynsky changed its title to "*Soumission*"), while for Lermontov resistance to confinement is an integral part of the cosmic rhythm of nature and life.[12]

The desire to resist confining walls is quite natural, and its manifestations hardly qualify anyone as a hero. Mtsyri, however, resists not only threatening and confining walls, but also protective and comforting ones. Having escaped the walls of the monastery, Mtsyri immediately confronts walls promising comfort and peace. The temptation of comforting walls is presented in Mtsyri's encounter with the beautiful Georgian girl.

MTSYRI'S EROTICISM: REFUSAL TO ENTER THE HUT

Soon after escaping from the monastery and its suffocating walls, Mtsyri, while searching for water, encounters a beautiful Georgian woman. Mtsyri observes the woman, without making himself seen. This episode does not lead anywhere and as such it is usually slighted by critics. Nevertheless, it is central to the poem not only thematically but also structurally: the episode occupies the three middle chapters (twelve to fourteen) in this poem of twenty-six chapters. It is the key example of Mtsyri's heroic refusals.

In many narrative poems of this period, including Lermontov's, an erotic encounter plays a central role in the hero's process of self-discovery. In "Mtsyri," however, Lermontov deliberately eschews the narrative opportunities that the meeting in the mountains offers. It is clear that this nonencounter is a signal on Lermontov's part.[13]

Mtsyri is an adolescent monk; the sight of the beautiful Georgian woman confuses him to such a degree that he faints:

И мрак очей был так глубок,
Так полон тайнами любви,
Что думы пылкие мои
Смутились, помню только я
Кувшина звон когда струя
Вливалась медленно в него,
И шорох . . . больше ничего.
(2:83)

(And the darkness of her eyes was so deep, so full of the mysteries of love, that my inflamed thoughts became confused. I only remember the sound of the jug, when the stream poured slowly into it, and a rustle . . . nothing else.)

Although Mtsyri feels a powerful attraction to this woman, he avoids contact with her. There is more at stake here, however, than a youth's innocence. Mtsyri's fainting is the sign of violent inner conflict. The woman is erotically attractive to Mtsyri, as suggested by the sexual undertones of his words and imagery: "darkness," "mysteries of love," "burning thoughts," a jug into which liquid pours. Mtsyri's emotions, however, are not limited to erotic desire. They also include spiritual longings. For instance, Mtsyri introduces the young Georgian's dwelling as a wonderful image of unity and harmony, as if suggesting what desire for an attractive young woman really implies:

Недалеко, в прохладной мгле
Казалось приросли к скале
Две сакли дружною четой;
Над плоской кровлею одной
Дымок струился голубой.
Я вижу будто бы теперь,
Как отперлась тихонько дверь . . .
И затворилася опять! . . .
Тебе я знаю не понять
Мою тоску, мою печаль;
И если б мог,—мне было б жаль:

Воспоминанья тех минут
Во мне, со мной пускай умрут.
(2:84)

(Nearby in the cool darkness two huts, forming a friendly couple, seemed to grow into a cliff. Above a single flat roof blue smoke was rising. I see it as if it were now, how the door opened slowly and then closed again! I know you would not understand my yearning and my sadness; and if you could—I'd be sorry. The memories of those minutes are inside me; let them die with me.)

Even though Mtsyri does not want his listener to understand his desires, he betrays them in the telling image of two huts standing under one roof. The image suggests not only the unity of lovers but also protection and care from above. The roof encloses the huts with a motherly embrace; this harmony is underscored by the image of blue smoke rising above and uniting the huts. It is to this loving, secure, comforting world that the door opens and closes, leaving Mtsyri outside. The eternal outsider's dream of entry is denied. The encounter with the beautiful Georgian invokes in Mtsyri a deep-seated yearning for home; for a state of care, security, and motherly love.

Mtsyri continues to be haunted by the girl: "and again I had a dream of the young Georgian girl. And my chest was aching with a sweet and strange pain" (*i snova videl ia vo sne gruzinki obraz molodoi. I strannoi sladkoiu toskoi opiat' moia zanyla grud'*) (2:84). Mtsyri then attempts—and fails—to verbalize what the encounter with the girl means for him: "I wanted to . . . but I did not dare to enter" (*khotelos' mne . . . no ia tuda vzoiti ne smel*) (2:85). The complexity and confusion of Mtsyri's desires are rendered by the ellipsis after "I wanted to" (*khotelos' mne*). He does not state what he wants because it is too mysterious, personal, and confusing.

We encounter the description of a similarly mysterious desire in Lermontov's unfinished prose piece, usually entitled by editors "I Would Like to Tell You" (*Ia khochu rasskazat' vam*). This narrative, which describes the emotional life of another orphan, a young motherless boy, states explicitly—as opposed to "Mtsyri"—the object of this boy's "sweet and strange" yearning, of his "I wanted to" (*khotelos'*):

> He got bored with the toys and began to dream. Being only six years old, he would already experience reverie while staring at the sunset, bedecked in pink clouds, and a mysteriously sweet feeling would already agitate his soul, the full moon shining through the window onto his childhood bed. *He wanted* (*emu khotelos'*) someone to caress him, to kiss him, to cuddle, but the old nurse's hands were so rough. (4:333)

The boy in this passage is haunted by an incomprehensible, yet sweet feeling: he wants a tender caress, a warm, motherly embrace. The persistent occurrence of such words as "strange," "puzzling," "miraculous," "sweet," in "Mtsyri," as well as in other Lermontov writings, reveals how deeply Lermontov's view of eroticism is connected with the child's and orphan's yearning for tenderness, for a motherly embrace, for former bliss. In "Mtsyri" Lermontov brings the implications of such a connection to the surface and allows Mtsyri to conquer the powerful and mysterious spell of eroticism.

The encounter with the woman reawakens in Mtsyri the orphan, "sweet" desires for home and family. The attraction of the beautiful girl is as powerful as the desire for food; nevertheless, Mtsyri conquers his desire: "I overcame the torment of hunger as best I could" (2:85). During his childhood captivity, Mtsyri had already proudly refused food, even at the expense of life: "he turned down the food with a gesture, and was dying quietly and proudly" (2:75). Is there a similarity between Mtsyri's childhood refusal of food and his later refusal to enter the hut of the young Georgian?

Mtsyri discloses the complexity of his erotic desire by associating the girl with her home. This home, whose doors open and close, suggests enclosure, that is, the creation of walls. Mtsyri is confronted with two opposite desires that pull him in opposite directions: the desire to belong and go on, to be securely embraced, and the desire to be outside the walls of confinement. Unable to resolve the conflict, he faints. Mtsyri is afflicted with the same painful syndrome that Richard F. Gustafson in his book on Tolstoy aptly calls "resident and stranger."[14]

Thus Mtsyri has to make a tragic choice between two goods: between being a resident and being a stranger, between hiding behind walls and remaining a *mtsyri* (an outsider). He made this choice once when he ran away from the monastery: now he has to choose again. But this time Mtsyri is dealing with the comfortable hut of a beautiful woman and not with the cold monastery walls.

It is doubtful whether Mtsyri is really aware of all the contradictory desires raging within him. Mtsyri himself explains his decision in very vague terms:

> Хотелось мне . . . но я туда
> Взойти не смел. Я цель одну—
> Пройти в родимую страну
> Имел в душе и превозмог
> Страданье голода, как мог,
> И вот дорогою прямой
> Пустился, робкий и немой.
> (2:85)

(I felt like it (*khotelos' mne*) . . . but I did not dare enter there. I had only one purpose in my soul—to reach the dear motherland—and I managed to overcome the torment of hunger; and now, timid and mute, I took off along the straight road.)

This ambiguous explanation is hardly adequate. Significantly, almost every line of this explanation features an enjambment. The clash of opposite forces, ambivalence, and confusion in Mtsyri is rendered by sentences that are split between the lines: "but there / I did not dare enter; having overcome / the torment of hunger; my journey / I continued." Mtsyri's confusion is expressed on other levels as well. His declaration of the high purpose of reaching his motherland is undercut by his phrase "but I did not dare enter" (*no ia tuda vzoiti ne smel*). If one really has a mission, one would say "I could not enter" rather than "I dared not enter."

And yet amid the confusion Mtsyri's choice of words reveals his most important characteristic: refusal to use others. Having declared that he does not dare enter the woman's hut, Mtsyri suddenly mentions the hunger he is trying to overcome, which clearly connects his desires for food with desire for the girl. Physical hunger, however, needs to be satisfied, and will be felt again and again. Hence the "insatiable heart" of Pechorin (41) and the Demon's constant sensation of loss. In contrast to such characters, Mtsyri confesses that he does not dare to use another person in order to satisfy his hunger. Because he has not yet reached the dear motherland, Mtsyri knows he will be hungry again. He thus refuses to use the girl only as *priiut,* as a temporary shelter. The youthful Mtsyri appears to be more sober and restrained than, say, Pechorin, who entertains the illusion that Bela is an "angel sent . . . by compassionate fate" (40) and thus destroys her. Mtsyri, however, is at his best at that moment: no matter what the Georgian woman means for him or how strongly he desires her, he does not dare to use her in order to resolve his own conflicts.

Mtsyri gives up the idea of entering the hut after he witnesses a scene of nature that alerts him to his own intentions. Waking from a dream in which he is haunted by the beautiful Georgian girl, he notices the moon, pursued by a cloud that is preparing to embrace it:

Уж луна
Вверху сияла—и одна
Лишь тучка кралася за ней,
Как за добычею своей,
Объятья жадные раскрьв.
(2:84)

(The moon was already shining high above—and only a single cloud was stealthily following it, having widened its greedy embrace as if following its prey.)

Mtsyri recognizes his own predicament in this picture of the predatory cloud. The cloud informs Mtsyri of his own desires and its possible outcome. To embrace the girl would be to act like such a cloud; that is, to darken the moon, to impose oneself upon it, to extinguish the source of one's own dreams and aspirations. The beautiful Georgian girl whose song Mtsyri overhears is similar to Bela and Tamara both in her beauty and artistic nature.

Yet Mtsyri overcomes the temptation to which both Pechorin and the Demon succumb.[15]

As the scene with the moon continues, we are presented with imagery that is clearly cosmic:

> Мир темен был и молчалив;
> Лишь серебристой бахромой
> Вершины цепи снеговой
> Вдали сверкали предо мной
> Да в берега плескал поток.
> (2:84)

(The world was dark and silent; only far ahead of me the edges of a snowy ridge sparkled like silvery tassels, and the stream splashed against the shore.)

In the face of a dark and silent world, Mtsyri's existential predicament is brought to the surface. He confronts "the silence of these infinite spaces" that frightened Pascal so much. And yet the world's silence is interrupted for Mtsyri by the sound of a stream splashing against the shore. This sound encourages Mtsyri; it reminds him of the eternal rhythm of nature's resistance to confinement.

Mtsyri's existential predicament is underscored by Lermontov's use of the image of light. In this silent and dark world Mtsyri sees two spots of light and has to choose between them: the distant shimmer of mountaintops and the flickering light of the Georgian hut: "in the familiar hut the light was flickering. In the same manner a bright star dies in heaven at the midnight hour" (*v znakomoi sakle ogonek to trepetal, to snova gas, na nebesakh v polnochnyi chas, tak gasnet iarkaia zvezda*) (2:84). The light of the hut, even so near, is flickering: it can go out. Possession of the girl will extinguish the light without achieving anything. Mtsyri chooses the light of the distant mountains.[16]

In "Mtsyri" the sense of an all-powerful and all-resolving eros is overcome. The protagonist intuits the futility of recapturing ever-vanishing paradise through erotic love. Mtsyri is aware that the light of the mountaintops is different from the flickering light of the hut: the two lights cannot be used interchangeably. The latter indicates possession here and now, while the former points the way toward his distant motherland.

Even though he avoids temptation, Mtsyri does not succeed in achieving his ostensible purpose: reaching home. The lines following his courageous decision state that Mtsyri begins to lose his way. Such a sequence of events is indicative both of Mtsyri's predicament and of Lermontov's general outlook. Lermontov's heroes fail to regain their lost bliss either through women or anything else. The mountains of one's former blissful existence are impossible to reach; the bliss of erotic passion is an illusion. There is no way home.

While he values his homeland more than paradise, Mtsyri inadvertently confesses that this homeland will not satisfy him either, for it too is surrounded by walls:

> Увы!—за несколько минут
> Мэжду крутых и темных скал,
> Где я в ребячестве играл,
> Я б рай и вечность променял . . .
> (2:92)

> (Alas! For the sake of several minutes among the stiff and dark cliffs where I played as a child I would have given both paradise and eternity . . .)

Mtsyri's homeland of childhood is hidden between dark and steep cliffs; that is, it is surrounded by protective, yet confining walls. It is obvious that Mtsyri, similar to the Demon, who felt a sense of loss in paradise, would experience confinement even at home.

If "The Demon" explores the mysterious wound that makes every experience a "paradise lost," "Mtsyri" shifts the focus. How to react to the fact that wounds never heal, that paradise always lies beyond the horizon? Disappointed in their erotic quests, Arbenin and the Demon tend to resort to aggression and violence. Mtsyri also gets angry upon losing his way:

> Напрасно в бешенстве порой
> Я рвал отчаянной рукой
> Терновник. . . .
> Тогда на землю я упал
> И в исступлении рыдал
> И грыз сырую грудь земли.
> (2:85)

> (In vain fits of rage did I tear a thorny bush with my desperate hand. . . . Then I fell down on the earth and in my madness I sobbed and gnawed the earth's raw breast.)

Mtsyri, however, transcends his frustration and violence. He directs his violent energy at the wild beast that attacks him first, thus ridding himself of his own violence and, on a symbolic plane, conquering it.

THE VICTORY OVER THE LEOPARD

In the middle of the night, lost in an endless forest, Mtsyri sees a leopard and immediately decides to challenge him: "suddenly my heart was set on fire with the desire for struggle and blood" (2:86). This decision of the otherwise nonviolent Mtsyri can be seen as a confrontation with the demonic temptation of violence and aggression. If the encounter with the girl was Mtsyri's temptation by an angel, by the semblance of paradise, the later adventure represents temptation by an evil spirit. The dynamics of Mtsyri's two encounters can be read allegorically. Mtsyri avoids the temptation of the good, refusing to introduce an evil element of possession into the peaceful scene of the girl and her home. By contrast, Mtsyri does not avoid the fight with the leopard. The struggle with the leopard suggests that temptation by evil should not be avoided, but rather confronted face to face.

The confrontation between a lost man and a wild leopard in the middle of a forest has several literary subtexts, the most obvious being Dante's *Divine Comedy*. The leopard of the very first page of the *Inferno* represents the self-indulgent sins of youth (incontinence), as Dorothy Sayers remarks in her commentary to Dante's *Inferno* (Dante 1977, 75). Likewise, one can read Mtsyri's victory over the leopard as his triumph over self-indulgence and aggression.

Many of Lermontov's protagonists are threatening and violent. Mtsyri can be as violent as they are, but he resorts to violence only during the confrontation with this wild beast, who is more dangerous and threatening than Mtsyri. Significantly, Mtsyri neither strikes first nor retreats like a coward. Instead, he courageously prepares himself for battle and emerges victorious. The text twice mentions that Mtsyri carefully waits for the leopard's attack: "I waited for the moment of battle, having grabbed a forked tree branch. . . . I waited. And finally it smelled an enemy in the darkness of the night" (2:86).

The two opponents exhibit striking similarities: Mtsyri emits an animal shriek; both combatants struggle, "having intertwined like two snakes and embracing each other more firmly than two friends" (*i my spletias' kak para zmei, obniavshis' krepche dvukh druzei*) (2:87). On some level, the leopard is Mtsyri's alter ego, his violent self: "I was terrifying at that moment; like the snow leopard, I was wild and fierce" (*ia byl strashen v etot mig, kak bars pustynnyi, zol i dik*) (2:86–87). Mtsyri, who was a stranger to evil, partakes of it for the first and only time: *zol* means in Russian both fierce/angry and evil. It should be stressed, however, that Mtsyri, who has declared that he will not do evil to people, remains true to his word; he kills, but only the wild beast against whom he has to defend himself.

While both opponents are characterized as *moguchii* (powerful), in the case of Mtsyri, the epithet is applied to his spirit, and the victory does indeed go to his indomitable spirit. We are alerted to Mtsyri's superiority by the fact that while the leopard "moans like a human being" (*on zastonal kak chelovek*) (2:86), Mtsyri, even as a child, does not: "he suffered without a complaint; not even a weak moan escaped his child's lips" (*bez zhalob on tomilsia, dazhe slabyi ston iz detskikh gub ne vyletal*) (2:75). The victory of Mtsyri's powerful spirit over the leopard's powerful body implies that spirituality can and should vanquish the violent and amoral power of nature.

The leopard, however, is not a completely evil figure in itself. The beast is courageous; it confronts loss face to face, as a warrior; it is described as both fierce and playful. In its animal splendor and energy the leopard appears to be beyond good and evil:

Какой-то зверь одним прыжком
Из чащи выскочил и лег,
Играя, навзничь на песок.
То был пустыни вечной гость—
Могучий барс. Сырую кость
Он грыз и весело визжал;
То взор кровавый устремлял,
Мотая ласково хвостом,
На полный месяц.

(2:86)

(An animal in one leap burst out of the bushes and fell down, playfully, on the sand. It was a perennial guest of the desert—a powerful mountain lion. Chewing a fresh bone he first squealed with merriment, then raised his bloody gaze toward the full moon, while gently wiggling his tail.)

Mtsyri, by contrast, is not beyond good and evil.[17] In fact, he consistently chooses good, which contrasts with numerous Romantic heroes, such as Byron's Cain or Lermontov's own Arbenin who, while trying to balance good and evil, eventually surrender to the dark force. A renegade monk who challenges the monastery and the world it represents, a courageous conqueror of a wild leopard—Mtsyri clearly exhibits features of a Byronic hero. Nevertheless, he conquers rather than succumbs to his own aggressiveness. Mtsyri's victory over the leopard finds a parallel in Lermontov's victory over the temptation of the Romantic cult of power, violence, and revolt. With the completion of "Mtsyri," Lermontov substantiated his earlier claim that he was different from Byron.

By slaying the leopard, Mtsyri conquers his own violence. Mtsyri's victory makes him similar to another epic hero, Aeneas, who puts an end to his own violence by slaying his sworn enemy, the wild and violent Turnus. Here is the description of Turnus's rage, a rage that Aeneas has to confront both inside and outside himself:

Insane he raves
For arms, he searches bed and halls for weapons.
Lust for the sword and war's damnable madness
Are raging in him and—above all—anger:
Just like when burning, loudly crackling twigs
Are heaped beneath a seething caldron's ribs,
The liquid dances with heat; within,
The water rages, violent, and pours
A stream of smoke and foam; it will not rest
But flies with dense steam.

(7:607–16)

Like Mtsyri, who fights the leopard with a forked tree branch, Aeneas fights Turnus with a spear; having received the first blow from Turnus, he mortally wounds him: "And now Aeneas charges straight at Turnus, he brandishes a shaft huge as a tree" (12:1178). Comparing the results of the two victories, however, we see immediately that Lermontov has rewritten the epic plot. While Aeneas's victory ends *The Aeneid*—having conquered his violence, the hero has passed his initiation and is now ready to establish the greatest empire on earth, Pax Romana—Lermontov's protagonist finds himself in a different situation: having conquered his own violence, Mtsyri can only hope for inner peace.

THE REFUSAL TO CURSE: MTSYRI AND THE ORDEAL OF JOB

Mtsyri's two victories, rather than leading to glory, in fact present him with the biggest challenge of his life: contending with the cruelty of fate: "but I argued with fate in vain, for it just mocked me" (2:88). Or as he puts it later:

> И страшно было мне, понять
> Не мог я долго, что опять
> Вернулся я к тюрьме моей;
> Что бесполезно столько дней
> Я тайный замысел ласкал,
> Терпел, томился и страдал,
> И все зачем?
>
> (2:88)

(And I felt frightened, and for a long time I could not comprehend that I had returned to my prison, that in vain had I cherished for so many days my secret plan; endured, languished, and suffered. But what was the purpose of all that?)

The theme of fate's mockery is first introduced in the epigraph. Lermontov uses epigraphs rather frequently, especially in his narrative poems. The majority of his epigraphs originate in literature, and from Byron in particular. The epigraph for "Mtsyri," however, appears to be the only one taken from the Bible, and conveys a solemn and majestic tone to the poem itself. Lermontov chose it after deliberation, crossing out the first epigraph, the French proverb "On n'a qu'une seule patrie." What made Lermontov use as the epigraph to his poem the biblical words pronounced by the young Jewish hero Jonathan: "*Vkushaia vkusikh malo meda, i se az umiraiu*" (I did but taste a little honey . . . and lo, I must die)?[18]

The epigraph refers to an episode in the Jewish war with the Philistines (1 Sam. 14:43). Jonathan, the son of the first Jewish king, Saul, destroys almost single-handedly an army of Philistines. Inspired by his success on the battlefield, Saul rashly imposes a one-day fast on his subjects to enable them to destroy even more enemies. Jonathan, however, does not hear the prohibition and eats a bit of wild honey. Recognizing signs of God's displeasure, Saul seeks out its source. When he finds the culprit, his own son, he decides to have him executed. The son accepts the cruel verdict yet bemoans his fate by referring to the "little honey": it is this reference that Lermontov uses for his epigraph.

The biblical context of Jonathan's words provides its readers with another example of fate's cruel mockery. At first glance, Jonathan's complaint of untimely death seems to be unjustified. It turns out that Jonathan, whom his father Saul has condemned to death, is spared by the will of the people; they protest Saul's rash decision and, in the words of the Bible, "ransom Jonathan." Thus the episode ends on an optimistic note: the son is forgiven and continues to live, which cannot be said of the hero of Lermontov's poem. Is there a contradiction then? I would suggest that there is none, as there is a deeper irony concealed in the biblical text, an irony that Lermontov clearly utilizes: a few chapters and several battles later the young hero Jonathan is caught and killed by Philistines. In the long run the prophecy of Jonathan's untimely death proves correct.

More broadly, the epigraph recalls one of Lermontov's favorite and most common plotlines: the initial fulfillment of a miracle, a prayer, or a desire followed by defeat. Vulich in *A Hero of Our Time* is saved from a bullet only to be killed on the same night by a drunken Cossack; Kalashnikov wins over Kiribeevich only to be executed by the order of Ivan the Terrible; and even the Demon gets Tamara only to lose her again. Similar to Jonathan, who is saved from death only to be killed shortly afterward, Mtsyri runs away, kills the leopard, and finds a way out of the surrounding forest only to be returned to his prison once more.

In fact, beyond Jonathan's bitterly ironic story lies an even more important biblical subtext of man's trial by injustice, that is, the story of Job. It is important to recall that Job, tormented by persecution, receives from his wife the famous bit of advice: "curse God and die" (Job 2:9). Job rejects his wife's advice, but later enters into an argument with God and begins to accuse him. Mtsyri, however, stoically perseveres through his torment, dying without a curse. In fact, it can be argued that, confronted by so much injustice, he dies in order not to curse.

There is another sign indicating how much the idea of fate's cruelty and irony preoccupied Lermontov. Lermontov, who rarely dated his work, made a point of dating the manuscript of this poem: 5 August 1839. Clearly, he saw something significant in this date, something worth preserving. In fact, the date refers to the eve of one of the most important Orthodox holidays, the Feast of the Transfiguration. This feast celebrates the miracle of the transfiguration of Jesus on Mount Tabor. Celebrating the possibility of change and transcendence, it promises the transfiguration of human nature into the divine. The promise of Transfiguration became essential to the literary imagination of another great Russian writer, Gogol, as was noted recently by Robert Maguire (1990, 48). Lermontov, however, came to see only bitter irony in this promise. The given promise remained unfulfilled, and thus the allusion to the eve of this important holiday is a bitter commentary on the events of the plot: the promise was there, but not the event; the miracle did not occur.

This favorite motif of Lermontov, which could be characterized as "re-losing of paradise regained," pervades the text on many levels: for example, Georgia is saved only to decay, and the prison flower is replanted from the dungeon to a beautiful garden only to be crushed by the sun: "the sun had hardly appeared when its burning rays scorched the flower, which had been raised in prison" (*edva zashla zaria, paliashchii luch ee obzheg v tiur'me vospitannyi tsvetok*) (2:89). The cruelty of fate is underscored by several literary allusions as well. Mtsyri loses his way in the middle of the forest: "there was forest, eternal forest all around, and it was getting thicker and more terrifying by the hour" (*vse les byl, vechnyi les krugom, strashnei i gushche kazhdyi chas*) (2:85). Mtsyri's disorientation clearly refers to the beginning of Dante's *Inferno,* and the reference becomes even more pronounced when Mtsyri encounters the leopard. But while for Dante the forest with its wild animals is but the prologue to a journey through the Inferno to Paradise, for Mtsyri the forest is the end. He has no Virgil or anyone else to guide him out of it. The promise is not fulfilled; instead, Mtsyri gets out of the forest only to find himself back in front of the monastery.[19] The contrasting outcomes of Mtsyri's and Aeneas's victories over their wild antagonists underscores a similar point.

The stanza describing the endless forest contains still another reference alerting us to the irony and sardonic failure of promises. Having realized that he is lost, Mtsyri bursts into tears. However, he refuses to appeal for help, stating that had a cry for help betrayed him, "he would have torn out his weak tongue" (*Ia b vyrval slabyi moi iazyk*) (2:85). This phrase refers to another encounter in the wilderness, that of Pushkin's "Prophet": "and [he] tore out my sinful tongue" (*vyrval greshnyi moi iazyk*). However, in Pushkin's case, as well as in Dante's, the poets/prophets lost in the middle of the wilderness receive help from above. A seraph appears before Pushkin's prophet, tears out his sinful tongue, and inserts a new one that will enable him to address people in the voice of a prophet. In "Mtsyri," however, the youth is ready to inflict such pain upon himself only in order *not* to address people prophetically.

Although Lermontov uses this turn of events to demonstrate the cruelty of the universe, this demonstration is not his ultimate aim. Instead, he shifts our attention away from the cruelty of fate, which plays tricks on

Vulich, the Demon, and Mtsyri, onto the courage of the individual who has to face such cruelty. By the time of the composition of "Mtsyri," Lermontov had apparently come to see captivity as humanity's inescapable fate: we are all doomed to wander and languish in this vale of tears, as he describes it in his lyrical masterpiece, "Angel" (1831). What remained to be explored, however, was the way each individual deals with such an evil fate. Should one seduce and kill as Pechorin and the Demon do? Or become a passive and obedient plaything of evil, like Grushnitsky and Baroness Strahl? In "Mtsyri" Lermontov returns to a solution he first offered in "The Song": regardless of all the injustice of fate Mtsyri makes a choice based on personal integrity, courage, and his proud resolve to resist evil even in the form of evil feelings.

In the biblical story the father's curse does not make sense to Jonathan. Having been told of the curse, Jonathan answers: "My father hath troubled the land: see, I pray you, how my eyes have been enlightened, because I tasted a little of this honey. How much more, if haply the people had eaten freely today of the spoil of their enemies which they found? For had there not been now a much greater slaughter among the Philistines?" (1 Sam. 14:29–30). Nevertheless, Jonathan accepts his father's cruel verdict and refuses to rebel. Although perhaps disagreeing with the prohibition, he does not challenge his father's right to punish. No matter what, Jonathan will eat his honey, the food that brightens his eyes, and will die. Mtsyri's attitude toward his cruel lot is similar.

The poem's last phrase is "and with this thought I will die and won't curse anyone" (*i s etoi mysliu ia umru i nikogo ne proklianu*) (2:93). The refusal to curse is a significant symbol in Lermontov. One can contrast the last line of "Mtsyri" with the last line of his early poem "Angel of Death": "and his kiss is a curse" (*I potselui ego—prokliatie!*) (2:209). Even more to the point are the words of Vadim, hunchback and orphan, uttered against the monastery that gave him shelter: "They took me into a *monastery* out of compassion. . . . Within the church *walls* I spent my best years, mistreated only because I was depraved by nature. . . . They *forced* me to *thank God* for my ugliness. . . . To pray! . . . My heart contained only *curses*" (*Vadim*, 1832–34) (4:169; my emphasis). Curses are usually accompanied by or substituted for the yearning for revenge, familiar to us from such characters as Arbenin or even Kalashnikov. In Lermontov's "Death of a Poet," the hero of the poem dies with "the thirst for revenge" (1:22); in fact, the phrase is repeated twice in the poem.[20]

By contrast, Mtsyri does not curse, nor does he aspire for revenge. Instead he dies stoically, remaining true to the convictions that he cherished all his life. In fact, Mtsyri's stoicism and pride are disclosed from the start. The first thing we learn about him is that, regardless of his frail body, the captured boy has a powerful spirit that enables him to face death proudly and quietly:

Без жалоб он томился,
Даже слабый стон
Из детских губ не вылетал,
Он знаком пищу отвергал
И тихо, гордо умирал.
(2:75)

(He suffered without complaints; even a weak moan did not leave his lips, by a sign he rejected food, and was dying quietly and proudly.)

Lermontov's attitude toward God and his world cannot be interpreted as open rebellion alone (*bogoborchestvo*), although this has been a commonplace ever since Russian symbolists like Merezhkovsky and Solov'ev took up the question. In fact, it is heroic resignation and stoicism, rather than rebellion, that are articulated in many Lermontov's poems. Mtsyri-like stoicism is most eloquently expressed in the famous poem of 1840 "Valerik," a poem that deals with war and tragedy:

Мой крест несу я без роптанья—
То иль иное наказанье?
Не все ль одно. Я жизнь постиг.
Судьбе как турок иль татарин,
За все я ровно благодарен.
У Бога счастья не прошу
И молча зло переношу.
(1:63)

(I carry my cross without complaint; this or another punishment, isn't it all the same? I understand life; like a Tartar or a Turk I am grateful to fate for everything; I do not ask God for happiness, and silently endure evil.)

Kalashnikov is another example of similar defiance. He does what he must do with the tsar's servant Kiribeevich and then dies with dignity and in silence. Kalashnikov's and Mtsyri's behavior is as heroic and paradoxical as that of Jonathan, who stoically accepts his unfair lot.

Alfred de Vigny, a poet whose sensitivity and outlook frequently coincide with that of Lermontov, especially on such issues as religious skepticism and aristocratic honor, praises a similarly defiant stoicism in his famous poem "La Mort du Loup" (1843). De Vigny writes about the hunted wolf who fights to the last and then proudly and silently accepts his lot: "Seul le silence est grand; tout le reste est faiblesse" (Vigny 1921, 225). Lermontov fully shares such a view of greatness.[21] Praising the proud death of his friend, the Decembrist Alexander Odoevsky, Lermontov concludes: "you died like many, without noise, but with resoluteness" "On the Death of Odoevsky" (1839) (1:45).

TRANSCENDENCE THROUGH SOUND: MTSYRI'S RECOVERY OF A PARADISE LOST

> Look how the floor of heaven
> Is thick inlaid with patents of bright gold,
> There's not the smallest orb which thou behold'st
> But in his motion like an angel sings,
> Still quiring to the young-eyed cherubins;
> Such harmony is in immortal souls,
> But whilst this muddy vesture of decay,
> Doth grossly close it in, we can not hear it . . .
> —Shakespeare, *The Merchant of Venice*

> The secret of writing consists in listening to the eternal and involuntary music within one's soul. If one lacks it, one can only "make a writer out of oneself," but one is not a writer.
> —Vassily Rozanov, *Solitaria*

What sustains and informs Mtsyri's stoicism and courage? What helps him to protect his soul from malice and enmity, the emotions that plague the majority of Lermontov's characters? Shakespeare's Lorenzo is convinced that the sounds of heaven cannot be heard while entrapped in one's "muddy vesture of decay." Even though Mtsyri feels entrapped by his own body, which he calls a "prison," his universe is not always silent; his soul is capable of hearing the harmony of heavenly sounds, a harmony that sustains him in his courageous life. As he escapes from the monastery's walls, Mtsyri also manages to transcend "the muddy vesture of decay," the encircling walls of his body, to hear the beautiful harmonies beyond.

It is precisely Mtsyri's artistic nature, his flights of fancy inspired by song, that nourish and sustain his proud stoicism, his courageous resistance, and, finally, his refusal to curse existence. Mtsyri hopes to hear a sound that will make him reexperience his most cherished dreams:

> Оттуда виден и Кавказ!
> Быть может он с своих высот
> Привет прощальный мне пришлет,
> Пришлет с прохладным ветерком
> И близ меня перед концом
> Родной опять раздастся звук!
> И стану думать я что друг

Иль брат, склонившись надо мной,
Отер внимательной рукой
С лица кончины хладный пот
И что вполголоса поет
Он мне про милую страну . . .
И с этой мыслью я засну,
И никого не прокляну!

(2:93)

(The Caucasus can also be seen from there. Maybe they will send me a farewell greeting from their heights, send it with a cool breeze; and before my end a familiar sound will resound near me. And I will think that a friend or a brother bending over me is wiping off the cold sweat of death, and that he is singing softly about our dear land . . . and soothed by that thought I will fall asleep, and won't curse anyone.)

Mtsyri's unwillingness to curse is directly related to song, the song of his motherland, which he hopes to hear in the sound of the wind.

In fact, references to sounds, songs, and listening pervade the poem. In the description of his flight, Mtsyri re-creates life outside the monastery mainly through references to sounds. Description of murmurs, howling, noise, songs, and speech dominate his passionate monologue:

И снова я к земле припал
И снова *вслушиваться* стал
К *волшебным странным голосам;*
Они *шептались* по кустам,
Как будто *речь* свою вели
О тайнах неба и земли;
И все природы голоса
Сливались тут; не *раздался*
В торжественный хваленья час
Лишь человека *гордый глас.*

(2:82; my emphasis)

(And again I pressed against the earth, and began to *listen to miraculous and strange voices;* they *whispered* among the bushes, as if *discussing* the secrets of heaven and earth. And all the *voices* of nature merged there; only the *proud voice* of man *was not heard* at that solemn hour of praise.)

The harmony of the world is presented as the harmonious fusion of various sounds of nature. By contrast, human alienation is rendered as man's failure, or rather as a proud demonic refusal to join the choir of praise.

The lack of sounds is connected with death in the poem. In the prologue we are told that no one sings in the abandoned monastery; Mtsyri complains of the silence of the grave; his final defeat is characterized by the dead silence of midday:

Мир Божий спал
В оцепенении глухом
Отчаянья тяжелым сном.
Хотя бы крикнул коростель,
Иль стрекозы живая трель
Послышалась, или ручья
Ребячий лепет

(2:90)

(God's world was lying in the deep stupor of the heavy slumber of despair. If only a corncrake would cry, or the living song of a dragonfly or childlike murmur of a brook could be heard.)

When neither corncrake (*korostel'*), nor "singing" (*trel'*), nor "the childlike murmur of a brook" (*ruch'ia rebiachii lepet*) are able to interrupt the reigning silence, Mtsyri faints. At that moment, however, he has a vision of a singing goldfish: "and it seemed that the echoing stream melded its murmur with the words of a goldfish" (*i mnilos' zvuchnaia struia slivala tikhii ropot svoi s slovami rybki zolotoi*) (2:92). Thus what is absent in real life is granted to Mtsyri in dream: the harmony of his favorite sounds transcends the power of silence. In fact, the same dynamic has already been introduced in the scene with the Georgian girl: the silence of the world has been broken by the sounds of the stream, sounds that help Mtsyri to persevere in his brave decision.

Among the sounds that dominate the universe of the poem, the sounds of waves are the most cherished. Indeed the poem is full of suggestive references to water: in remembering his childhhood Mtsyri recalls the streams of his motherland in which he played; he meets the Georgian woman near the stream; in his trance he imagines himself lying on the bottom of a river. It is not a coincidence that the very first image of the poem refers to the sound of rivers: "Several years ago, at the place where the two rivers Aragva and Kura noisily flow into each other, embrace each other like two sisters, there stood a monastery" (2:74). Upon his escape Mtsyri listens to the sounds of water:

Внизу глубоко подо мной,
Поток, усиленный грозой
Шумел, и шум его глухой
Сердитых сотне голосов
Подобился. Хотя без слов
Мне внятен был тот разговор,
Немолчный ропот, вечный спор
С упрямой грудою камней.

(2:81)

(Deep down below me a stream thundered, strengthened by the storm, and its inarticulate roar sounded like hundreds of angry voices. Even without words I understood its speech, the constant murmur, the perennial dispute with the stubborn pile of stones.)

In fact, rhythmical repetitive sounds, of water in particular, play an important role in Lermontov's oeuvre. Throughout his poetry the sounds of waves tend to put the lyrical hero in a mystical trance. The poem "When the Yellow Field Is Agitated" (*Kogda volnuetsia zhelteiushchaia niva*) describes this state vividly:

Когда студеный ключ играет по оврагу
И, погружая мысль в какой-то смутный сон,
Лепечет мне таинственную сагу
Про мирный край, откуда мчится он,
Тогда смиряется души моей тревога,
Тогда расходятся морщины на челе,—
И счастье я могу постигнуть на земле,
И в небесах я вижу Бога.

(1:28)

(When the cold brook plays in the ravine and, drowning my thoughts in a hazy dream, murmurs to me a mysterious saga about the peaceful land from where it flows, then the anxiety in my soul is appeased; then the wrinkles on my forehead vanish, and I understand happiness on earth, and see God in heaven.)

The rhythmic murmur of the brook eases the torment of the poet's soul by submerging it into a dreamlike state. Only in such a state is the poet able to conquer his anxiety and perceive the goodness of life and of God. This dreamlike state is clearly ambivalent: the moment of deathlike passivity, the "murky dream" (*smutnyi son*) cannot be sustained without turning into death, but it is moments like these that provide nourishment for the tormented souls of Lermontov's protagonists, including Mtsyri. Significantly, Lermontov placed this poem immediately after "Mtsyri" in his 1840 collection of verse, though it was written two years before "Mtsyri."

It is hardly surprising that the most transcendent moment in the poem is connected with the harmonious sounds of waves and song. Mtsyri's dream of a singing goldfish occurs at the very end of his adventures. Mtsyri faints and dreams of lying on the bottom of the river. The golden fish swims above him and sings him a song of love. In this trance, Mtsyri hears his favorite sounds, the stream's murmur merging harmoniously with the song of a golden fish. Mtsyri experiences the vision in a passive state of delirium; this passivity is one of the reasons why this transcendent moment is neglected by critics, drawn as they are to the active side of the Romantic hero.[22]

To lie on the bottom of the river and to hear the melodic, rhythmical, peaceful murmur of waves is equivalent to lying in a cocoon, or in the fluid world of a mother's womb. Thus it is not surprising that the song of the goldfish takes the form of a mother's lullaby. The singer addresses Mtsyri as "my child" (*ditia moe*) (2:91); this apostrophe is reminiscent of "my dear child, sleep!" (*Spi, ditia moe rodnoe*) (1:38) from Lermontov's "The Cossack Lullaby" (1838). And indeed, the fish continues:

Усни, постель твоя мягка,
Порзрачен твой покров.
Пройдут года, пройдут века
Под говор чудных снов.
О, милый мой! не утаю,
Что я тебя люблю,
Люблю как вольную струю,
Люблю как жизнь мою.
(2:91)

(Go to sleep; your bed is soft, your blanket transparent. Years will pass, and so will the centuries, accompanied by the murmur of mysterious dreams. Oh, my dear, I cannot hide that I love you—love you as much as I love a free stream, as much as I love my own life.)

In "Mtsyri" and in numerous other poems Lermontov depicts a recurrent desire: to hear a tender song whose source is hovering above the protagonist. In "Mtsyri" it is not just a goldfish that gives expression to this paradigm. Mtsyri recalls his sisters leaning over his cradle: "my young sisters, the rays of their sweet eyes and the sound of their songs and words over my cradle" (2:79). Likewise, on his deathbed, Mtsyri expresses a similar desire: to have a brother or friend sing a song while leaning over him.

The desire for a lullaby is also expressed in Lermontov's celebrated poem "Alone I Walk Out on a Road" (1841):

Я б желел навеки так заснуть . . .
Чтоб всю ночь, весь день мой слух лелея,
Про любовь мне сладкий голос пел,
Надо мной чтоб вечно зеленея
Темный дуб склонялся и шумел.
(1:86)

(I would like to go to sleep forever . . . but in such a way that all night and all day, caressing my ears, a sweet voice would sing to me of love, and so that a dark eternally greening oak would lean over me and rustle.)

The poem returns again to the paradigmatic images of leaning over, caressing, and singing.[23]

Mtsyri's desire is an organic part of Lermontov's oeuvre. The only thing that truly pacifies the anxiety of Lermontov's lyrical hero is sweet, tender, caressing sounds that transcend the hero's present enslavement. Through poetic reverie Mtsyri finds a way to recover lost bliss; Mtsyri's recovery comes not through the violence of erotic possession, or rivalry, but through harmonious sounds. There are certain songs, sounds, and rhythms that can sing a lullaby to Mtsyri's soul and thus return all that has been lost, at least temporarily.[24]

Mtsyri's Refusals

Mtsyri is as strong, courageous, and anxious as Lermontov's other demonic heroes. Similar to Tamara, though, Mtsyri has a soul made of "living strings" (*zhivye struny*) (2:72). This fact enables him to transcend "the muddy vesture of decay," the walls that enclose his soul, and to recover his "dear land" again: "and I shall think that a friend or a brother . . . quietly sings to me about my dear country. And with this thought I'll fall asleep and shall not curse anyone" (*i stanu dumat' ia, chto drug il' brat . . . vpolgolosa poet on mne pro miluiu stranu. I s etoi mysliu ia zasnu, i nikogo ne proklianu*) (2:93). Mtsyri's poetic reveries provide his anguished soul with the tranquillity and nourishment for which the Demon and Pechorin so vainly strive. Mtsyri is thus able to live and die stoically and peacefully; no violence is committed in the process. Mtsyri, indeed, passes the initiatory test that Lermontov sets up for his ultimate hero.

Afterword: "The Man That Hath No Music in Himself . . ."

> Since naught so stockish, hard, and full of rage,
> But music for the time doth change his nature,—
> The man that hath no music in himself,
> Nor is not moved with concord of sweet sounds,
> Is fit for treasons, stratagems and spoils,
> The motions of his spirit are dull as night,
> And his affections dark as Erebus:
> Let no such man be trusted: —mark the music.
> —Shakespeare, *The Merchant of Venice*

MODIFYING WESTERN MODELS, utilizing various perspectives and literary genres, Lermontov produced a unique gallery of heroes, all striving to conduct themselves with integrity, self-reliance, and courage, but drastically different in two separate yet related aspects: their artistic sensibility and their attitudes toward other individuals. Thus Lermontov's characters cover a range of characteristics, from Arbenin and the Demon, who easily resort to evil and violence, to the person of Mtsyri, who flatly rejects any imposition of his will upon others.

Lermontov's ultimate hero, the orphan and exile Mtsyri, yearns for his lost motherland and is tormented by the same wound as are the Demon and Pechorin. Mtsyri, however, refrains from any evil action; he learns to accept his anxiety of loss courageously and stoically. As the analysis of his encounters with the beautiful girl and leopard reveals, Mtsyri declines to seek a solution to his inner loss through possession or aggression. Lermontov's poem underscores that Mtsyri's stoicism and integrity are sustained by his poetic nature. Mtsyri's aesthetic experiences during his escape allow him temporarily to regain his lost bliss, thus giving him the strength and courage to continue stoically until his death.

All of Lermontov's protagonists manifest a highly individualistic and antagonistic attitude toward the existing world and its creator. Whether in heaven, a monastery, or aristocratic society, they perceive themselves as prisoners and are tormented by a sense of loss: be it of love, honor, the motherland, or paradise. Both the soul that pines for lost heavenly sounds in "Angel," and the Demon tormented by memories of better days, suffer from the same affliction: the experience of "paradise lost," that is, of simultaneous bliss and loss. The resulting anxiety and pessimism appear to be a permanent feature of Lermontov's heroes.

Yet Lermontov, as psychologist, articulates a real insight when he demonstrates how the same intellectual outlook can produce drastically different results in different personalities. For Lermontov, philosophical outlook has less influence on actions than do personality traits. Such indifference to philosophical and ideological outlooks partly explains Lermontov's disdain for metaphysical discussions in *A Hero of Our Time*.

The reaction to losses differs drastically from Kalashnikov to Pechorin, from the Demon to Tamara, from Arbenin to Mtsyri. It is a person's artistic sensibility that seems to be key in defining personal conduct. A creative personality counterbalances or mediates the loss through art and song. The personality that lacks creativity is fruitless; it can only rebel and destroy. Those who lack the ability to transcend the anxieties, tensions, and inner void of their existence through art, resort instead to meaningless competition and amorous conquests.

Mtsyri's behavior amply demonstrates Lermontov's belief that interaction with the aesthetic dimension of existence in part determines one's conduct and even fate. Furthermore, I argue that even in such texts as *A Hero of Our Time*—that is, texts whose problematics are seemingly unrelated to issues of aesthetic experience—the conduct of the protagonists is still shaped by their artistic sensibility. It is important to stress and articulate this dimension of Lermontov's thought because it has not yet been adequately recognized in Lermontov scholarship.

I thus reconsider an oft-neglected character in *A Hero of Our Time*, one who, nevertheless, casts an important light on the aesthetic dimension of the novel, and thus on Pechorin's predicament: Doctor Werner, the character who comes as close as possible to being Pechorin's friend. Werner understands Pechorin better than anyone else, and also manifests a certain sympathy for him. Their differences, however, are illuminating. One of the first things we learn about the doctor is that "he is a skeptic and materialist, like almost all medical men, but he is also *a poet*, and this I mean seriously, he is *a poet in all his actions* and frequently in his utterings, although in all his life he never wrote two lines of verse" (91; my emphasis). There seems to be perfect understanding between Pechorin and Werner; they have similar convictions and attitudes: both are caustic, witty, cynical, contradictory. Both despise Grushnitsky. And yet, Werner is terrified by Pechorin's cruelty at the duel. Initially Werner "turn[s] away in horror" from Pechorin upon hearing his cruel comment "Finita la commedia!" (171) and then refuses to shake hands with Pechorin. Or as Pechorin describes it: "The doctor came in; his brow was furrowed; contrary to his custom, he did not give me his hand" (176). Pechorin tries to downplay it later, but in the process he adds this most damaging condemnation of himself: "That's the human being for you! . . . They help you, they advise you, they even approve of it . . . and afterwards they wash their hands of it, and turn indignantly from him who had the courage to take upon himself the entire burden of responsibility. They are all like that, even the kindest, even the most intelligent ones" (177).

Pechorin's wording is correct: Werner is a "human being" and thus he turns indignantly from Pechorin, not regardless of his kindness ("they are all like that, even the kindest"), but *because* of it. He also turns away because he is "a poet in all his actions" and thus cannot shake "the merciless hand" of a murderer, even if he shares Pechorin's convictions as well as the same attitude toward Grushnitsky. In Lermontov's world, "the merciless hand" cannot belong to a poet: it can belong only to those who kill poets. In his poem "Death of a Poet" (*Smert' poeta*) Lermontov attributes such a hand to Onegin and D'Anthès, that is, to the two duelists who killed Lensky and Pushkin, fictional and real-life poets. Werner, better than anyone, explains why at his own duel the poet Lermontov did not even take aim at his murderer, Martynov.

The fact that Werner is called a poet is crucial to an understanding of the novel. For one, it is Pechorin who calls him a poet, which is especially significant since Pechorin is much more likely to deny a person self-proclaimed qualities than to attribute nonexistent ones. Also, behind Pechorin's words stands Lermontov himself, who as a poet would of course not use the word indiscriminately. Werner, we learn, has in fact never written a line of verse; thus his being characterized a "poet" obviously refers not to his profession, but rather to his psychological makeup. Through the image of Werner, Lermontov stresses that a poet (which literally means "maker") is a creator and as such must exhibit a revulsion toward destruction. It is also telling that Werner is a doctor: he might draw caricatures of his patients, but he heals them and cries over them.

The significance of Werner, one of the most important figures in "Princess Mary," is usually downplayed by scholars. S. Durylin, B. M. Eikhenbaum, and I. L. Andronnikov dutifully report that Werner's prototype was one Doctor Meyer, a friend of the Decembrists, as if the existence of a literary prototype could explain anything by itself. One of the greatest Lermontov scholars, Victor Manuilov, states confidently in his commentary on the novel: "Doctor Werner is the only character in the tale who has a definitive prototype" (Manuilov 1966, 182). Such commentaries, insufficient at best, appear in fact to be erroneous. According to Nikolai Ogarev (1956), the real Doctor Meyer was an extremely religious man; he was also madly in love with a woman whose departure broke his heart (389–90). These facts have no correspondence in the text of the novel: in fact they are contradicted by it. Nor is there anything more than a superficial physical resemblance between Meyer and Werner. One is also surprised to learn that Doctor Meyer, upon reading Lermontov's novel, managed to be offended by such a warm and wonderful character as Werner and said of Lermontov: "Pauvre sire, pauvre talent" (quoted in Manuilov 1966, 186). The attitude expressed by this comment indicates convincingly that the similarities between Doctor Meyer and Werner, especially in the intellectual and moral areas, have been exaggerated. Werner, in my opinion, is more similar to Lermontov himself than to an obscure doctor with Decembrist leanings, a doctor who as a friend of Marlinsky entertained the latter in his house when Marlinsky visited Kislovodsk. It is Werner's actions that carry the moral weight capable of condemning Pechorin. The presence of Werner within the novel reveals that Lermontov finds Pechorin wanting for the same reason that he found the Demon wanting: not so much because of his strength, pride, or excessive individualism—faults traditionally ascribed to Lermontov's heroes—but because of his sterility, insensitivity toward creation, and thus, his unrestrained potential toward violence. By juxtaposing Werner and Pechorin, Lermontov reveals that the failure to partake of or appreciate the harmony of the world (consider the Demon's indifference to the beauty of creation), quickly turns into violence and destruction. To downplay the significance of Werner by reducing him to his false prototype is to miss entirely Lermontov's point.

In fact, the exploration of the conflict between two like-minded people, one of whom is gentle and artistic, the other active and heartless, is not limited to Lermontov's novel. His early play, *Two Brothers* (1835), features two brothers, Iuri and Alexander, both sarcastic and disillusioned, who nevertheless react differently to the same predicament: the loss of the woman they both love. Alexander resorts to lies and treachery in his despair: his more poetic brother Iuri, having confronted evil and deception, faints rather than create more destruction.

Alexander Radin, the demonic protagonist of the play, like so many Lermontovian heroes, has a monologue that lays bare the tragic flaw of all Lermontov's destructive characters:

> Alone, always alone, ostracized like Cain, God knows for what crime. And then for once, to encounter something like love—only once and even then to know that I owe it to my skills, or to chance . . . and finally, against one's will, to surrender to a miraculous and sweet feeling—then to lose it all, to be alone again with the same poisonous doubt in my breast, with the eternal doubt, which does not recognize any borders. . . . Why are my most ordinary feelings dead? Why, even now, at the most decisive moment of my life, is my heart calm, my mind refreshed, my head cool. . . . It seems that I was created this way, it seems that some *resounding string is somehow missing* from my heart. (3:372; my emphasis)

Alexander's predicament is reenacted in Arbenin, Pechorin, the Demon: an ostracized and lonely hero hopes to transcend loss through love. Alexander falls in love against his own better judgment; the ensuing failure leads to an even greater loss. Alexander's monologue echoes the Demon's own cruelty and inability to forget, the cold reasoning of Arbenin, and Pechorin's remarks on his icy head and heart.

Alexander, however, reveals a cause of his plight: a "resounding string" (*zvuchnaia struna*) is absent from his heart. It is a rather convincing diagnosis, and one that recalls Shakespeare's warning:

> The man that hath no music in himself,
> Nor is not moved with concord of sweet sounds,
> Is fit for treasons, stratagems and spoils,
> The motions of his spirit are dull as night,
> And his affections dark as Erebus.

Alexander is aware that he is not a selfish villain. Nevertheless, because the string is absent, he must replay the fate of all his demonic doubles: loneliness, an attempt at salvation through love, crime, destruction, and a new loss. The resounding string is a metaphor for the potential to respond creatively to the challenges of loss. Tamara's soul is described as made of special "living strings" (*zhivye struny*): "The Creator has made the living strings [of their souls] from the best ether" (*Tvorets iz luchshego efira sotkal zhivye struny ikh*) (2:72). Lermontov's diction is important here. The strings are characterized as "living"; they bring the soul to life. By contrast, Alexander's soul lacks this string; his emotions have withered, making him nothing more than a murderous Cain, as he characterizes himself in his monologue.

In his translation of Byron's poem "Hebrew Melody" Lermontov introduces an image absent from the original and thus obviously crucial for Lermontov. Translating Byron's phrase "And let thy gentle fingers fling its [the lute's] melting murmurs o'er mine ear" into "let your fingers, having run upon it [the lute] awaken *the sounds of paradise within the strings*" (*Puskai persty tvoi, promchavshisia po nei, probudiat v strunakh zvuki raia*) (1:282), Lermontov creates an image of strings that have the power to awaken the sounds of paradise. These strings can produce sounds capable of relieving Saul's pain, a pain that arises in his "dark soul" (1:282). Unfortunately, neither the Demon, Alexander Radin, nor Pechorin possesses the resounding string that can reawaken the sense of paradise and thus assuage the demonic torment of their "dark souls."

For Lermontov, it is poetry, the paradisiacal sounds of strings, that can resolve the ancient tension among truth, goodness, and beauty. In his celebrated poem "When the Yellow Field Is Moving" (*Kogda volnuetsia zhelteiushchaia niva*) (1837) Lermontov speaks explicitly about this merging of moral, philosophical, and aesthetic experience:

> И счастье я могу постигнуть на земле,
> И в небесах я вижу Бога.
>
> (1:28)

> (And I can comprehend happiness on Earth, and see God in Heaven.)

Thus, the happiness that constantly eludes Lermontov's characters is granted to the lyrical persona alone, in aesthetic experience.

Lermontov perceived poetry in terms reminiscent of Baratynsky's famous dictum: "the suffering spirit is cured by singing" (*boliashchii dukh vrachuet pesnopenie*) (Baratynsky 1989, 167). Creating poetry about the most grave matters mitigates, alleviates, and harmonizes one's perception of the world. It is in his own poetic texts that Lermontov achieves this simultaneous awareness of both good and evil that so frequently eludes his protagonists. Similar to his creation Tamara, who responds to demonic temptation with song and dance, Lermontov overcomes the temptations of his demons through art. He thus manages to resist both the historical pessimism that pervades his "Song of Kalashnikov, and the religious, social, and intellectual pessimism that pervades his other texts. Yet, if poetry is the only sustaining force in Lermontov's universe, then the poet's plight is inevitably precarious. Lermontov's well-known poem "I Am Sad and Weary" (*I skuchno i grustno*) (1840) expresses the predicament of a lyrical persona who is no longer "moved by the concord of sweet sounds." Granted that Lermontov describes this persona in poetry, one may still wonder what would happen to a poet when poetic words are no longer to be found. As Lermontov's great contemporary Nikolai Gogol once asked: "If even music were to abandon us, what would happen to our world?" (1952, 8:13). Lermontov's death, which occurred some two years after the composition of "I Am Sad and Weary," suggests a rather grim answer. One can also recall here the tragic death of Alexander Blok—whom Korney Chukovsky called "the Lermontov of our epoch" (Chukovsky 1976, 129)—and Blok's complaint that "all sounds have stopped" (Chukovsky 1980, 247).

Notes

All citations in Russian come from Lermontov (1984). Volume and page references appear in the text. All quotations from *A Hero of Our Time* are taken from Nabokov (1988, vol. 6). Page references appear in the text. Prose citations from Russian are given only in translation. Except where noted, all translations are my own. When I quote from a multivolume edition of a Russian author, the volume and page references appear in the text. For complete authors' names, titles, and publication data on works cited, see the Selected Bibliography.

CHAPTER ONE

1. There is a growing interest in the problem of individualism in the former Soviet Union. Terrified by the abuses of Soviet-style socialism and Soviet-style Marxist studies, Russian scholars have begun to explore alternative traditions; see Obolonsky (1994) or Kantor (1994). Both books contain what might be called a post-perestroika revisionism of traditional Soviet interpretations of Russian literature, history, and culture.

One can also refer to A. Ia. Gurevich (1990a, 1990b) or to P. S. Gurevich (1995).

Among the prerevolutionary Russian studies of the issues related to individualism and literature, one should single out Andreevich (1905) and Ivanov-Razumnik (1911).

2. In Golstein (1997), I argue that Gogol was much less willing to dismiss his hard-working characters than were his readers (243–57).

3. On Bulgakov see Meerson (1996).

4. According to Berdiaev (1939), "individuum is a naturalistic, biological, and sociological category. . . . It is characterized as the subordinated part of the whole and as the part that egoistically asserts itself" (31). Personality (*lichnost'*), on the other hand, is "not a naturalistic, but spiritual category . . . it is not a cell, and it does not enter into the organism as part of the whole. It is the primal integrity and unity . . . it is not part of the world, but it is correlated to the world, and it is correlated to God" (35). Berdiaev claims that "human being is a personality because God is a personality, and vice versa" (44). By establishing inexorable ties between God and man, Berdiaev fore-

grounds the connection between the very concept of the human person and the existence of God. He then defines heroism as true service to God: "asceticism is the response to the calling of God . . . a true asceticism connected with personality is the heroic element in man" (43). The well-known Russian theologian, Vladimir Lossky, admits that he has not "found what one might call an elaborated doctrine of the human person in patristic theology" (1985, 112). Lossky therefore models his view of personality on the idea of divine persons or hypostases in Trinitarian theology; the analogy with the Trinity results in the following dichotomy: "a person can be fully personal only in so far as he has nothing that he seeks to possess for himself, to the exclusion of others, i.e. when he has a common nature with others . . . otherwise we are in the presence of individuals, dividing nature among themselves" (106). In his earlier text, *Mystical Theology of the Eastern Church* (written in 1944), Lossky (1976) explains what "individ" means:

> the man who is governed by his nature and acts on the strength of his natural qualities, of his "character," is the least personal. He sets himself up as an individual, proprietor of his own nature, which he pits against the natures of others . . . thereby confusing person and nature. This confusion, proper to fallen humanity has a special name in the ascetic writing of the Eastern Church—*filavtia,* or, in Russian, *samost'.* (122)

5. In fact, the losses of the nineteenth century created a paradoxical situation. Depiction of heroism is possible in the climate of shared values: a hero is someone who embodies social and cultural values, be it the martyr of Christianity or a warrior of paganism. When such systems of values collapse, however, as they did during Romanticism, the search for heroes becomes endless, as nobody seems to agree about what constitutes one. Hence, Byron's ironic comment on the need for heroes at a time when "every year and month sends forth a new one." It is clear that the Byronic or "demonic" hero, as Goethe understood the term, could not reign for long and was bound to give way to various anti-heroes of modern literature. As Peter Thorslev (1962) has written, the Romantic period was "our last great age of heroes" (14–24).

6. On de Maistre in Russia see M. Stepanov (1937), Edwards (1977), and Berlin (1979, 57–81; 1991, 150–58).

7. According to Lukes (1973), Saint-Simon's disciples were the first to use the term *individualisme* systematically in order to refer to the set of ideas and attitudes underlying the modernity. They characterized the contemporary moment as the clash of opposing values: "disorder, atheism, individualism, and egoism" on the one hand, and "order, religion, association and devotion" on the other (7).

8. Furthermore, Tocqueville associated American democracy and individualism with a decline in artistic standards, prefiguring Russian aristo-

cratic dismissals of the West as a tyranny of the petite bourgeoisie with their petty property-oriented concerns and small artistic achievements.

Particularly revealing is the turnaround of Alexander Herzen, who began as a revolutionary leader and staunch defender of the individual rights of Russians. In exile, face to face with the Western bourgeoisie, he rapidly modified his position. Enraged by bourgeois culture and private property (which he saw as inexorably connected) Herzen was only too eager to dismiss Western achievements. Siding with the Slavophiles, he began to see the Russian peasant commune as a fertile ground for achieving "individual'nost'." On the development of Herzen's views, see Malia (1961).

9. Russian writers were destined to resuscitate the Counter-Reformation project well into the nineteenth century, as they continued to explore the dangers of separation, egotism, and autonomy, and continued to stress the need of some external guidance for human affairs. Indeed, Dostoevsky's famous novella, *Notes from the Underground* (1864), features what Watt (1996) describes as "a hero who was an emblem of individualism which fails" (137). Joseph Frank (1986) has recently underscored the Underground Man's connection to other champions of individualism/anti-individualism: "The term 'underground man' has become part of the vocabulary of contemporary culture, and this character has now achieved—like Hamlet, Don Quixote, Don Juan, and Faust—the stature of one of the great archetypal literary creations" (310).

Dostoevsky, we recall, characterized the Underground Man as an "anti-hero." Similar to the early myths of Faust and Don Juan, which were intended to undermine Renaissance heroism, Dostoevsky undermined the heroes of Romanticism (including those of Lermontov, to whom the Underground Man explicitly refers) by presenting an anti-hero who parodies and trivializes them. While defending the individual's freedom and autonomy, the Underground Man reenacts in his own life all the negative aspects traditionally ascribed to individualism: its self-centeredness, disorientation, alienation, and blind caprice. Echoing the fate of the early individualistic heroes who were glorified during the cultural upheavals of the Romantic period, Dostoevsky's paradoxical protagonist has acquired a new resonance within twentieth-century Western culture. Yet, in terms of the Russian situation, *Notes from the Underground* reinforced the Russian tendency to dismiss individualism as a dangerous Western import.

10. In a letter to V. P. Botkin of 9 February 1840, Belinsky (1978) writes: "the external circumstances are terrible, and the thought of them stings the soul. . . . What is in store for us? Only one thing: tears and grief for a lost paradise, and even that only at moments, and the usual state of awareness of one's fall into death and eternity" (9:307).

11. This belated development, as well as the powerful intellectual and cultural charge that Russians inherited from Romanticism, explains why

Romanticism remained a productive force in Russia, and produced great Romantic poets and individualists such as Mayakovsky or Tsvetaeva well into the twentieth century. The Western origin of individualism also explains why any proponent of individualism is frequently labeled as "non-Russian," and his or her views are frequently dismissed as nothing but pale copies of Byron, Stirner, or Nietzsche.

12. For a more detailed analysis of Russian attitudes toward human person, as articulated in the polemics between Westernizers and Slavophiles, see Ivanov-Razumnik (1911), as well as Walicki (1989).

13. The source of Slavophile doctrines might be the Russian religious and cultural tradition itself, as they themselves claimed, or the writings of German conservative Romantics, as suggested by various scholars, including Walicki (1989, 160–78), or it might be a combination of both. But even if the Slavophiles themselves were not at the origin of the Russian fears of separation and individualism, they dressed these fears in contemporary religious and philosophical terminology, and therefore left a lasting legacy on Russian cultural attitudes. Khomiakov (1994), for example, insisted on the impossibility of individual salvation: "nobody can be saved alone. The one who is saved, saves himself within the church, in unity with other members of the church" (15). He thus foreshadowed many other utopian dreams of communal salvation, be it Solov'ev's fascination with *vseedinstvo* (all-unity), or Fedorov's idea of the "common task" for all of the humanity, or Bolshevik insistence on the need for world revolution in order to achieve the ideal communist society. The results of the Slavophiles' powerful rhetoric can be seen in the Russian tendency to adorn words by adding the root "all" (*vse*) to them: (*vseobshchii, vsemirnyi, vsestoronnii, vsenarodnyi, vseob'emliushchii*), which is quite opposite to, say, English, where the tendency is to coin words with the root "self": the self, self-reliance, self-help. That such words are notoriously difficult to translate into other languages is quite revealing of the respective cultural attitudes.

14. Confirming Dumont's observation, Walicki (1989) points to certain similarities between the Slavophile dichotomy of a group of individuals versus the Orthodox unity of believers (*sobornost'*) and a similar opposition of *Gemeinschaft* (community) versus *Gesellschaft* (society, collective) found in the work of a German sociologist, Ferdinand Tonnies (168–78). I suggest, however, that these oppositions should be considered within an even wider context of what I would call the Romanticist revival of antinominalism; that is, an attempt on the part of the "holist" ideology to multiply and posit the existence of mysterious entities, far beyond necessity, thereby ignoring a still very useful intellectual tool known to philosophy: Occam's razor.

It is this Romanticist project that lies behind the creation of mysterious entities, such as "narod" (folk) imposed upon that of the nation, or *sobornost'* imposed upon that of a group. Later it will find expression in the opposition between the concepts of "individ" (individual) and "lichnost'" (person, personality).

This antinominalist impulse is nourished and supported by the doctrines of theology (such as Trinitarian and Christological doctrines, or the view of the Church as the mystical Body of Christ). Kantorowicz (1957) explores how the doctrine of the dual nature of Christ found its way into the very elaborate political and legal doctrine of the King's Two Bodies. Western political thought had obviously moved far beyond its medieval roots, so it is now very reluctant to apply theological doctrines to the legal or political spheres. Russian political and social thought, however, preserved many of the medieval features.

The medieval dimension of Russian thought was made particularly visible by the Slavophiles in their striving for holistic knowledge and their refusal to see the religious, political, social, and private spheres as truly separate. It is thus hardly surprising that the admirer of Slavophile thought I. A. Essaulov proudly insists that the medieval Russian text "The Sermon on Law and Grace" with its rejection of legalism in favor of love and grace already contains all the components of the Slavophile doctrine (1995, 28–33). Likewise, in his 1914 study of Dostoevsky, Viacheslav Ivanov (1994) utilizes the concept of *sobornost'* to describe the status of an individual during the Middle Ages, while connecting the Renaissance with the disintegration of this divine harmony:

> During the Middle Ages the human person (*lichnost'*) experienced itself as but a link in the hierarchy of *sobornost'*-like subordination (*sobornoe sopodchinenie*) to a common structure, which was presumed to reflect the hierarchical harmony of the Divine world. During the Renaissance, it [the person] tore itself away from this heavenly and earthly harmony, and felt itself as alienated, and, in this haughty alienation, as self-reliant and self-centered. (284)

Russian fascination with the Middle Ages, that is, with the period of preindividualist, holistic existence, can also be seen in Nikolai Berdiaev, who, in his 1924 essay "New Middle Ages," called for the establishment of the new ("irrational and trans-national") cultural paradigm modeled on the Middle Ages (1990, 3–35).

15. Andreevich (1905) approaches Russian literature specifically from the perspective of the "idea of individuality" (*ideia lichnosti*) and claims that throughout the nineteenth century the general attitude of Russian writers toward individuality and its freedom was that of hostility and suspicion.

16. Former and present literary figures, both in Russia and the West, might complain of the burdens and dangers of an overdeveloped ego, yet the historians and philosophers of the twentieth century are confronted by a more terrifying phenomenon: "the revolt of the masses" (Ortega y Gasset 1968). It is precisely the masses of nonindividualized people lacking ideolo-

gies or values of their own who create and support the terrible regimes responsible for endless destruction of human life.

CHAPTER TWO

1. For a recent analysis of this phenomenon see Russell (1986).

2. Dostoevsky (1972–90) often refers to Lermontov as "a demon," as, for example, in the following commentary:

> Another Demon—but we liked him even more than the first [Gogol]. . . . He cursed and suffered. He avenged and forgave, he wrote and burst into laughter, was magnanimous and ridiculous. . . . He was telling us his life, his love-adventures: it all looked as if he was mystifying us, now saying something seriously, now mockingly. . . . Finally he got bored with us, nowhere could he get along with anyone, he cursed us and laughed at us "with a bitter mockery of a deceived son at his bankrupt father" [Lermontov's "Meditation"]. . . . We followed him for a long time, but finally he perished somewhere—without a purpose, capriciously, and even ridiculously. (18:59)

It is curious that Dostoevsky's assessment contains the phrases used by the crowd in Lermontov's "The Prophet" (1841): "He was proud and could not get along with us" (*On gord byl, ne uzhilsia s nami*) (1:88). Lermontov was indeed a prophet to predict such a reaction toward himself, but even he would hardly predict such dismissal from a fellow writer, and a fellow prophet, for that matter. Solov'ev (1901) is even more categorical and judgmental and provides the following moralizing comment on Lermontov's tragic fate:

> I think that everyone would agree that to enjoy doing evil is already a non-human feature. Such demonic voluptuousness did not leave Lermontov till his bitter end . . . even his last tragedy occurred because Lermontov's joy at tormenting weak people had encountered, instead of a young lady, a brave major Martynov. . . . Soon this evil element took another direction in the life of Lermontov. As time went on, the demon of bloodthirstiness weakens, yielding the main part of its strength to its brother, the demon of impurity. (454)

3. N. P. Dashkevich (1914) and Boris Eikhenbaum (1987) provide valuable, if dated, explorations of Lermontov's connection with both the Western and Russian literary traditions. Boris Udodov's *M. Iu. Lermontov* (1973) is the most recent and most thorough book written on the same lines.

4. This feature of Lermontov's poem has been observed by Shaw (1958, 163–65) and Mann (1976, 131–33).

5. Lermontov endows his Demon with a very human psychological conflict: "Only in a man can the holy meet the sinful, all his torments are caused by it" (*lish' v cheloveke vstretit'sia mogli sviashchennoe s porochnym, vse ego muchen'ia proiskhodiat ottogo*) ("11 June") (1:208).

6. Eikhenbaum (1987) laments this fact, claiming that Lermontov's work is more primitive than that of its European precursors. In his "Literary Position of Lermontov," he writes: "Having been replanted into Russian soil, without its ties to the epic and narrative poems of the Middle Ages, this plotline has lost its richness, its theological metaphysical nature, and become much more primitive" (218). It is unclear why the lack of metaphysical philosophizing automatically makes a literary work more primitive. It does not occur to Eikhenbaum that Lermontov might be interested in psychology rather than metaphysics, and that to judge his plot by comparing it to something that Lermontov does not even try to emulate is shortsighted.

7. Most Soviet works fall, predictably, into this category, as the scholarship of Andronnikov or Udodov attests. Udodov collects vast background material on the cultural life of the period (1973, 213–435). His conclusions, however, are buried under the weight of this information. Furthermore, because of his propensity to explain everything through Marxist dialectics, Udodov converts Lermontov's poem into a poetic rendition of Herzen's, Hegel's, and Belinsky's thought.

8. The debates on the dates of various variants of "The Demon," as well as the more general question of whether the poem should be considered completed or not, seem to have abated. A majority of Soviet scholars agree now that the final version of Lermontov's poem was written at the end of 1838 (not in 1840 or 1841 as was thought for more than a century) and that Lermontov did not return to the poem after 1838. In his essay "The Last Variant of 'The Demon,'" Naidich (1971) argues this point convincingly (76).

9. The Demon admits to Tamara: "The gloomy amusement of malice did not please me for long" (*no zloby mrachnye zabavy nedolgo nravilisia mne!*) (2:63).

10. In the 1830 variant the Demon's emotions run the already familiar pattern: recovery of hope and love, an encounter with the angel, hostility and malice that is directed not at the angel but at the object of their contest:

И мщенье, ненависть и злоба
Взыграли демонской душой....
Красавице погибнуть надо,
Ее не пощадит он вновь—
Прежняя любовь
Не будет для нее оградой
(2:425)

(And revenge, hatred, and malice sent the Demon's soul into commotion. . . . The beauty has to perish, he is not going to save her again, their former love is not going to protect her.)

The poet adds that it is the encounter with the angel that turns the Demon back to evil: "But it is too late. The sinless son of paradise has awakened the rebellious mind, and it now boils with jealousy" (*no pozdno! Syn bezgreshnyi raia vdrug razbudil miatezhnyi um, kipit on revnost'iu pylaia*) (2:425–26). This comment on the fatal role of the angel should put to rest all the qualms of Shan-Girei. The interaction between love and anger that accompanies the psychic life of Lermontov's heroes is clearly brought to the surface.

11. Lermontov was long familiar with such tangled emotions, as "Justification" (*Opravdanie*) (1841) reveals: "the heart where blood was boiling, where love waged such insane, such vain battle with enmity" (*serdtse gde kipela krov', gde tak bezumno, tak naprasno s vrazhdoi borolosia liubov'*) (1:69).

12. The predicament of an exile is crucial to Lermontov's sensitivity: he populates his poetry with exiles, from the soul in "Angel" to Napoleon on Saint Helena, and to the poet who, according to his 1830 poem "Enough Excuses for Corruption" (*O, polno izviniat' razvrat*), should "be proud of being exiled from his motherland" (*izgnaniem iz strany rodnoi khvalis' povsiudu kak svobodoi*) (1:179). The literary predecessor of the exiled and ostracized Romantic outlaws is Cain. Byron, besides writing his mystery "Cain," referred to Cain in practically all of his works, revitalizing the image of this ostracized and rebellious character. Lermontov stresses not so much the crime of Cain's pride and rebellion, as the theme of exile and loneliness. As one of his characters observes: "I am alone, always alone, ostracized like Cain" (*Two Brothers*) (3:372). The Demon is the same kind of stranger and outsider.

13. The sense of loss and separation is echoed in the description of Tamara: the fate of a stranger and an exile awaits her after her marriage.

14. Lermontov's incessant anxiety (*trevoga*), which Blok (1962) interprets as his dominant emotion (29), is familiar to all Lermontov's readers. Compare Rozanov's (1990) remark on Lermontov: "Lermontov does not arrive anywhere, he simply goes away. . . . You always see him 'from the back.' No matter what 'harmony' you give him, no matter into what 'paradise' you place him, you'll see him heading for the door. . . . Pushkin would have been happy even in prison. *Lermontov would have been miserable even in paradise*"(192; my emphasis).

15. Granting that "paradise lost" is a popular literary trope and that the world will hardly disappoint anyone who views it tragically, Lermontov had his own personal reasons to be interested in this trope. The early death of Lermontov's mother personalized his vision of this Romantic topos. Lermontov lost his father at the same time, not to death but to the family arrangement that led him to move away and leave his child to the care of the grandmother. Lermontov's tragic vision, his awareness of the world's disunity and pain, probably received its initial jolt from his childhood trauma: the idealized bliss of the past is replaced by the misery and loneliness of the present; an appeal is answered with rejection, hope with despair. Taken by

itself, political tyranny or oppression does not automatically make a tragic poet. As Rozanov (1990) suggests, both Pushkin and Lermontov shared the same political and social situation, yet their outlook is quite different. The Demon experienced loss and anxiety even in paradise, after all.

Many psychological works have concentrated on the experience of bereavement and loss in childhood. A specialized field of research explores the dynamics of attachment and loss, a field pioneered by the British psychiatrist, John Bowlby. Bowlby's (1969–80) major work is a three-volume study, *Attachment and Loss.* Volume 1 is subtitled *Attachment;* volume 2, *Separation: Anxiety and Anger;* and volume 3, *Loss: Sadness and Depression.* In contrast to Freud, Bowlby sees attachment as the primal element of human psyche. According to him, a child's need for attachment is unconnected to its need for nourishment; the mother provides not just material objects, like food or shelter, but also "bonding." Bowlby's research shows that many psychic problems are caused not by the "subconscious trauma" construed by Freud, but by the way the bond between the mother figure and the child is maintained on an everyday basis. According to Bowlby's empirical studies, early loss of the figure of attachment has many grave consequences, including the inability to create new bonds due to the fear of another loss.

16. Here another similarity with Cain is relevant: the Demon is called "first born" (*pervenets tvorenia*), and so his hatred for the angel is the hatred for an interloper who takes what rightfully belongs to the Demon. Lermontov selected lines from Byron's "Cain" as the epigraph to one of the earlier variants of "The Demon."

17. Referring to Pechorin's confession to princess Mary, Debreczeny (1973) correctly observes: "This confession, like the Demon's speech, should not be taken at face value since it is made with the explicit purpose of impressing the heroine. . . . Yet to say that Pechorin didn't mean what he says would be oversimplification" (95).

18. The desire to regain paradise through love is typical of various speakers in Lermontov's poetry. The speaker of "Stanzas to D°°°" (1831) declares to his beloved: "Did others search for their paradise in you alone as I did?—Hardly!" (*Kak ia, uzhel' oni iskali svoi rai v tebe odnoi?—edva li!*) (1:233), while that of "Tormented by Anxiety and Affliction" (*Izmuchennyi toskoiu i nedugom*) (1832) reveals to his lover that she "meant for [him] what the happiness of paradise meant for a demon, this exile of heaven" (*Ty dlia menia byla kak schastie raia dlia demona, izgnannika nebes*) (1:258).

19. In his essay on "The Demon" Mann (1976) observes the complex nature of Lermontov's image of poison, which includes the poisonous kiss, but he fails to explain it (225–26).

Tamara's namesake in the Bible, beautiful Tamar, is raped by her brother Amnon, who then loathes her: "Then Amnon hated her exceedingly; so that the hatred wherewith he hated her was greater than the love wherewith he had loved her" (2 Sam. 13:15). Like the Demon, Amnon confuses the state of bliss with the sexual possession. He realizes his mistake, but it is already too late; Tamar is ruined and Amnon is eventually killed by his brother, Absalom.

20. In his 1837 poem "To the Neighbor" (*Sosedu*) Lermontov connects confinement and a song. In this poem a prisoner responds to the songs of another prisoner. The emotions of the listener come alive, the sense of bliss is resurrected in his soul:

> Я слушаю и в мрачной тишине
> Твои напевы раздаются.
> О чем они—не знаю; Но тоской
> Исполнены, и звуки чередой,
> Как слезы, тихо льются, льются. . . .
> И лучших лет надежды и любовь—
> В груди моей все оживают вновь,
> И мысли далеко несутся,
> И полон ум желаний и страстей,
> И кровь кипит—и слезы из очей,
> Как звуки, друг за другом льются
> (1:27–28)

> (I listen, and in dark silence your songs resound. What are they about?—I don't know; but they are filled with yearning, and their sounds pour quietly like tears. . . . And the hopes and love of better days reawaken in my breast, and my thoughts are borne to places far away, and my mind is full of desires and passions, and my blood is boiling, and the tears, like the sounds, keep on pouring from my eyes.)

In contrast to the prisoner, the Demon sheds only one tear: "And what a miracle—a heavy tear rolls out of his darkened eyes" (*i chudo: iz pomerkshikh glaz sleza tiazhelaia katitsia*) (2:59). It is at that moment that the Demon wants to reject his plan to seduce her, but one tear is not enough to revive his soul and to break the cycle of loss and possessiveness.

21. Tamara's song in the 1834 version of the poem is in a different meter from the rest of the poem. Its rhythmic scheme—alternate anapestic and amphibrachic lines—repeats the rare and sophisticated rhythmic scheme of "The Mermaid" (1832). Lermontov also uses this scheme in his most personal poems, such as "Hebrew Melody" (1830) or "Angel" (1831).

CHAPTER THREE

1. Z. S. Efimova (1927) quotes Russian scholars Borozdin, Vladimir Fisher, and Boris Eikhenbaum, all of whom view the play as a failure and attribute the play's shortcomings to the Romantic disposition of its author. Compare Fisher's comment that "lyricism of his spirit prohibited Lermontov

from creating an original drama" or Borozdin's that "Lermontov's talent, like that of Byron, was rather incompatible with the dramatic form" (Efimova 1927, 26).

2. *"Je sens que mon âme s'est tout-a-fait développée, je puis créer"*—Pushkin to N. N. Raevsky in July 1825 (Pushkin 1962, 10:163).

3. On the proliferation of texts that accompanied the gambling mania of the period, see Vinogradov " (1936, 74–148).

4. In his study of "Queen of Spades," Iuri Lotman (1992) explores the role of cards in Russian culture and society. Lotman, however, pays more attention to the gambling mania of the eighteenth century and its connection to the cultural climate created by Catherine the Great than to the post-Decembrist situation (389–416). Lotman quotes the gamblers of *The Masquerade*, yet he prefers to stress the randomness of the card-domain, neglecting the fact that in Lermontov's play gambling presupposes control, manipulation, and calculation. By contrast, Iuri Mann (1987) correctly notices that gambling in the play has little to do with the exploration of "randomness," but much to do with the art of deception (209–37).

5. I. N. Ignatov, a scholar of Russian theater, commenting on the incredibly popular 1828 staging of Ducange's *Thirty Years or the Life of a Gambler*, writes:

> Romanticism arrived, saw, and conquered the Russian scene—from that moment on robbers, villains, poison, knives, daggers, murders, and betrayals take over. . . . It seems that the natural evolution from Shakhovskoi, Zagoskin, Fedorov, and others toward Griboedov will culminate in the emergence of a solid and realistic Russian theater. . . . But 1825 ends, a new era begins, the frightened spectator shrinks and returns to his slumber, the demand disappears, and the Russian theater does not materialize. (quoted in Efimova 1927, 27)

6. The latest discussion of Lermontov's treatment of theatricality is presented in Todd (1986, 152–61). Earlier Lermontov scholars, such as V. Vinogradov, N. Diakonova, John Mersereau, Richard Peace, and C. J. G. Turner have also touched upon the theme of theatricality.

7. Iuri Mann appears to be the only scholar who takes Lermontov's play seriously (1987, 209–27). Even though my analysis differs, I profited from his insightful reading of the play.

8. An early scholar of Decembrism, Iulian Oksman, noted that Belinsky's writings contain not a single reference to the Decembrist uprising. This is surprising, as Belinsky was a courageous person, and the Decembrists were among the most prominent people of the period, well known to anyone in the cultural scene (quoted in Belinkov 1987, 194).

9. For the generic features of a Byronic hero, see Thorslev (1962).

10. For Lermontov's debt to Griboedov, see A. V. Fedorov (1967, 171–95).

11. On the division of Romanticism into what he calls "high Romanticism" and its later, more subdued period, see Nemoianu (1984).

12. It is most likely that the initial impetus for Arbenin's self-revelation came from a popular book titled *Life of a Gambler Described by Himself, or the Revelation of the Secrets of Gambling. Russian Composition* (*Zhizn' igroka, opisannaia im samim, ili Otkrytie khitrosti kartochnoi igry. Rossiiskoe sochinenie*) (1827). This book provides the following recipe for success in gambling:

> Only someone cunning, deft, and unscrupulous is capable of it [success in gambling]. He must be shrewd, cautious, prudent, and modest in regard to his skill. He has to give the impression of being a connoisseur of everything. . . . He has to be—depending on circumstances—a prankster or philosopher, a spendthrift or a tightwad. He has to be tender, angry, explosive, meek, good-natured, or magnanimous. (quoted in Shakhovskoi 1961, 794)

13. One might question the relevance of all the parallels discussed by Vadim Vatsuro (1994), yet it is telling that Salieri uses poison as his murder weapon. Salieri claims to know it all—"I know it, I"—and strives to improve upon both earthly and heavenly laws. He compares himself to a snake: "I am like a snake, crushed by people, biting in vain the sand and dust." He evokes the imagery of Genesis: "Upon thy belly shalt thou go, and dust shalt thou eat all the days of thy life. And I will put enmity between thee and the woman, and between thy seed and her seed; it shall bruise thy head, and thou shalt bruise his heel" (Gen. 3:14–15).

According to the biblical account the serpent was not only the wisest of all beasts, but also introduced the first couple to the knowledge of good and evil. In other words, the connection between wisdom and knowledge on the one hand and poison on the other goes back to the first chapters of human history. Pushkin and Lermontov only highlight what was there from the beginning: intellectual pride turns both Salieri and Arbenin into vessels of a poison that ruins them as it poisons others.

14. On the subject of literature and gnostic thought, especially in its American manifestation, see Bloom (1976, 1982). Cantor (1984) explores the relationship of gnosticism and English Romanticism; Cantor's work is by far more relevant to the problematics of Russian Romanticism than is Harold Bloom's. Butler (1989) discusses the attraction of dualistic Manichaeism for both Shelley and Byron.

The classic book on gnosticism is Hans Jonas, *The Gnostic Religion* (1963). A recent work that incorporates Nag Hammadi discoveries is Rudolph (1983). In my discussion I follow Cantor's terminology. He uses the term "gnosticism" to describe a general heretical outlook now and then resurfacing in the history of religious thought, as opposed to "Gnosticism," the teachings of the original Gnostics.

15. Lermontov's 1831 poem "Angel," his first masterpiece, describes a soul that preserves forever the memory of the heavenly music it heard when being transported into this world.

16. On Byron and gnosticism, see Cantor (1984, esp. 135–55 and 214–16). Cantor cites a letter in which Byron calls himself Manichean. It is also well known that Blake studied Gnostic writings.

CHAPTER FOUR

1. Yazykov (1988), responding to the proliferation of fairy tales, begins his "Fairy-Tale about the Shepherd and the Wild Boar" (*Skazka o pastukhe i dikom vepre*) (1835) in the following manner: "Why don't I write a fairy tale? Nowadays this type of poetry is in fashion in our land. And it is not a sin to take from your own people a half-forgotten short story" (*Dai napishu ia skazku! Nynche moda na etot rod poezii u nas. I grekh li vziat' u svoego naroda poluzabytyi nebol'shoi rasskaz*) (380). Lermontov himself once remarked: "But if ever I become interested in folk poetry, I surely shall not search for it anywhere else except in Russian songs" (4:353).

2. I am not aware of any other article devoted solely to "The Song" except Mersereau (1960). The author is correct in insisting that Pushkin's duel is related to the genesis of "The Song," yet I do not find convincing either Mersereau's conjecture that "The Song" is an allegory of Pushkin's death, or the motives he attributes to Lermontov for wanting to write such an allegory. Garrard (1982) discusses "The Song" along with other narrative poems by Lermontov. My reading of the poem questions several of Garrard's observations, including: "['The Song'] stands out among Lermontov's narrative poems for its consistent narrative viewpoint"; "For once, we need not filter a work of Lermontov's through his personality"; and "Furthermore, far from being rebellious, Kalashnikov is a devoted subject of the Tsar" (113–19). Schulz (1992) also offers insightful comments on "The Song."

3. See Vatsuro (1976), Azadovsky (1941), Shtokmar (1941), and Mendel'son (1914).

4. For example, this is how Lominadze (1985) justifies the execution of Kalashnikov: "In other words, 'sacred Russia' needs the living Kalashnikovs, but for Russia's sake and with fateful inevitability they have to be executed from time to time" (157).

5. The organization of poems in this collection is not chronological, although all the poems date from 1836 or later. Apparently some other ordering principle is at play in the organization and selection of material. Strangely, the content and order of the collection have been neglected in all editions of Lermontov, despite the complaints of scholars such as Vatsuro or Lominadze. Even they fail to provide the table of contents of the original collection. The organization of the collection is an important tool for Ler-

montov research. Even if the editor, Kraevsky, contributed to the organization of the collection, credit for the bulk of the selection and organization belongs to Lermontov. Thus, major conclusions should not be drawn from the early poetry that Lermontov never intended to publish.

Here is the list of Lermontov's poems as they appeared in his collection:

1. The Song of the Tsar Ivan Vasilievich (1837)
2. Borodino (1837)
3. Prisoner (*Uznik*) (1837)
4. The Prayer (*Molitva: Ia, Mater' Bozhiia, nynche s molitvoiu . . .*) (1837)
5. Meditation (*Duma*) (1838)
6. Mermaid (*Rusalka*) (1836)
7. The Branch from Palestine (*Vetka Palestiny*) (1837)
8. Don't Believe Yourself (*Ne ver' sebe*) (1839)
9. Hebrew Melody (*Evreiskaia melodiia*) (1836)
10. Like a Lonely Grave (*Kak odinokaia grobnitsa*) (1836)
11. Three Palm Trees (*Tri palmy*) (1839)
12. A Prayer (*Molitva: V minutu zhizni trudnuiu*) (1839)
13. Gifts of Terek (*Dary Tereka*) (1839)
14. To The Memory of Prince Odoevsky (*Pamiati A. Odoevskogo*) (1839)
15. How Often Surrounded by the Multicolored Crowd . . . (*Kak chasto, pestroiu tolpoiu okruzhen . . .*) (1840)
16. A Cossack Lullaby (*Kazachiia kolybelnaia*) (1840)
17. Journalist, Reader, and Writer (*Zhurnalist, chitatel' i pisatel'*) (1840)
18. The Aerial Ship (*Vozdushnyi korabl'*) (1840)
19. It is Sad and Tedious . . . (*I skushno i grustno . . .*) (1840)
20. To a Child (*Rebenku*) (1840)
21. Why? (*Otchego?*) (1840)
22. Gratitude (*Blagodarnost'*) (1840)
23. From Goethe (*Iz Gete*) (1840)
24. Mtsyri (1839)
25. When the Yellow Field Is Wavering (*Kogda volnuetsia zhelteiushchaia niva*) (1837)
26. The Neighbor (*Sosed*) (1837)
27. We Separated, but Your Portrait . . . (*Rasstalis' my no tvoi portret . . .*) (1837)
28. Clouds (*Tuchi*) (1840)

6. Violation of an established order and mood also form the basis of the next two confrontations: Alyona is not at home after church and thus fails to perform her duties, and Kalashnikov destroys the festivities by killing Kiribeevich and turning the holiday entertainment into a personal vendetta.

7. See the discussion of problems connected with the dating of "The Song" in Andronnikov's commentary to the poem (2:490–91).

8. On his deathbed Pushkin received a note from Nicholas I in which the tsar promised the poet complete financial support for his family. Nicholas also compensated the widow of his other poet-victim, the Decembrist Ryleev (O'Meara 1984, 309).

9. Mersereau here reiterates the idea first developed in his 1960 article on "The Song."

10. "According to Lermontov's words, his poetry was distributed in the city by one of his friends whom he refused to identify" (quoted in Manuilov 1964, 72).

11. In Lermontov's defense it must be added that Raevsky had already been arrested and admitted his participation in the dissemination of the poem. He even wrote a letter to Lermontov advising him on what to admit. The letter was intercepted and became the main cause of the tsar's anger against Raevsky. At the time Lermontov knew nothing of this, and so continued to write and ask Raevsky's forgiveness. Lermontov's grandmother, who saw his torment, tried to use her influence to ameliorate Raevsky's situation, and was ultimately successful.

12. Nicholas I's ongoing attempt to control the inner world of his subjects was demonstrated in his handling of the Decembrist investigation. Nicholas played the role of God or at least spiritual father to his subjects, by eliciting the most private information from them and by using even their confessions to priests to resolve the problems of the state (Mazour 1964, 203–9). Not only does Lermontov's Kalashnikov preserve his integrity and honor in dealing with the tsar, something that most of the Decembrists failed to do, but also the poem's tsar, Ivan, seems to respect such integrity, unlike Nicholas I. As leader of a state Ivan the Terrible punishes Kalashnikov, but he does not try to play the role of religious confessor.

On the sacralization of the monarch, which was very much alive in Russia even at the time of Nicholas I, see Cherniavsky (1961), as well as Wortman (1995). Zhivov and Uspensky (1987) also contains some fascinating observations.

13. In a comment that should highlight Kalashnikov's pride and dignity Golovin (1970) refers to the joy experienced by one whose wife was chosen by a member of the royal family (59). When Kiribeevich announces to Alyona that he is a servant to the tsar he simply uses the most powerful argument available to a seducer.

14. The exact date of the composition of "Borodino" is not known. It has usually been thought that the poem was written before Pushkin's death. See, for example, Manuilov (1981) who dates the poem before Pushkin's death, judging solely "by the mood and the tone of the poem" (68). From these two features it would be more apt to draw the opposite conclusion. In the latest edition of Lermontov's collected works the editor, Andronnikov, places "Borodino" after "The Death of the Poet" on the strength of Raevsky's

draft explanation to the authorities where Raevsky writes that Lermontov, inspired by the success of his "Death of the Poet," also composed "Borodino." Although Raevsky may not be the most trustworthy witness (in the same letter he mistakenly attributes an earlier poem to the same period), I am inclined to trust him in this instance. That "Borodino" was published in Pushkin's *Sovremennik* (May 1837) in the second issue after Pushkin's death also suggests that Lermontov meant the poem as a response to Pushkin's death.

15. Tolstoy detects a similar seriousness and lack of interest toward "fun" in Lermontov himself. Tolstoy once remarked: "He began at once as one endowed with power. He has no cute jokes. . . . It is not difficult to write such jokes, but each of his words was the word of a man with power" (quoted in Leusheva 1964, 413).

16. Compare

Пусть монастырский ваш зкаон
Рукою Бога утвержден,
Но в этом сердце есть другой,
Ему не менее святой:
Он оправдал меня—один
Он сердца полный властелин!
(2:331)

(Even if your monastery law was established by the hand of God, this heart has another one, no less sacred. It [the law] has acquitted me, and it is the full master of my heart.)

17. To exemplify Lermontov's stance vis-à-vis earthly and heavenly power Lominadze makes an ingenious comparison between "There are Speeches" (*Est' rechi*) (1840) and Pushkin's "A Poet and the Rabble" (*Poet i tolpa*) (1828):

Pushkin:
Не для житейского волненья,
Не для корысти, не для битв.
Мы рождены для вдохновенья,
Для звуков сладких и молитв.

(Neither for everyday commotion
Nor for greed or battles.
We are born for inspiration,
For sweet sounds and prayers)

Lermontov:
Не кончив молитвы
На звук тот отвечу,
И брошусь из битвы
Ему я на встречу.

(Before I have finished the prayer
I'll respond to that sound,
And I'll abandon the battlefield
To rush toward it)

Lominadze correctly observes that while in Pushkin prayers are preferred to and opposed to battles—that is, the divine realm is elevated above the worldly—in Lermontov there is something else (sounds of speech) opposed to both realms, that of prayer and that of battle (Lominadze 1985, 85).

18. Lermontov, like Kalashnikov, uses in his explanation the notion of "a guilty head" (*povinnaia golova*). Both he and Kalashnikov adhere to and defend their truths, but they also experience a certain guilt. They accept that their unusual actions can be viewed by the world as criminal. The Russian proverb "A sword does not cut the head of anyone who admits his guilt" (*povinnuiu golovu mech ne sechet*), suggested by the expression *povinnaia golova,* is ironic in Kalashnikov's case—his head *is* chopped off after all.

19. Having decided to fight, Kalashnikov must ask his brothers to challenge Kiribeevich in case of his failure, since they "are less sinful and maybe God will spare [them]" (*Na vas men'she grekhov nakopilosia, tak avos' Gospod' vas pomiluet*) (2:15). Before the execution he asks them to pray for his "sinful soul." He also acknowledges his guilt before the tsar: "Order for me to be executed and bring my guilty head to the execution block" (*Prikazhi menia kaznit'—i na plakhu nest' mne golovushku povinnuiu*) (2:18).

20. Kalashnikov's proud answer to the tsar is a marked signal not only within the text (it differs from the two other responses to interrogation) but also deviates from folk songs that feature similar encounters with the tsar. Vladimirov (1892) refers to a number of folk songs in which criminals respond to the interrogation of the tsar, who either executes or forgives them, yet all of them make a response (18–19). Here is one example, similar yet so different from Lermontov's poem:

Повели младца в каменну Москву,
Ко Грозну Царю.
Как и стал Царь младца спрашивати:
"Ты скажи, скажи, удалый молодец,
Ты за что убил мово подручника,
Молодого мово опричника?
—Я скажу тебе, православный Царь.
Я за то убил зла Татарченка,
Молодого твово опричника:
Я убил его за дурны дела.

(They took the young lad to Moscow, to Ivan the Terrible. And the tsar began his interrogation: "tell me you, stout fellow, why did you kill my servant, my young oprichnik?"—I'll answer you, orthodox tsar. I killed the evil Tartar, your young oprichnik, for his evil deeds.)

21. The upbeat mood of terms such as "warrior," "cheerfully," "young," "daredevil," and "carefree" give way to the tender "dear head" (*golovushka*) and the implied sorrow, violence, and shame of terms such as "vicious," "shameful," "hapless," "death," "blood," or "execution block."

22. A nameless grave often functions as a source of inspiration for Lermontov. Many heroes of his verse, such as Napoleon or Alexander Odoevsky, are buried in unknown graves. In his translation of Byron's "Lines Written in

an Album at Malta" (1809), Lermontov changes Byron's "As o'er the cold sepulchral stone some name arrests the passer-by" into "as the lonely grave arrests the attention of the passer-by" (*kak odinokaia grobnitsa vnimanie putnika zovet*) (1:283).

23. In *A Hero of Our Time* Lermontov sustains his critique and has Pechorin state that his contemporaries cannot even have convictions, let alone act according to them:

> What strength of will they [past generations] derived from the certitude that the entire sky with all its countless inhabitants was looking upon them with mute but permanent sympathy! Whereas we, their miserable descendants, who roam the earth without convictions or pride . . . we are no longer capable of great sacrifice, neither for the good of mankind, nor even for our own happiness, because we know its impossibility, and pass with indifference from doubt to doubt, just as our ancestors rushed from one delusion to another. (188)

24. An excellent survey of other literary and historical sources can be found in Shtokmar (1941). The song "Mastruk Mastrukovich" from Kirsha Danilov's collection of folk songs, *Ancient Russian Poems* (*Drevnie russkie stikhotvoreniia*) (1818) appears the most relevant. This song tells of a fist-fight organized by Ivan the Terrible. The proud and seemingly invincible champion Mastruk, the brother of a Tartar wife of the tsar, does not participate in the tsar's festivity. When reproached by the tsar, he complains that he wants to fight but nobody dares to challenge him. Finally he is challenged by two Russian brothers who beat him into unconsciousness and take his clothing away. After the tsar's wife complains to the tsar of her brother's treatment, Ivan benevolently answers that he is proud of the Russian fighters and would have rewarded them even if they had killed the Tartar champion:

> А не то у меня честь в Москве,
> Что татары-то борются,
> То-то честь в Москве,
> Что русак тешится!
> Хотя бы ему голову сломил,
> Да, любил бы я, пожаловал
> Двух братцев родимыех,
> Двух удалых Борисовичев.
> (*Drevnie Rossiiskie stikhotvoreniia*, 32)

> (And in Moscow the great honor goes not to the fighting Tartars, but to a Russian who is having fun. Had one of them even broken his [Tartar] head, I would still have loved and supported the two brothers: two stout sons of Boris.)

25. The fight scene already provides a hint of the tragic outcome. Kiribeevich is the first to strike, hitting Kalashnikov in the chest. The blow is so powerful that it bends Kalashnikov's copper cross. The blow symbolizes

Kiribeevich's actions: it is directed against the Christian faith, but it fails, only bending the cross. There is another, rather sardonic aspect to the cross episode. The cross exacerbates the pain experienced by Kalashnikov: "the cross was bent and it protruded into the chest and the blood began to drip from beneath it like dew" (*I pognulsia krest i vdavilsia v grud'; kak rosa iz-pod nego krov' zakapala*) (2:18).

26. However, the majority of the critics, especially Soviet ones, see in the work only a masterly imitation of folklore and thus tend not to question the events of the song. In his study of the poem, Garrard (1982) echoes this attitude: "Theirs is a society in which certain things are done and others are not, in which authority is accepted" (116).

27. It is doubtful that Lermontov, author of the poem "Motherland" (*Rodina*) (1840), which discloses his deeply private love for his country, would take seriously a concept such as "sacred Russia," a staple of the art inspired by the "Orthodoxy-Autocracy-Nationhood" policy of his time. It was left to such writers as Nestor Kukol'nik to spice up plays with incessant references to "Sacred Russia," or "Sacred Moscow." At the time of Lermontov, Kukol'nik dominated Russian theater with chauvinistic historical plays, such as *The Hand of the Almighty Saved the Fatherland* (1832) and *Prince Skopin-Shuisky* (1835). The popularity of Kukol'nik's nationalist rhetoric and pious platitudes is the background against which to consider the heroism of Kalashnikov and the author. Lermontov resented the success of this hack playwright, while his own *Masquerade* was constantly rejected by the censor. One of Lermontov's few known epigrams mocks Kukol'nik's *Prince Skopin-Shuisky*. Kukol'nik, nevertheless, enjoyed complete support from the government: Nikolai Polevoi's important journal, *Moskovsky Telegraf*, was closed for criticizing a Kukol'nik play.

28. Lermontov's oeuvre explores not only ways of overcoming a gnostic outlook, but also particular reasons for falling into it. One, as "The Song" and *The Masquerade* suggest, is historical and social experience: Arbenin is in fact surrounded by treacherous and manipulative people, while Kalashnikov's heroism remains unrecognized and ignored. Another reason for such a decisive embrace of the gnostic outlook might be traumatic personal experience. "The Demon" explores how the experience of loss and defeat leaves a wound that is always ready to open, ready to shape the world in terms of treachery, loss, and evil.

CHAPTER FIVE

1. Such a dual strategy in the approach to the novel was introduced by Belinsky. His excesses, however, as well as the exaggeration of his views in Soviet criticism, have led to an obvious reaction in the West. Thus, while the majority of Soviet studies tend to blame Pechorin's time, the majority of

Western ones blame Pechorin himself. Because it avoids such unproductive separation of a hero from his time, Belinsky's approach remains not only the more fruitful, but probably the correct one.

2. Manuilov, in his commentary to the novel, shows clearly how much this flower passage echoes similar confessions of Melmoth, the protagonist of Charles Maturin's book *Melmoth the Wanderer* (1820), and Octave, the protagonist of *Confession d'un enfant du siècle* by Alfred de Musset (1835) (1966, 213).

3. Practically all contemporary critical works take the flower passage at its face value and condemn Pechorin's demonism (Faletti 1978, 367; Peace 1967, 26), his hunger for power (Turner 1984, 22–23), or attempt at self-aggrandizement (Barratt and Briggs 1990, 68), without ever considering the ironic and parodic dimension of such a confession.

4. The study of cultural background seems to be a preoccupation of various Soviet scholars, from Eikhenbaum to Udodov.

5. Barratt and Briggs (1990) present Pechorin as a psychopath, whose main source of inadequacy is attributed to his failure to incorporate Jung's teachings on a harmonious personality. To account for Pechorin's predicament they utilize such concepts as "mental sickness" (93), "healing power" (97), "persona-inflation" (67), "pathological," "hero's fantasy system" (68), "shadow," and "conscious integration" (80). Where modern scholars see the source of Pechorin's "problem" in his failure to consult a psychoanalyst, criticism of the previous century saw simply a lack of faith caused by Western upbringing. In 1841 Shevyrev (1907) explained the main source of Pechorin's apathy in the following manner:

> The main root of all evil is Western education, which lacks any experience of faith. . . . But whence and from what sources could the disease that torments the West develop here? . . . Pechorin does not have anything essential that is related to a purely Russian life. . . . He is a shadow cast to us from the West. (168–71)

Barratt, Briggs, Shevyrev, and Co. seem blissfully unaware that the real Russia inhabited by Lermontov as well as the imagined one inhabited by Pechorin provides ample opportunities for development of apathy, anger, and pessimism. Calling Pechorin sick or Western is a rather simplistic way to dismiss Lermontov's challenge without ever confronting it.

6. Gordin (1989) describes various abuses that the concept of "honor" underwent in Russia and observes that in the 1830s honorable behavior was rapidly falling out of fashion. See especially his chapter "*Russkaia duel', ili Agoniia dvorianskoi chesti*" (443–58).

7. Vigny (1935) elaborates the point ever further: "Le gentleman ou gentilhomme est l'homme d'honneur même qui, par les convenances, est retenu dans les limites de bonne conduite et de bienséance que la religion

n'atteindrait pas; car il y a des choses que ferait un prêtre et que jamais ne pourrait faire un galant homme" (307).

8. See Mersereau (1962, 132–44), Gershtein (1976, 51–61), and Vinogradov (1964). I would especially single out Vinogradov, who approaches "The Fatalist" in terms of an atheistic predicament and provides a most rewarding and stimulating discussion on the subject.

9. See Vinogradov (1986) on the importance of the theme of fate in the literature and culture of the period.

10. For a somewhat different treatment of the issues raised by "The Fatalist" see a recent discussion of the tale in Morson (1994, 67–69). I agree with Morson that Vulich's test is inconclusive and that, furthermore, the tale reveals that "psychologically, if not logically, neither fatalism nor skepticism has any necessary consequences" (69). Yet, in my reading of the novel, Lermontov attacks, maybe not the necessary, but at least the very probable and typically Russian connection between fatalism, immaturity, naive hopes, and passivity.

11. Pushkin explores Hermann's desperate striving for certainty in his "Queen of Spades." There are obvious references to Pushkin in the text of "The Fatalist": Vulich looks like Hermann; he is more interested in cards than in sex; of two cards mentioned in Lermontov's text, we recognize Pushkin's "seven and ace."

12. Similarly, Turner (1984) contends that "Pechorin's motivation is unclear: he could be literally 'testing fate' either for himself or in emulation of Vulich . . . he could be simply finding another and more extreme diversion from his boredom" (44), while Richard Gregg (1984) joins the cant: "as for the dashing and quite unnecessary exploit which concludes the tale, it bears no more relation to altruism than did Vulich's game of Russian roulette a few hours earlier" (392). Likewise, Mersereau (1962) remarks that " 'The Fatalist' doesn't reveal anything essentially new with respect to Pechorin's personality. It only reiterates his qualities of audaciousness and contentiousness" (135), while Barratt and Briggs (1990) state confidently: "In his final 'heroic' deed, as always, Pechorin acts in obedience to a purely egotistical motive. . . . The important thing for Pechorin is . . . the emulation of Vulich" (114).

13. It has already become a critical cliché to accuse Pechorin of using references to fate as a means of avoiding personal responsibility. This approach was initiated by John Mersereau, and many scholars repeat it without question. According to Mersereau (1962), Pechorin makes fate "the scapegoat" for his own irresponsible actions, and invokes fate only when he needs to avoid responsibility; elsewhere he acts as if he were a free agent (137–41). Pechorin is thus accused of casuistry and self-deception. However, is it not clear that Pechorin makes more of an effort to avoid self-deception than anyone else in the novel? Indeed, might not the entire book be read as Pechorin's attempt to understand his own motivations and emotions, his striving for

an honest and adequate view of himself? To accuse him of self-deception is to miss the point of Lermontov's novel. Pechorin, for example, has enough courage to admit to himself that he made a deal with his conscience not to spare Grushnitsky. Why should he be so perceptive at one moment and blind at another? If Pechorin is such a skillful dodger of responsibility, why is nobody fooled by it? In fact, he deliberately foregrounds his responsibility; describing the duel, he meticulously records his own evil and cruel actions. Pechorin's world lacks any authority figure before whom he might have wanted to appear less guilty than he is, while Pechorin's conscience hardly bothers him enough to force him to engage in self-deception.

14. My analysis of the moral seriousness, responsibility, and pragmatic approach to conduct that Lermontov proposes is indebted to several works, all of which strive to reformulate the problems of morality into questions of everyday conduct, and thus to bring morality from its heavenly heights down to the ordinary and concrete questions of choosing and learning: Letwin (1982), Morson (1987), Oakeshott (1975), and Todd's "Eugene Onegin: Life's Novel" (in Todd 1986, 106–37).

15. Compare Vladimir Odoevsky's (1981) assessment of the period:

> My youth belongs to that époque when metaphysics was as much part of the atmosphere as is political science today. We believed in the possibility of a unifying theory, with the help of which it would be possible to build (we used to say—construct) all the events of nature, as today they believe in the possibility of such social form that would satisfy all the needs of man. (307)

16. One can argue whether Lermontov's view of the world's ability to frustrate expectations and thus cause apathy and passivity has a universal relevance. However, in terms of Russian history, it is clear that Lermontov is more often right than not. Chaadaev woefully remarks on the futility and the debilitating effect of hopes in Russia: "The main thing is that henceforth we shall not hope for anything. . . . Nothing exhausts so much, nothing is so conducive to pusillanimity as insane hope. . . . What boundless stupidity it is to hope when with every movement it makes one sink deeper and deeper into the mire" (1837 letter to M. F. Orlov) (quoted in Budgen 1990, 34).

17. In his first "Philosophical Letter" Chaadaev (1989) calls the uprising "a great misfortune that has thrown Russia back by half a century" (48).

CHAPTER SIX

1. The fact is convincingly demonstrated by Levin (1972).

2. On the significance of "Taman'" see Peace (1967), as well as Lominadze (1989).

3. The list of the gullible includes not only Soviet biographers of Marlinsky—such as V. Kardin, S. Golubov, or L. Rakovsky, who were clearly con-

stricted in their possibilities of criticizing him—but even contemporary Western scholars. While Lauren Leighton at least provides pertinent facts about his behavior, Bagby (1995) leaves the myth of a heroic Decembrist practically unchallenged.

4. Compare the testimony of one Lutskoi: "he went from one detail to another in order to convince us to prefer death to surrender" (Oksman 1926, 321).

5. Marlinsky (Bestuzhev-Marlinsky 1981) in his 1826 letter to the tsar, is enough of a toady to declare Nicholas greater than Peter the Great (2:493).

6. Kardin (1984) refers to the fact that Benkendorf was aware of Bulgarin's connection with Marlinsky, but did not mind it at all (289–90).

7. Even though the details of Marlinsky's concrete behavior began to appear in print only in the 1860s, there is no doubt that Lermontov, who personally knew many prominent Decembrists (including Alexander Odoevsky, whom Marlinsky recruited and then betrayed) could not help knowing many of the details. The Decembrists were forced to confront each other during interrogations and thus a person could easily know who had denounced whom. Marlinsky's quick release from Siberia also could not have passed unnoticed.

8. Vatsuro (1964) observes that in his mature work Lermontov often took positions opposed to Marlinsky (347). Several other scholars also explored the Lermontov-Marlinsky connection: Vinogradov (1986), Eikhenbaum's "Literaturnaia pozitsiia Lermontova" (in Eikhenbaum 1986, 94–186), and Ginzburg (1940). These works, formalist in their orientation, concern themselves with literary connections and with the ubiquitous "overcoming" of one literary form by another. What I explore, instead, is Lermontov's attitude toward marlinism as a cultural phenomenon. On the cultural influence of Marlinsky see Alekseev (1989).

9. Shevyrev (1907) who was not always receptive toward Pechorin and Lermontov, nevertheless observes: "Pechorin's dislike of Grushnitsky results from that feeling which makes us dislike someone who mimics us, thus turning into an empty *mask* that which for us is a living essence" (161). Shevyrev's statement, undoubtedly correct, has been echoed by numerous critics, all of whom acknowledge that Grushnitsky is a copy or parody of Pechorin. Durylin (1986), for example, sees Grushnitsky as "a mask" (*lichina*) and Pechorin as a "personality" (*lichnost'*) (120), while Gershtein (1976) simply calls the one "an original" and the other "a copy" (79). In other words, all these critics fail to move in their analysis beyond the concept of a double.

Significantly, Shevyrev, hostile toward Pechorin, is even more hostile toward Grushnitsky. He accuses Grushnitsky of a lack of honor (161) and acknowledges the fundamental difference between the two; the rest of the critics, who stress the imitative aspect of Grushnitsky, imply that Grushnitsky is different from Pechorin only in degree.

10. In his 1926 study of Marlinsky's style, the Russian formalist scholar N. Kovarsky stresses Marlinsky's indebtedness to Karamzin (Kovarsky 1985, 109–27).

11. Princess Mary and Grushnitsky are portrayed in a fundamentally different manner from other secondary characters of the novel. Pechorin does not search for transcendence in his relationship with Mary; regardless of all her attractiveness she never becomes an object of love in the manner of Bela, Vera, or even *Undine.* Likewise, there is no deadly competition with Grushnitsky; Pechorin knows that Grushnitsky is not his match, as are, say, Kazbich, Yanko, and the Cossack.

12. Todd (1986), whose suggestive and insightful analysis of the play of literary and cultural patterns in Pushkin's *Eugene Onegin* (106–37) influenced my own approach to the issue of generic expectations in *A Hero of Our Time*, has surprisingly missed a similar strategy in Lermontov's novel:

> *A Hero of Our Time* not only limits the role that literature plays in shaping the lives of its characters . . . it also constricts the forms of literary life that appears in the novel. In contrast to *Eugene Onegin,* which reflected upon almost all of the institutional possibilities of Russian literature . . . *A Hero of our Time* deliberately suppresses almost all sense of writing as a public activity. (145)

13. This analysis should help to explain why Grushnitsky becomes the target of Pechorin's wrath and hostility, although he alone is not responsible for all these ills. While condemning Pechorin's personal vendetta we should still remember that, in Grushnitsky, Pechorin attacks the profound ills of an entire society, its lack of freedom, its complacent embrace of falsehoods, its dangerous discouragement of individualism.

14. Lermontov, following Pushkin, was well aware of the pressure that the expectations of the audience could put upon a narrator. As the narrator in Lermontov's second preface remarks, Rousseau could not help lying to the friends to whom he read his *Confessions.* He lied because he had to fulfill the expectations of his listeners. Some twenty-five years after Lermontov, Tolstoy underscored the corrupting impact of such pressure in his depiction of Nicholas Rostov's inability to describe truthfully the military attack in which he participated.

CHAPTER SEVEN

1. While Mann (1976) views "Mtsyri" as the "culmination of a tradition [of a Romantic narrative poem]" (197), according to Pul'khritudova (1979), "Mtsyri" belongs to "the pinnacle of Russian Romanticism" (282). This approach to "Mtsyri" was pioneered by Eikhenbaum (1987): "Neither in the history of Lermontov's art nor of Russian poetry does 'Mtsyri' constitute a new genre; nor did it open a new vista. In fact, it is a last word, the

culmination of a particular line of development in Russian lyrical poetry" (217).

2. Reid's (1986) appears to be the only specialized study of the poem.

3. Mann, for example, in his book on Russian Romanticism, discusses generic features of Lermontov's poems, yet this discussion, informative as it is, leaves many unique features of the poem unexplored. To observe that the protagonists of Lermontov's poems are as ostracized and alienated as are the protagonists of other Russian Romantic poems is not to say very much. Mann also observes the poem's tensions and contradictions, noting that the monastery is presented in the poem as both friendly and hostile. Mann, however, explains—or perhaps explains away—the poem's complexities by positing something he calls "the subtle artistic dialectics of the poem" (1976, 205). Such a rephrasing of the poem's contradictions hardly explicates the meaning of Lermontov's text.

Similarly, Lominadze (1985) expresses his puzzlement at the contradictory nature of Mtsyri's desires and actions, but explains it as a sign of the inner conflict of both Mtsyri and Lermontov. Such an explanation is obviously true, but hardly adequate.

4. My approach to the problems of Mtsyri's name and his initiation is inspired by George E. Dimmock's brilliant essay, "The Name of Odysseus" (Dimmock 1956, 52–70).

5. David Quint (1993) observes that, along with the epics of winners—that is, epic texts glorifying the winners of the historical process and written in the form of teleologically coherent narratives—there also exists a body of texts written from the perspective of those who lost. Such epics of losers, according to Quint, are composed of repetitive stories of endless wanderings. Eventually losing their narrative interest, they are thus doomed to lose even in the struggle for readers' attention. Lermontov's narrative poem "Mtysri", with its endless wandering and its nonevents, is clearly part of this latter tradition.

6. Mann (1976) views this description as the "center (*uzel*) of the poem's . . . dialectic": but rather than interpreting it in terms of the predicament of freedom he prefers to see in it the beginning of Mtsyri's fall; he thus concludes that "the fall of the evil spirit is the background to Mtsyri's history" (205).

7. Lermontov underscores the paradoxical heroism of Mtsyri by making him an escapee from a monastery. In his adventures Mtsyri is thus poised between two extremes: the total license of the very popular Romantic monk of Matthew Lewis's novel *The Monk,* and the traditional morality of Ivan Kozlov's poem "A Monk" (*Chernets*) (1825). While Lewis's protagonist commits all sorts of "earthly" crimes in the monastery, Kozlov's monk returns to the monastery in order to renounce earthly passions. Mtsyri, on the other hand, escapes the monastery yet lives like a monk. He remains a novice, never fully joining either domain.

8. In his interpretation of Homer's *Odyssey* Dimmock (1956) suggests that Odysseus's main task is to live up to his name (which originates from the Greek verb "to suffer") and thus to learn both to bear and inflict pain. Having learned this, Odysseus returns home to his Ithaca (52–70). In order for him to live up to his name, Mtsyri has to remain an outsider, both physically and spiritually; his journey, paradoxically, cannot be completed.

9. Lermontov was very much preoccupied with the theme of Jewish captivity. An early variant of "The Demon" was set in Babylon during the Jewish captivity; in this variant the Demon falls in love with a captive Jewish girl. Lermontov also translated and wrote variants on Byron's "Hebrew Melodies;" one poem in that group deals directly with the theme of Jewish loss ("*Plach', plach' Izrailia narod, ty poterial zvezdu svoiu*") (1831) (1:162). Lermontov's first drama, *The Spaniards*, depicts the plight of the Jews in Spain at the time of the Inquisition. The protagonist of the play, the orphan Fernando, seeks and ultimately finds his Jewish parents in the course of the play. This text also contains a song in which the Jews mourn the loss of Jerusalem.

10. The ruined monastery, a common Romantic topos, became a highly charged theme for Lermontov. In "The Demon," for example, Lermontov stresses that although Tamara's castle is destroyed, the church in which she hoped to escape the Demon still stands: "but the church . . . saved by sacred power, is still seen among the clouds standing on the steep top of the mountains" (2:73). In his play, *The Spaniards*, there is a song about another ruined monastery: a Muslim comes to a monastery to be converted but is treacherously murdered by monks; of the monastery only ruins remain. Thus the ruins of the monastery, like the ruins of the Temple in Jerusalem, suggest that God was not pleased with them.

11. In Lermontov's poetry the image of a heavy, burdensome crown occurs several times, and in his "Hebrew melody" (*Evreiskaia melodiia*, 1836), which is a free translation of Byron's "My Soul is Dark" (1815), it is used in connection with the first Jewish king, Saul. Lermontov renders the complaint of the tormented king in the following manner: "the sounds of merriment are as burdensome to me as my crown" (*kak moi venets mne tiagostny veselia zvuki*) (1:282). Significantly, Byron does not refer to a crown in his poem. Lermontov uses the same image of a heavy crown in his 1832 poem, "Like the Star's Flame Falling into the Night" (*Kak v noch zvezdy paduchei plamen'*): "like a tsar's crown, happiness became burdensome for me (*i tiagostno mne schastie stalo, kak dlia tsaria venets*) (1:252), referring to Saul and also to Pushkin's more contemporary use of the image in his "Boris Godunov." The image of the heavy crown refers thus to the inner conflicts of Saul and Boris. The decision of the Georgian king to give up his crown appears futile: external walls cannot ward off the inner demons that torment kings.

12. Dostoevsky parodies Romantic challenges to confinement in his portrayal of the Underground Man who is ready to stick his tongue out at any wall. Such parodying, though, hardly does justice to the tensions that Lermontov explores in "Mtsyri."

13. Significantly, in the previous variants of the poem ("Confession" and "Boyarin Orsha"), the protagonist is a typical Romantic character, with violent and deadly passions, engaged in traditional romantic adventures. In "Confession" the protagonist decides to renounce paradise because he cannot be there with his beloved. The hero of "Boyarin Orsha" remains in humiliating and confining service because of his erotic love. In these variants, Mtsyri's prototypes commit all sorts of evil: they lie, sham, join up with robbers or rebels, enter into illicit love affairs. In fact, "Boyarin Orsha" is written in the same notebook as an early variant of "The Demon," thus underlining the initial proximity of both plotlines; that is, their common focus on an erotic adventure.

14. One should not be surprised by similarities in Lermontov's and Tolstoy's sensitivities. Both writers lost their mothers at a very early age, and thus probably experienced at its most acute the human desire both to belong and escape. Tolstoy felt tremendous sympathy toward Lermontov, going so far as to declare that among Russian writers only he and Lermontov were more than just literary figures: "Turgenev is a *littérateur* (*literator*), Pushkin was also one; Goncharov, even more of a *littérateur* than Turgenev; Lermontov and I are not *littérateurs*" (quoted in Leusheva 1964, 413). Although what Tolstoy means by *literator* may not be clear, it is nevertheless quite possible that he senses anxieties and aims in Lermonotv similar to his own.

In his late seventies Tolstoy (1935–64) expresses a desire for motherly tenderness that sounds surprisingly similar to the desire of Lermontov's protagonists, to Mtsyri's *khotelos'*:

> During the entire day—a state of anxiety and stupor. By the evening this state has changed into a feeling of tenderness—desire for a caress, for love. I *wanted* (*khotelos'*), as in childhood, to cling to a loving, pitying creature and tenderly cry and be comforted . . . to become small and [cling] to the mother, as I imagine her. Yes, yes, mother, whom I never called by that name, not yet being able to talk. . . . My best, weary soul yearns for it. *You, mother, you caress me.* All that is madness, but all that is true (written in 1906). (15:374; my emphasis)

15. Both the Demon and Arbenin destroy the objects of their passion. A similar paradigm is replayed in the famous ballad "The Sea-Princess" (*Morskaia tsarevna*) (1841), in which the knight seizes the beautiful mermaid and takes her out of the water, only to discover that he is holding a corpse.

16. Mtsyri's encounter in the Caucasus can be contrasted with two other encounters, that of the Demon with Tamara, and Pechorin with Bela. Similar to Mtsyri, both Pechorin and the Demon are tormented by the

yearning for a lost bliss that finds expression only in erotic conquest, death, and destruction. Mtsyri, however, resists the temptation.

17. Significantly, in the drafts to *A Hero of Our Time* Pechorin was compared to a tiger: "magnanimous or cruel, depending on the mood of the moment, always ready for lasting battle, sometimes forced into retreat, but incapable of submission" (quoted in Gershtein 1976, 37). Mtsyri thus seems to be struggling not only with a wild animal, but with the spell of Pechorin and the Demon, with their aggressive and courageous energy. Mtsyri, in fact, is wounded by the leopard, and it is this wound that is partly responsible for his failure to escape. Even though the leopard is destroyed, he leaves his deadly mark on Mtsyri.

18. The epigraph has been touched upon in a number of articles: both Lubovich (1964) and Meshchersky (1976) refer to the text of the Bible but leave many significant connections between the poem and its biblical subtext unexplored. Vagin (1978) suggests that Lermontov's source is not the Bible but the Latin rendition of the biblical phrase used in George Sand's anti-clerical novel, *Spiridion.* In fact, Lermontov relies on the biblical subtext of his epigraph to a greater degree than any of the previous critics would allow.

19. The reference to Dante is acknowledged in scholarship, although its irony has not been explored. Maksimov in his chapter on "Mtsyri" observes only that Lermontov refers to the forest to utilize Dante's symbolism of "the dark forest of life in which one can be easily lost" (1964, 231).

20. Mtsyri's gaze, which is fixed on the East, together with the Jewish setting of the epigraph, bring to mind another curse pronounced by another group of exiles. In Psalm 137, the captured Jews vow never to forget Jerusalem; the vow, however, ends on a tragic note: they pronounce a cruel and bitter curse against Babylon.

21. One can also recall the heroic resignation and courage of the mother who waits hopelessly for her son in Lermontov's "The Cossack Lullaby": "I will be suffering from anxiety, and will hopelessly wait" (*Stanu ia toskoi tomit'sia, bezuteshno zhdat'*) (1:38). Even though the mother knows that the son must go and will never come back, she resigns herself to a patient waiting against all odds.

22. Mtsyri's vision reveals why mermaids enjoyed such popularity both with Lermontov and numerous other Romantic poets: their imagination associated mermaids with the devotion of motherly love. Gaston Bachelard (1969), in fact, considers mermaids the constant subject of what he calls "cosmic reveries," "or reveries toward childhood" (97–143; 196–205). According to Bachelard such reveries "put us in the state of the soul being born" and "situate us in the world . . . of stability and tranquillity" (14–15). Bachelard also stresses that "cosmic reverie causes us to inhabit a world. It gives the dreamer the impression of being at home (*chez soi*) in the imagined universe" (177). Bachelard, who views such reveries as the center of the

poetic vision, partly discloses the reasons behind Mtsyri's and Lermontov's reaction to water. According to Bachelard, the function of these reveries is to remove the poet's soul from the here and now, to transcend the walls of narrow facticity. The reveries about childhood, inspired by the sounds of water, resurrect the home of the past and thus carry the dreamer away from the narrow confinement of the present dwelling. For a classic description of the process, see Lermontov's poem "How Surrounded by a Multicolored Crowd I Frequently . . ." (*Kak chasto pestroiu tolpoiu okruzhen . . .*) (1840), in which the poet escapes the present by dreaming of his childhood and its dreams.

Lermontov's own poem "The Mermaid" (*Rusalka*) (1836) contains a song, sung by a mermaid, that tells of her dedication and love for a drowned knight who lies at the bottom of the river, indifferent both to mermaids and to the golden fish that swim above him (1:276). Mtsyri's deathlike state, however, as well as the poem "The Mermaid," suggests that Lermontov was quite aware of the deathlike aspect of such a return to the womb. It is thus not surprising that another "mermaid," Undine from "Taman" tries to drown Pechorin.

23. There is a striking correspondence between Lermontov's ideal of happiness and Tolstoy's. In *War and Peace,* Tolstoy (1935–64) describes the wounded prince Andrei and makes him reexperience the happiest moments of his life:

> all the best and happiest moments of his life—especially those of early childhood, when he had been undressed and put to bed, and when the nurse, had sung lullabies to him (*nad nim*) and he had burried his head in the pillow and felt happy just to be alive—rose to his mind, not as something past, but as a present reality. (11:257)

24. The capacity of sounds to recover lost bliss is mentioned frequently in Lermontov's work. While I treat the subject in greater detail in the Afterword, for the time being let me quote from the 1831 poem "Sounds" (*Zvuki*):

> Что за звуки! неподвижен внемлю
> Сладким звукам я;
> Забываю вечность, небо, землю
> Самого себя.
> Всемогущий! Что за звуки, жадно
> Сердце ловит их,
> Как в пустыне путник безотрадной
> Каплю вод живых!
> И в душе опять они рождают
> Сны веселых лет
> И в одежду жизни одевают
> Все, чего уж нет.
>
> (1:182)

> (What sounds! Motionless do I listen to these sweet sounds. I forget eternity, heaven, earth, and myself. Almighty God! What sounds! My heart greedily grabs them, as a hapless wanderer in the desert grabs a drop of life-giving water! And in my soul they again give birth to dreams of my happy years. And they dress in the cloth of life everything that is no more.)

The sweet sounds allow the listener to forget his torment: "I forget eternity, heaven, earth, and myself," and thus transcend time, space, and the self. The sounds resurrect not only the listener's soul but also everything that he has lost: "and they dress in the cloth of life everything that is no more." The torment is transcended; former bliss is recalled and recovered.

Selected Bibliography

Abbott, H. Porter. 1984. "The Expressive Text and Textual Self-Consealment: Lermontov's *A Hero of Our Time.*" In *Diary Fiction: Writing as Action,* 55–72. Ithaca: Cornell University Press.

Abrams, M. H. 1971. *Natural Supernaturalism: Traditions and Revolution in Romantic Literature.* New York: Norton.

———. 1981. *The Mirror and the Lamp: Romantic Theory and the Critical Tradition.* New York: Oxford University Press.

Aikhenval'd, Iu. 1929. "Lermontov." In *Siluety russkikh pisatelei,* 1:120–53. Berlin.

Aivazyan, K. V., and V. A. Manuilov, eds. 1974. *Lermontov i literatura natodov Sovetskogo Souiza.* Erevan.

Aizlewood, Robin. 1990. "*Geroj Nashego Vremeni* as Emblematic Prose Text." In *From Pushkin to Palisandria: Essays on the Russian Novel in Honor of Richard Freeborn,* edited by Arnold McMillan, 39–52. New York: St. Martin's.

Alekseev, M. P. 1989. "Etiudy o Marlinskom" and "Turgenev i Marlinsky." In *O mirovom znachenii russkoi literatury,* 81–162. Leningrad.

Andreevich (E. A. Solov'ev). 1905. *Opyt filosofii russkoi literatury.* Saint Petersburg.

Andreev-Krivich, S. A. 1978. *Vsevedenie poeta.* Moscow.

Andreevsky, S. A. 1913. "Lermontov." In *Literaturnye ocherki.* Saint Petersburg.

Annensky, Innokentii. 1979. "Iumor Lermontova." In *Knigi otrazhenii,* 136–41. Moscow.

Arkhipov, Vladimir. 1965. *M. Iu. Lermontov: Poeziia poznaniia i deistviia.* Moscow.

Ashukin, N. S. 1941. "Istoriko-bytovoi kommentarii k drame Lermontova 'Maskarad.'" In *Maskarad Lermontova. Sbornik statei,* edited by P. I. Novitsky, 211–49. Leningrad.

Asmus, V. 1941. "Krug idei Lermontova." *Literaturnoe nasledstvo* 43–44: 83–129.

Azadovsky, M. 1941. "Fol'klorism Lermontova." *Literaturnoe nasledstvo* 43–44:227–63.

Bachelard, Gaston. 1969. *The Poetics of Reverie: Childhood, Language, and the Cosmos.* Translated by Daniel Russell. Boston: Beacon.

Bagby, Lewis. 1978. "Narrative Double-Voicing in Lermontov's *A Hero of Our Time.*" *Slavic and East European Journal* 22:265–86.

———. 1995. *Alexander Bestuzhev-Marlinsky and Russian Byronism.* University Park: Pennsylvania State University Press.

Bakhtin, Mikhail. 1968. *Rabelais and His World.* Translated by Helene Iswolsky. Cambridge: MIT Press.

Baratynsky, E. A. 1989. *Polnoe sobranie stikhotvorenii.* Leningrad.

Barratt, Andrew, and A. D. P. Briggs. 1990. *A Wicked Irony: The Rhetoric of Lermontov's* A Hero of Our Time. Bristol: Bristol University Press.

Barzun, Jacques. 1975. *Classic, Romantic, and Modern.* Chicago: University of Chicago Press.

Bayle, Pierre. 1984. *Pensées Diverses sur la Comète.* Vol. 2. Paris: Société des Textes Français Modernes.

Belinkov, Arkady. 1987. "Strana rabov, strana gospod." *Vremia i my* 95:165–207.

Belinsky, V. G. 1978. *Sobranie sochinenii v deviati tomakh.* Moscow.

Bentley, Eric. 1957. *A Century of Hero-worship: A Study of the Idea of Heroism in Carlyle and Nietzsche, with Notes on Wagner, Spengler, Stefan George, and D. H. Lawrence.* 2d ed. Boston: Beacon.

Berdiaev, Nikolai. 1918. *Sud'ba Rossii.* Moscow.

———. 1939. *O rabstve i svobode cheloveka.* Paris: YMCA Press.

———. 1971. *Russkaia Ideia.* Paris.

———. 1990. *Novoe srednevekov'e.* Moscow.

Berlin, Isaiah. 1979. "The Hedgehog and the Fox." In *Russian Thinkers,* edited by Henry Hardy and Aileen Kelly, with an Introduction by Aileen Kelly, 22–82. New York: Penguin Books.

———. 1991. "De Maistre and the Rise of Modern Fascism." In *The Crooked Timber of Humanity: Chapters in the History of Ideas.* New York: Knopf.

Bestuzhev-Marlinskii, A. A. 1981. *Sochineniia v dvukh tomakh.* Moscow.

Billacois, François. 1990. *The Duel: Its Rise and Fall in Early Modern France.* New Haven: Yale University Press.

Blok, Alexander. 1962. *Sobranie sochinenii v vos'mi tomakh.* Vol. 5, *Proza: 1903–1917.* Edited by V. N. Orlov. Moscow.

Bloom, Harold. 1970. *Romanticism and Consciousness.* New York: Norton.

———. 1976. *Poetry and Repression.* London: Oxford University Press.

———. 1982. *Agon: Towards a Theory of Revisionism.* London: Oxford University Press.

Botkin, V. P. 1984. *Literaturnaia kritika. Publitsistika, Pis'ma.* Moscow.

Bowlby, John. 1969–80. *Attachment and Loss.* 3 volumes. New York: Basic Books.

Brombert, Victor. 1978. *The Romantic Prison: The French Tradition.* Princeton: Princeton University Press.

Brown, William Edward. 1986. *A History of Russian Literature of the Romantic Period.* Vol. 4. Ann Arbor, Mich.: Ardis.

Budgen, David. 1990. "Pushkin and Chaadaev: The History of a Friendship." In *Ideology in Russian Literature,* edited by Richard Freeborn and Jane Grayson, 7–47. New York: St. Martin's.

Bulgakov, Sergei. 1993. "Geroizm i podvizhnichestvo." In *Sochineniia v dvukh tomakh,* 2:302–42. Moscow.

Burachok, S. 1840. "Geroi nashego vremeni." *Maiak* 4:210–19.

Burckhardt, Jacob. 1958. *The Civilization of the Renaissance in Italy.* New York: Harper and Row.

Burckhardt, Sigurd. 1968. *Shakespearean Meanings.* Princeton: Princeton University Press.

Butler, Marilyn. 1989. "Romantic Manichaeism: Shelley's 'On the Devil and Devils' and Byron's Mythological Dramas." In *The Sun is God: Painting, Literature, and Mythology in the Nineteenth Century,* edited by B. Bullen, 13–39. London: Oxford University Press.

Camus, Albert. 1956. *The Rebel: An Essay on Man in Revolt.* New York: Vintage Books.

Cantor, Paul. 1984. *Creator and the Creature: Myth-making and English Romanticism.* London: Cambridge University Press.

Castle, Terry. 1986. *Masquerade and Civilization.* Berkeley and Los Angeles: University of California Press.

Chaadaev, P. Ia. 1989. *Stat'i i pis'ma.* Moscow.

Chekhov, Anton. 1974–83. *Polnoe sobranie sochinenii i pisem.* 30 vols. Moscow.

Cherniavsky, Michael. 1961. *Tsar and People: Studies in Russian Myths.* New Haven: Yale University Press.

Chernyshevsky, Nikolai. 1939–53. *Polnoe sobranie sochinenii v 16-ti tomakh.* Moscow.

Chesterton, G. H. 1989. *Collected Works.* Vol. 15, *Chesterton on Dickens.* San Francisco, Calif.: Ignatius Press.

Chistova, I. S., ed. 1985. *Lermontovskii sbornik.* Leningrad.

Chukovsky, K. 1976. *Kniga ob Aleksandre Bloke.* Paris: YMCA Press.

———. 1980. "Aleksandr Blok." In *Aleksandr Blok v vospominaniiakh sovremennikov. V dvukh tomakh,* 2:210–52. Moscow.

Cornwell, Neil. 1986. *V. F. Odoevsky: His Life, Times, and Milieu.* Athens: Ohio University Press.

Cox, Gary D. 1982. "Dramatic Genre as a Tool of Characterization in Lermontov's *Hero of Our Time.*" *Russian Literature* 11:163–72.

Custine, Marquis de. 1951. *Journey for Our Time: The Russian Diary of Marquis de Custine.* Edited and Translated by Phyllis Penn Kohler. Chicago: Henry Regnery.

———. 1989. *Empire of the Czar: A Journey Through Eternal Russia.* New York: Doubleday.

Dante Alighieri. 1977. *The Divine Comedy: Hell.* Translated by Dorothy L. Sayers. New York: Penguin Books.

Dashkevich, N. P. 1914. "Motivy mirovoi poezii v tvorchestve Lermontova." In *Stat'i po novoi russkoi literature,* 411–514. Saint Petersburg.

Debreczeny, Paul. 1973. "Elements of the Lyrical Verse Tale in Lermontov's *A Hero Of Our Time.*" In *American Contributions to the Seventh International Congress of Slavists. Warsaw, August 21–27, 1973,* edited by Victor Terras, 93–117. The Hague: Mouton.

Diakonova, Nina. 1982. "Byron and Lermontov: Notes on Pechorin's 'Journal.'" In *Lord Byron and His Contemporaries: Essays from the Sixth International Byron Seminar,* edited by Charles E. Robinson, 144–66. London: Associated University Presses.

Dimmock, George E., Jr. 1956. "The Name of Odysseus." *Hudson Review* 9:52–70.

Dostoevsky, F. M. 1972–90. *Polnoe sobranie sochinenii v tridtsati tomakh.* Leningrad.

Driver, Sam. 1989. *Pushkin: Literature and Social Ideas.* New York: Columbia University Press.

Dumont, Louis. 1986. *Essays on Individualism: Modern Ideology in Anthropological Perspective.* Chicago: University of Chicago Press.

———. 1994. *German Ideology: From France to Germany and Back.* Chicago: University of Chicago Press.

Durylin, S. 1934. *Kak rabotal Lermontov.* Moscow.

———. 1986. *Geroi Nashego Vremeni M. Iu. Lermontova.* Ann Arbor, Mich.: Ardis. Reprint.

Eagle, Herbert. 1975. "Lermontov's 'Play' with Romantic Genre Expectations in *A Hero of Our Time.*" *Russian Literature Triquarterly* 10:299–315.

Edwards, David. 1977. "Count Joseph Marie de Maistre and Russian Educational Policy, 1803–1828." *Slavic Review* 36:54–76.

Efimova, Z. S. 1927. "Iz istorii russkoi romanticheskoi dramy. 'Maskarad' M. Iu. Lermontova." In *Russkii romantism,* edited by A. I. Beletsky, 26–50. Leningrad.

Eidel'man, N. Ia. 1990. *Byt' mozhet za khrebtom Kavkaza: Russkaia literatura i obshchestvennaia mysl' pervoi poloviny XIX v. Kavkazskii kontekst.* Moscow.

Eikhenbaum, B. M. 1986. *O Prose, o poezii: sbornik statei.* Leningrad.

———. 1987. "Lermontov. Opyt istoriko-literaturnoi otsenki." In *O literature: Raboty raznykh let.* Moscow.

Elias, Norbert. 1983. *The Court Society.* Translated by Edmund Jephcott. Oxford: Basil Blackwell.

———. 1991. *The Society of Individuals.* Translated by Edmund Jephcott. Oxford: Basil Blackwell.

Engelberg, Edward. 1989. "Rebels Without Cause: Lermontov, Turgenev, Brontë." In *Elegiac Fictions: The Motive of the Unlived Life.* University Park: Pennsylvania State University Press.

Essaulov, I. A. 1995. *Kategoria sobornosti v russkoi literature.* Petrozavodsk.

Evgeniev, A. P., ed. 1977. *Drevnie rossiiskie stikhotvoreniia. Sobranie Kirshi Danilova.* Moscow.

Faletti, Heidi E. 1978. "Elements of the Demonic in the Character of Pechorin in Lermontov's *Hero of Our Time.*" *Forum for Modern Language Studies* 14:365–77.

Faryno, J. 1979. "Dve modeli liricheskogo 'ya' u Lermontova." In *Russian Romanticism: Studies in the Poetic Codes,* edited by Nils Åke Nilsson, 167–86. Stockholm.

Fedorov, A. V. 1967. *Lermontov i literatura ego vremeni.* Leningrad.

Fedotov, George P. 1975. *A Treasure of Russian Spirituality.* Belmont, Mass.: Nordland.

Fischer, Hermann. 1991. *Romantic Verse Narrative: The History of a Genre.* Cambridge: Cambridge University Press.

Frank, Joseph. 1986. *Dostoevsky: The Stir of Liberation, 1860–1865.* Princeton: Princeton University Press.

Frye, Northrop. 1982. *A Study of English Romanticism.* Chicago: University of Chicago Press.

Furst, Lilian. 1979. "Individualism." In *Romanticism in Perspective,* 53–117. London: Macmillan.

Garrard, John. 1982. *Mikhail Lermontov.* Boston: Twayne.

Gasparov, M. L. 1984. *Ocherk istorii russkogo stikha: Metrika, ritmika, rifma, strofika.* Moscow.

Gerasimov, O. P. 1890. "Ocherk vnutrennei zhizni Lermontova po ego proizvedeniyam." *Voprosy filosofii i psikhologii* 3:1–44.

Gershtein, Emma. 1941. "Lermontov i 'kruzhok shestnadtsati.'" In *Zhizn' i tvorchestvo M. Iu Lermontova,* edited by N. L. Brodsky, 77–124. Moscow.

———. 1976. *"Geroi nashego vremeni" M. Iu. Lermontova.* Moscow.

———. 1986. *Sud'ba Lermontova.* Moscow.

Gilroy, Marie. 1988. *Lermontov's Ironic Vision.* Birmingham Slavonic Monographs 19. Birmingham: University of Birmingham.

Ginzburg, L. Ia. 1940. *Tvorcheskii put' Lermontova.* Leningrad.

———. 1977. *O psikhologicheskoi proze.* Leningrad.

Gnug, Hiltrud. 1990. "The Dandy and the Don Juan Type." In *European Romanticism: Literary Cross-Currents, Modes, and Models,* edited by Gerhart Hoffmeister, 229–47. Detroit: Wayne State University Press.

Gogol, N. V. 1952. *Polnoe sobranie sochinenii.* Moscow.

Gol'denveizer, A. B. 1959. *Vblizi Tolstogo.* Moscow.

Golovin, Ivan. 1970. *Russia under the Autocrat, Nicholas the First.* New York: Praeger. (German original, 1845.)

Golstein, Vladimir. 1997. "Landowners in *Dead Souls;* or, The Tale of How Gogol Blessed What He Wanted to Curse." *Slavic and East European Journal* 41–42:243–57.

Golubov, S. 1938. *Bestuzhev-Marlinsky.* Moscow.

Goncharov, I. A. 1986. "Vospominaniia." In *Ocherki, stat'i, pis'ma.* Moscow.

Gordin, Ia. A. 1989. *Pravo na poedinok.* Leningrad.

Gregg, Richard. 1984. "The Cooling of Pechorin: The Scull Beneath the Skin." *Slavic Review* 43:387–98.

Griboedov, A. S. 1987. *Sochineniia v stikhakh.* Leningrad.

Grigor'ev, Apollon. 1990. *Sochineniia v dvukh tomakh.* Vol. 2, *Stat'i, pis'ma.* Moscow.

Grigor'ian, K. N. 1982. "Dramaturgiia Lermontova." In *Istoriia russkoi dramaturgii XVII–pervaia polovina XIX veka,* edited by L. M. Lotman et al., 368–402. Leningrad.

Gukovsky, G. A. 1965. *Pushkin i russkie romantiki.* Moscow.

Gurevich, A. Ia., ed. 1990a. *Chelovek i kul'tura. Individual'nost' v istorii kul'tury.* Moscow.

———. 1990b. *Odyssei. Chelovek v istorii.* Moscow.

Gurevich, P. S., comp. 1995. *Chelovek.* Moscow.

Gusky, Andreas. 1970. *M. Iu. Lermontovs Konzeption des literarischen Helden.* Munich.

Gustafson, Richard. 1986. *Leo Tolstoy: Resident and Stranger.* Princeton: Princeton University Press.

———. 1995. "Solov'ev's Doctrine of Original Sin." In *Freedom and Responsibility in Russian Literature: Essays in Honor of Robert Louis Jackson,* edited by Elizabeth Cheresh Allen and Gary Saul Morson, 170–81. Evanston: Northwestern University Press.

Hecht, Leo. 1976. "Lermontov and the German Poets." *Canadian-American Slavic Studies* 10:400–409.

Heller, Thomas C., ed. 1986. *Reconstructing Individualism: Autonomy, Individuality, and the Self in Western Thought.* Stanford: Stanford University Press.

Herzen, A. I. 1954–66. *Sobranie sochinenii v tridtsati tomakh.* Moscow.

———. 1982. *My Past and Thoughts: The Memoirs of Alexander Herzen.* Abridged by Dwight Macdonald. Berkeley and Los Angeles: University of California Press.

Hook, Sidney. 1943. *The Hero in History: A Study in Limitation and Possibility.* New York: John Day.

Hutcheon, Linda. 1989. "Modern Parody and Baxtin." In *Rethinking Bakhtin: Extensions and Challenges,* edited by Gary Saul Morson and Caryl Emerson, 88–105. Evanston: Northwestern University Press.

Ivanov, Viacheslav. 1987. "Lermontov." In *Sobranie sochinenii,* 4:367–83. Brussels: Foyer Oriental Chrétien.

———. 1994. *Rodnoe i vselenskoe.* Moscow.

Ivanov-Razumnik (R. V. Ivanov). 1911. *Istoriia russkoi obshchestvennoi mysli. Individualism i meshchanstvo i russkoi literature i zhizni XIX v.* Vol. 1. Saint Petersburg.

Ivanova, T. 1967. *Posmertnaia syd'ba poeta.* Moscow.

Jackson, Robert L. 1960–61. "Napoleon in Russian Literature." *Yale French Studies* 26:106–19.

Jonas, Hans. 1963. *The Gnostic Religion.* Boston: Beacon.

Kantor, Vladimir. 1994. *V poiskakh lichnosti. Opyt russkoi klassiki.* Moscow.

Kantorowicz, Ernst H. 1957. *The King's Two Bodies: A Study of Medieval Political Theology.* Princeton: Princeton University Press.

Karamzin, N. M. 1991. *Zapiska o drevnei i novoi Rossii.* Moscow.

Kardin, Vladimir. 1984. *Minuta probyzhdenia: Povest' ob Aleksandre Bestuzheve (Marlinskom).* Moscow.

Kavelin, K. D. 1989. *Nash umstvennyi stroi. Stat'i po filosofii russkoi istorii i kul'tury.* Moscow.

Keen, Maurice. 1984. *Chivalry.* New Haven: Yale University Press.

Kholodov, E., et al., eds. 1978. *Istoriia russkogo dramaticheskogo teatra.* Vol. 3, *1826–1845.* Moscow.

Khomiakov, A. S. 1994. *Sochineniia v dvukh tomakh.* Vol. 2, *Raboty po bogosloviiu.* Moscow.

Kiernan, V. G. 1986. *The Duel in European History: Honour and the Reign of Autocracy.* Oxford: Oxford University Press.

Kiukhel'beker, Wilhelm. 1967. *Izbrannye proizvedeniia v dvukh tomakh.* Vol. 2. Moscow.

———. 1979. *Puteshestvie, dnevnik, stat'i.* Leningrad.

Kliuchevsky, V. O. 1991. "Grust' (pamiati M. Ju Lermontova)." In *Literarturnye portrety,* 133–51. Moscow.

Kon, Igor' S. 1976. *Sotsiologiia lichnosti.* Moscow.

Korovin, V. I. 1988. "Geroi i mif. (Po drame M. Iu. Lermontova 'Maskarad')." In *Analiz dramaticheskogo proizvedeniia,* edited by V. M. Markovich, 122–35. Leningrad.

Kotliarevsky, N. A. 1907. *Dekabristy. Kn. A. Odoevsky i A. Bestuzhev.* Saint Petersburg.

———. 1915. *M. Iu. Lermontov. Lichnost' poeta i ego proizvedeniia.* Saint Petersburg.

Kovarsky, N. 1985. "The Early Bestuzhev-Marlinsky." In *Russian Prose,* edited by B. M. Eikhenbaum, translated by Ray Parrott, 109–27. Ann Arbor, Mich.: Ardis.

Kshitseva, Danushe. 1987. "Friedrich Nietzsche i M. Ju. Lermontov." *Studia Slavica Hungaricae* 33:119–29.

Kuhn, Reinhart. 1978. *The Demon of Noontide: The Theme of Ennui in Western Literature.* Princeton: Princeton University Press.

Lampert, Evgenii. 1957. *Studies in Rebellion.* London: Routledge and Kegan Paul.

Landa, E. V. 1990. "'Undina' v perevode V. A. Zhukovskogo i russkaia kultura." In *Undina,* by F. H. K. de la Motte-Fouqué, edited by S. V. Turaev, 472–537. Moscow.

Leighton, L. G. 1975a. *Aleksandr Bestuzhev-Marlinsky.* Boston: Twayne.

———. 1975b. *Russian Romanticism: Two Essays.* The Hague.

Lermontov, Mikhail. 1954–57. *Sobranie sochinenii v shesti tomakh.* Moscow.

———. 1984. *Sobranie sochinenii v chetyrekh tomakh.* Edited by I. Andronnikov. Moscow.

———. 1988. *A Hero of Our Time.* Translated by Vladimir Nabokov, in collaboration with Dmitri Nabokov. Ann Arbor, Mich.: Ardis.

Letwin, Shirley Robin. 1982. *The Gentleman in Trollope: Individuality and Moral Conduct.* Cambridge: Harvard University Press.

Leusheva, S. 1964. "Lermontov i Tolstoy." In *Tvorchesto Lermontova,* edited by U. Fokht, 395–417. Moscow.

Levin, V. Ia. 1972. "Dostoevskii, 'podpol'nyi paradoksalist' i Lermontov." *Izvestiia Akademii Nauk SSSR: Seriia Literatury i Yazyka* 31:142–56.

Levkovich, Ia. L. 1978. "Literaturnaia i obshchestvennaia zhizn' pushkinskoi pory v pis'makh A. E. Izmailova k P. L. Iakovlevu." In *Pushkin: Issledovaniia i materialy,* edited by Vadim Vatsuro, 8:151–94. Saint Petersburg: Izd-vo Akademii nauk.

Loginovskaia, Elena. 1977. *Poema M. Iu. Lermontova "Demon."* Moscow.

Lominadze, S. 1976. "Na fone garmonii. (Lermontov)." In *Tipologiia stilevogo razvitiia novogo vremeni,* edited by Ia. El'sberg, 343–86. Moscow.

———. 1985. *Poeticheskii mir Lermontova.* Moscow.

———. 1989. "Stranstvuiushchii ofitser (Zametki o 'Tamani')." In *O klassikakh i sovremennikakh,* 319–48. Moscow.

Lossky, Vladimir. 1976. *In the Image and Likeness of God.* Crestwood, N.Y.: St. Vladimir's Seminary Press.

———. 1985. *The Mystical Theology of Eastern Christianity.* Crestwood, N.Y.: St. Vladimir's Seminary Press.

Lotman, Iu. M. 1988. *V shkole poeticheskogo slova: Pushkin, Lermontov, Gogol'.* Moscow.

———. 1992. "'Pikovaia dama' i tema kart i kartochnoi igry v russkoi literature nachala XIX veka." In *Izbrannye stat'i,* 2:389–415. Tallin.

Lotman, Iu. M., and B. A. Uspenskii. 1984. *The Semiotics of Russian Culture.* Edited by Ann Shukman. Ann Arbor: Department of Slavic Languages and Literature, University of Michigan.

Lovejoy, Arthur O. 1924. "On the Discriminations of Romanticisms." *PMLA* 39:229–53.

Lubovich, N. 1964. "Mtsyri' v ideinoi bor'be 30–40-kh godov." In *Tvorchesto Lermontova,* edited by U. Fokht, 106–32. Moscow.

Lukes, Steven. 1973. *Individualism.* Oxford: Basil Blackwell.

Lutzeler, Paul Michael. 1990. "The Image of Napoleon in European Romanticism." In *European Romanticism: Literary Cross-Currents, Modes, and Models,* edited by Gerhart Hoffmeister, 211–29. Detroit: Wayne State University Press.

Maguire, Robert A. 1990. "Gogol and the Legacy of Pseudo-Dionysius." In *Russianness: Studies on a National Identity: In Honor of Rufus Mathewson, 1918–1978,* edited by Robert L. Belknap, 44–55. Ann Arbor, Mich.: Ardis.

Maksimov, D. E. 1964. *Poeziia Lermontova.* Moscow.

Malia, Martin. 1961. *Alexander Herzen and the Birth of Russian Socialism, 1812–1855.* Cambridge: Harvard University Press.

Mann, Iuri. 1976. *Poetika russkogo romantisma.* Moscow.

———. 1987. "O Poniatii igry kak khudozhestvennom obraze." In *Dialektika khudozhestvennogo obraza,* 209–37. Moscow.

Manuilov, V. A. 1964. *Letopis' zhizni i tvorchestva M. Iu. Lermontova.* Moscow.

———. 1966. *Roman M. Iu. Lermontova "Geroi nashego vremeni": Kommentarii.* Moscow.

Manuilov, V. A., et al., eds. 1960. *Lermontov.* Seminarii. Leningrad.

———. 1981. *Lermontovskaia entsiklopediia.* Moscow.

Marchenko, Alla. 1989. "Pechorin: znakomyi i neznakomyi." In *Stoleti'ia ne sotrut . . . : Russkie klassiki i ikh chitateli,* edited by A. A. Il'in-Tomich, 161–223. Moscow.

Markovich, V. M. 1967. "'Geroi nashego vremeni' i stanovlenie realizma v russkom romane." *Russkaia Literatura* 4:45–66.

———. 1981. "O liriko-simvolicheskom nachale v romane Lermontova 'Geroi nashego vremeni.'" *Izvestiia Akademii Nauk SSSR: Seriia Literatury i Iazyka* 40:219–302.

Marx, Karl. 1994. *Early Political Writings.* Edited and Translated by Joseph J. O'Malley. Cambridge: Cambridge University Press.

Martens, Lorna. 1985. *The Diary Novel.* London: Cambridge University Press.

Mazour, Anatole. 1964. *The First Russian Revolution, 1825: The Decembrists Movement: Its Origins, Development, and Significance.* Stanford: Stanford University Press.

Meerson, Michael. 1996. "Sergei Bulgakov's Philosophy of Personality." In *Russian Religious Thought,* edited by Judith Deutsch Kornblatt and Richard F. Gustafson, 139–54. Madison: University of Wisconsin Press.

Mendel'son, N. M. 1914. "Narodnye motivy v poezii Lermontova." In *Venok Lermontovu: Iubileinyi sbornik,* edited by S. Shuvalov, 165–95. Moscow.

Merezhkovskii, D. S. 1991. "Lermontov: poet sverchchelovechestva." In *V tikhom omute. Stat'i i issledovaniia raznykh let,* 378–416. Moscow.

Mersereau, John. 1960. "M. Yu. Lermontov's 'The Song of the Merchant Kalashnikov': An Allegorical Interpretation." *California Slavic Studies:*10–33.

———. 1962. *Mikhail Lermontov.* Carbondale: Southern Illinois University Press.

Mersereau, John, and David Lapeza. 1988. "Russian Romanticism." In *Romanticism in National Context,* edited by Roy Porter and Mikulas Teich, 290–316. London: Cambridge University Press.

Meshchersky, N. A. 1976. "Ob Epigraphe k poeme Lermontova 'Mtsyri.'" *Nauchnye doklady vysshei shkoly. Filologicheskie nauki* 5:103–8.

Mestr, Zhosef de (Maistre). 1937. "Pis'ma." In *Literaturnoe nasledstvo,* 33–44:577–726. Moscow.

Mikhailova, E. N. 1941. "Ideia lichnosti u Lermontova i osobennosti ee khudozhestvennogo voploshcheniia." In *Zhizn' i tvorchestvo Lermontova. Issledovaniia i materialy,* edited by N. L. Brodskii, 125–62. Moscow.

Mikhailovskii, N. 1989. "Geroi bezvremen'ia." In *Literaturnaia kritika. Stat'i o russkoi literature XIX–nachala XX veka,* 402–49. Leningrad.

Mil'don, V. I. 1992. "Zhit' nigde i nikogda." In *Otkrylas' bezdna. Obrazy mesta i vremeni v klassicheskoi russkoi drame,* 54–78. Moscow.

Miller, O. V. 1980. *Bibliographiia literatury o M. Iu. Lermontove: 1917–1977.* Leningrad.

———. 1990. *Literatura o M. Iu. Lermontove: 1825–1916.* Leningrad.

Mirsky, D. S. 1958. *A History of Russian Literature.* New York: Vintage Books.

Morson, Gary Saul. 1987. *Hidden in Plain View: Narrative and Creative Potentials in "War and Peace."* Stanford: Stanford University Press.

———. 1994. *Narrative and Freedom: The Shadows of Time.* New Haven: Yale University Press.

Morson, Gary Saul, and Caryl Emerson. 1990. *Mikhail Bakhtin: Creation of Prosaics.* Stanford: Stanford University Press.

Nabokov, Vladimir. 1988. "Translator's Foreword." In *A Hero of Our Time,* by Mikhail Lermontov, translated by Vladimir Nabokov, in collaboration with Dmitri Nabokov, v–xix. Ann Arbor, Mich.: Ardis.

Naidich, E. E. 1971. "Posledniaia redaktsiia 'Demona.'" *Russkaia literatura* 1:76–80.

Neiman, B. 1941. "Lermontov i dekabristy." In *M. U. Lermontov,* edited by N. A. Glagolev, 31–61. Moscow.

Nemoianu, Virgil. 1984. *The Taming of Romanticism: European Literature and the Age of Biedermeier.* Cambridge: Harvard University Press.

Neverin. 1839. "Maskarad." In *Biblioteka dlia chteniia,* 33:41–64. Saint Petersburg.

Nikitenko, A. V. 1955. *Dnevnik.* Vol. 1. Moscow.

Novitskii, P. I., ed. 1941. *"Maskarad" Lermontova: Sbornik statei.* Moscow.

Oakeshott, Michael. 1975. *On Human Conduct.* Oxford: Clarendon Press.

Obolonsky, Aleksandr. 1994. *The Drama of Russian Political Thought: The System Against the Individual.* Moscow.

Odoevsky, Vladimir. 1981. *Sochineniia v dvukh tomakh.* Vol. 1, *Russkie nochi. Stat'i.* Moscow.

Ogarev, N. N. 1956. "Kavkazskie vody." In *Izbrannye proizvedeniia v dvukh tomakh,* 2:375–92. Moscow.

Oksman, Iu., ed. 1926. *Dekabristy.* Moscow.

O'Meara, Patrick. 1984. *K. F. Ryleev.* Princeton: Princeton University Press.

Ortega y Gasset, José. 1968. "The Self and the Other." In *The Dehumanization of Art, and Other Essays on Art, Culture, and Literature,* 175–204. Princeton: Princeton University Press.

Otzoupe, Nikolai. 1956. "Vigny's Eloa and Lermontov's Demon." *Slavonic and East European Review* 34:311–37.

———. 1961. "Satana i Demon." In *Literaturnye ocherki,* 98–120. Paris.

Ovsianiko-Kulikovski, D. N. 1989. "Pechorin." In *Literaturno-kriticheskie raboty v dvukh tomakh.* Vol. 2, *Iz istorii russkoi intelligentsii. Vospominaniia,* 98–122. Moscow.

Paganuzzi, P. 1967. *Lermontov.* Montreal.

Pavlov, N. F. 1985. *Sochineniia.* Moscow.

Peace, Richard. 1967. "The Role of 'Taman' in Lermontov's *Geroj Nashego Vremeni.*" *Slavonic and East European Review* 55:12–29.

Praz, Mario. 1970. *The Romantic Agony.* 2d ed. Translated by A. Davidson. Oxford: Oxford University Press.

Pulkhritudova, E. M. 1979. "Romantism v russkoi literature 30-kh godov. Lermontov. In *Istoriia romantizma v russkoi literature: 1825–1840,* edited by S. E. Shatalov, 258–314. Moscow.

Pushkin, Alekander. 1937–59. *Polnoe sobranie sochinenii.* 17 vols. Moscow.

Quint, David. 1993. *Epic and Empire: Politics and Generic Form from Virgil to Milton.* Princeton: Princeton University Press.

Reed, Walter. 1974. *Meditations on the Hero: A Study of the Romantic Hero in Nineteenth-Century Fiction.* New Haven: Yale University Press.

Reid, Robert. 1982. "Lermontov's Demon: A Question of Identity." *Slavonic and East European Review* 60:189–210.

———. 1986. "Lermontov's 'Mtsyri': Themes and Structures." In *Problems of Russian Romanticism.* Aldershot, Hants, England: Gower.

Ricoeur, Paul. 1967. *The Symbolism of Evil.* Boston: Beacon.

Rodnianskaia, Irina. 1981. "Demon uskol'zaiushchii." *Voprosy literatury* 5:140–62.

Rosenshield, Gary. 1988. "Fatalism in *A Hero of Our Time:* Cause or Commonplace." In *The Supernatural in Slavic and Baltic Literature,* edited by A. Mandelker and R. Reeder, 83–102. Columbus, Ohio: Slavica.

Rostopchina, Evdokiia. 1986. *Stikhotvoreniia, proza, pis'ma.* Moscow.

Rozanov, Vassily. 1989. "Vechno pechal'naia duel'." In *Mysli o literature,* 217–32. Moscow.

———. 1990. "Pushkin i Lermontov." In *Pushkin v russkoi filosofskoi kritike,* edited by R. Gal'tseva, 191–93. Moscow.

Rudolph, Kurt. 1983. *Gnosis: The Nature and History of Gnosticism.* Translation edited by Robert McLachlan Wilson. San Francisco: Harper and Row.

Rudwin, Maximilian. 1973. *The Devil in Legend and Literature.* LaSalle: Open Court. (Originally published 1931.)

Russell, Jeffrey Burton. 1986. *Mephistopheles: The Devil in the Modern World.* Ithaca: Cornell University Press.

———. 1988. *The Prince of Darkness: Radical Evil and the Power of Good in History.* Ithaca: Cornell University Press.

Savodnik, V. F. 1911. *Chuvstvo prirody v poezii Pushkina, Lermontova i Tiutcheva.* Moscow.

Schalk, Ellery. 1986. *From Valor to Pedigree: Ideas of Nobility in France in the Sixteenth and Seventeenth Centuries.* Princeton: Princeton University Press.

Schulz, Rostislav. 1992. "Otzvuki Lermontova v poezii Alexandra Galicha." In *Norwich Symposia on Russian Literature and Culture.* Vol. 3, *Mikhail Lermontov, 1814–1989,* edited by Efim Etkind, 173–87. Northfield, Vt.: Russian School of Norwich University.

Semenov, L. P. 1914. "K voprosu o vliianii Marlinskogo na Lermontova." In *Filologicheskie zapiski,* 5–6:614–39. Moscow.

———. 1939. *Lermontov na Kavkaze.* Piatigorsk.

Shakhovskoi, A. A. 1961. *Komedii, stikhotvoreniia.* Moscow.

Shan-Girei, A. P. 1989. "M. Iu. Lermontov." In *M. Iu. Lermontov v vospominaniiakh sovremennikov,* edited by V. Vatsuro and N. Gei, 33–56. Moscow.

Shapiro, Barbara. *The Romantic Mother: Narcissistic Patterns in Romantic Poetry.* Baltimore: Johns Hopkins University Press.

Shaw, Joseph T. 1958. "Lermontov's 'Demon' and the Byronic Oriental Verse Tale." *Indiana Slavic Studies* 2:163–80.

Shchegolev, P. E. 1926. *Dekabristy.* Leningrad.

———. 1929. *Kniga o Lermontove.* Leningrad.

Shestov, Lev. 1990. "A. S. Pushkin." In *Pushkin v russkoi filosofskoi kritike,* edited by R. Gal'tseva, 194–207. Moscow.

Shevyrev, Stepan. 1841. "Vzgliad russkogo na sovremennoe obrazovanie v Evrope." In *Moskvitianin,* 1:219–96. Moscow.

———. 1907. "Geroi nashego vremeni." In *Russkaia kriticheskaia literatura o proizvedeniiakh M. Iu. Lermontova,* edited by V. Zelinsky, 152–73. Moscow.

Shtokmar, M. 1941. "Narodno-poeticheskie traditsii v tvorchestve Lermontova." *Literaturnoe nasledstvo* 43–44:263–353.

Shuvalov, S., ed. 1914. *Venok M. Iu. Lermontovu: iubileinyi sbornik.* Moscow.

Simpson, Mark S. 1983. *The Russian Gothic Novel and its British Antecedents.* Columbus, Ohio: Slavica.

Sokolov, A. N. 1956. *Ocherki po istorii russkoi poemy XVIII i pervoi poloviny XIX veka.* Moscow.

Solov'ev, Vladimir. 1897. "Zhozef De Mestr." In *Entsikopedicheskii slovar' Brokgauz-Efron,* 20:349–52. Saint Petersburg.

———. 1901. "Lermontov." *Vestnik Evropy* 2:441–59.

———. 1988. "Tri rechi v pamiat' Dostoevskogo." In *Sochineniia v dvukh tomakh,* 2:289–324. Moscow.

Stanton, Domna C. 1980. *The Aristocrat as Art: A Study of the Honnête Homme and the Dandy in Seventeenth- and Nineteenth-Century Literature.* New York: Columbia University Press.

Stepanov, M. 1937. "Zhozef De Mestr v Rossii." In *Literaturnoe nasledsvo,* 29–30:577–726. Moscow.

Stepanov, N. 1966. "Pisatel'-dekabrist. (A. Bestuzhev-Marlinsky)." In *Poety i prozaiki,* 180–218. Moscow.

Stepun, Fedor. 1936. *Russian Soul and the Revolution.* Translated by Ermine Huntress. London: Scribner.

Strakhov, Nikolai. 1970. "Tolstoy's *War and Peace.*" In *Literature and National Identity: Nineteenth-Century Russian Critical Essays,* translated and edited by Paul Debreczeny and Jesse Zeldin, 119–69. Lincoln: University of Nebraska Press.

Sutherland, Christine. 1984. *The Princess of Siberia: The Story of Mary Volkonsky.* New York: Farrar, Straus, and Giroux.

Taylor, Charles. 1989. *Sources of the Self: The Making of the Modern Identity.* Cambridge: Harvard University Press.

Thorslev, Peter L. 1962. *The Byronic Hero: Types and Prototypes.* Minneapolis: University of Minnesota Press.

Todd, William Mills, III. 1986. *Fiction and Society in the Age of Pushkin: Ideology, Institutions, and Narrative.* Cambridge: Harvard University Press.

Tocqueville, Alexis de. 1945. *Democracy in America.* Vol. 2. New York: Vintage Books.

Tolstoy, Leo. 1935–64. *Polnoe sobraniie sochinenii.* 90 vols. Moscow.

Tomashevsky, Boris. 1941. "Proza Lermontova i zapadno-evropeiiskaia traditsiia." *Literaturnoe nasledstvo* 43–44:469–517.

Trilling, Lionel. 1972. *Sincerity and Authenticity.* Cambridge: Harvard University Press.

Tsvetaeva, Marina. 1979. *Izbrannaia proza v dvukh tomakh.* Vol. 1. New York: Russica.

Turbin, V. N. 1978. *Pushkin, Gogol, Lermontov.* Moscow.

———. 1989. "Vospriiatie i interpretatsiia Lermontovym zhanrovoi struktury romana Pushkina 'Evgenii Onegin.'" *Vestnik moskovskogo universiteta* 5:17–27.

Turgenev, Ivan. 1968. *First Love and Other Stories.* Translated by David Magarshack. New York: Norton.

———. 1983. "Literaturnye i zhiteiskie vospominania." In *Polnoe sobraniie sochinenii i pisem v tridtsati tomakh,* 3:7–167. Moscow.

———. 1987. *Pis'ma: 1855–1858.* Vol. 3 of *Polnoe sobraniie sochinenii i pisem v tridtsati tomakh.* Moscow.

Turner, Brian S. 1984. *The Body and Society: Explorations in Social Theory.* New York: Basil Blackwell.

Udodov, B. T. 1973. *M. Iu. Lermontov: Khudozhestvennaia individual'nost' i tvorcheskie protsessy.* Voronezh.

Ulam, Adam. 1981. *Russia's Failed Revolutions: From the Decembrists to the Dissidents.* New York: Basic Books.

Ulph, Owen. 1972. "Unmaking the Masked Guardsman: A Case-Study of the Moral Man in the Immoral Society." *Russian Literature Triquarterly* 3:269–79.

Unbegaun, B. O. 1977. *Russian Versification.* Letchworth Herts, England: Prideaux.

Vagin, E. 1978. "Ob Epigrafe poemy 'Mtsyri.'" *Novyi zhurnal* 130:82–91.

Vatsuro, Vadim. 1964. "Lermontov i Marlinsky." In *Tvorchestvo M. Iu. Lermontova,* edited by U. R. Fokht, 341–64. Moscow.

———. 1976. "M. Iu. Lermontov." In *Russkaia literatura i fol'klor: Pervaia polovina XIX v,* 210–48. Leningrad.

———. 1979. "K Tsenzurnoi istorii 'Demona.'" In *M. Iu. Lermontov: Issledovaniia i materialy,* edited by V. Manuilov, 410–15. Leningrad.

———. 1994. "'Mozart i Salieri' v 'Maskarade.'" In *Zapiski kommentatora,* 234–91. Saint Petersburg.

Vatsuro, V., and N. Gei, eds. 1989. *Lermontov v vospominaniiakh sovremennikov.* Moscow.

Vatsuro, V. E., and M. I. Gillel'son. 1986. *Skvoz' umstvennye plotiny.* Moscow.

Venclova, Tomas. 1986. *Neustoichivoe ravnovesie: Vosem' russkikh poeticheskikh tekstov.* New Haven: Yale Center for International and Area Studies.

Veselitskii, V. V. 1964. *Razvitie otvlechennoi leksiki v russkom literaturnom iazyke pervoi treti XIX veka.* Moscow.

———. 1972. *Otvlechennaia leksika v russkom literaturnom iazyke XVIII–nach. XIX veka.* Moscow.

Viazemskii, P. A. 1992. *Zapisnye knizhki.* Moscow.

Vigny, Alfred de. 1921. *Oeuvres complètes: Poésies.* Paris: Librairie Delagrave.

———. 1935. *Le Journal D'un Poète.* Vol. 1. Paris: Louis Conard.

Vinogradov, Igor. 1964. "Filosofskii roman Lermontova." *Novyi mir* 10: 210–31.

Vinogradov, Viktor. 1936. "Stil' 'Pikovoi damy.'" *Vremennik pushkinskoi komissii* 2:74–148.

———. 1986. *Stil' prozy Lermontova.* Ann Arbor: Ardis.

Viskovatov, P. A. 1987. *Mikhail Iur'evich Lermontov: Zhizn' i tvorchestvo.* Moscow.

Vladimirov, P. V. 1892. *Istoricheskiie i narodno-bytovye siuzhety v poezii M. Iu. Lermontova.* Kiev.

Walicki, Andrzej. 1979. *A History of Russian Thought from Enlightenment to Marxism.* Stanford: Stanford University Press.

———. 1989. *The Slavophile Controversy: History of a Conservative Utopia in Nineteenth-Century Russian Thought.* Notre Dame: University of Notre Dame Press.

Watt, Ian. 1996. *Myths of Modern Individualism: Faust, Don Quixote, Don Juan, Robinson Crusoe.* Cambridge: Cambridge University Press.

Weber, Max. 1958. *The Protestant Ethic and the Spirit of Capitalism.* New York: Scribner.

Weintraub, Karl Joachim. 1978. *The Value of the Individual: Self and Circumstance in Autobiography.* Chicago: University of Chicago Press.

Wellek, René. 1949. "The Concept of 'Romanticism' in Literary History." *Comparative Literature* 1:1–23 and 147–72.

Wilson, James D. 1982. *The Romantic Heroic Ideal.* Baton Rouge: Louisiana State University Press.

Wortman, Richard S. 1995. *Scenarios of Power: Myth and Ceremony in Russian Monarchy. From Peter the Great to the Death of Nicholas I.* Princeton: Princeton University Press.

Yazykov, N. M. 1988. *Stikhotvoreniia i poemy.* Moscow.

Zamotin, I. I. 1906. *Literaturnye epokhi XIX-go stoletiia: ocherki po istorii russkoi literatury.* Warsaw.

———. 1907. *Romanticheskii idealism.* Saint Petersburg.

Zetlin, Mikhail. 1958. *The Decembrists.* Translated by G. Panin. New York: International Universities Press.

Zhivov, V. M., and B. A. Uspenskii. 1987. "Sakralizatsiia monarkha v Rossii." In *Iazyki kultury i problemy perevodimosti,* edited by B. A. Uspenskii, 47–154. Moscow.

Zis, A. Ia., et al., eds. 1991. *Dekabristy. Estetika i kritika.* Moscow.

Index